The *Art of* VINTAGE UKULELES

by
Sandor Nagyszalanczy

ISBN 978-1-57424-422-9

Dedication

This book is dedicated to the memory of my dear friend and "Uke Ellington" bandmate Rick Turner, who shared my passions for and supported my interests in vintage ukuleles.

Acknowledgements

As you might imagine, putting a book like this together isn't an easy matter for a single individual. In fact, it's neigh on impossible to do without the contributions of a small army of dedicated supporters. First of all, I'd like to thank the editors and staff at Ukulele Magazine who have published my articles and columns for many years, including Greg Olwell, Blair Jackson, Joey Lusterman and Nick Grizzle. I'd also like to thank all the various friends and colleagues who loaned me their precious ukuleles for research and photography (as well as those who contributed photographs): Jim Beloff, Joel Eckhaus, Frank Ford, Tony Graziano, Rick McKee, Gregg Miner, Gene Reese, Gary Schireson, and Shawn Yacavone at Ukulele Friend. I'd like to give special credit to my dear friend, one-time bandmate and fellow ukulele collector Rick "Ukulele Dick" McKee who was always ready to share a story and a smile. Special thanks, too, to fellow ukulele historian Jim Tranquada, co-author of the world's most complete and thoroughly researched book on the uke's origins: The Ukulele a History (University of Hawaii Press, 2012). Relying on his encyclopedic knowledge of the instrument helped me distinguish ukulele facts from fiction.

I'd also like to thank some of the folks that helped me acquire some of the lovely vintage ukuleles featured in the pages of this book: Norman Harris and Norm's Rare Guitars, Mario and Maria Maccaferri, Mike Longworth, Dick Boak and the Martin Guitar Company, John Bernunzio and Bernunzio Uptown Music, David Colburn at Vintage Fret Shop, Richard Gellis of Union Grove Music, Peter Thomas, Eric Schoenberg and Gregg Miner.

Finally, I'd be remiss if I didn't acknowledge the unqualified support of the people, past and present, who are nearest and dearest to me: My mother Maria, who not only devoted much of her life to my betterment, but also provided me with many of the skills I used in wheeling and dealing when acquiring vintage ukuleles (she was a very successful dealer of high-end antiques in Los Angeles); My ex-wife and still good friend Ann Gibb, who put up with a house full of ukuleles for decades and never gave me grief about my nearly unbridled uke collecting habits; and Karen Lehman, my girlfriend and musical partner, who aided in this book's creation by offering bountiful love and inspiration.

TABLE OF CONTENTS

FOREWORD
My First Ukuleles

When my parents and I escaped Hungary during the November Revolution of 1956, little did we know that we'd end up in America. We were supposed to go live with a rich relative in Switzerland who reneged on his promise to take us in. After a long flight to Boston and a short bus ride, we ended up at Camp Kilmer Army Base in northern New Jersey, which had been set up to house the 30,000 refugees who had fled Hungary. We soon moved to a tenement building in Newark which housed another dozen Hungarian families. Although I was only a child, I remember the kindness of the people who helped get us started on the path to our new life free from the tyranny of Russian Communism. One of those people was, a kindly older man I came to call "uncle Henry," who visited us regularly. One day he brought me a surprise gift: A small plastic musical instrument with four strings and a top adorned with images of a tropical land and the single word "Aloha." I had no idea that this little toy was called a ukulele (I don't think uncle Henry knew either). Whatever it was, I loved it and spent many happy hours banging away on that uke, although I had no idea how to actually tune it or play it. Decades later, I discovered an old Polaroid photo that my dad had snapped of me as a child strumming my little Carnival brand "Aloha" model uke.

Although that was technically my first ukulele, it was a toy that I never actually learned how to play properly. I didn't get my first "real" ukulele until I went to college in the early 1970s. I was lucky enough to attend the University of California Santa Cruz on a campus that is one of the most beautiful in the entire world. Although I didn't study music there (I was a design major), I always enjoyed playing my guitar, the same one I'd had since I started playing at age 11—a 1927 koa wood Martin. I'd often sit outside and strum between classes when I probably should have been studying. My girlfriend at the time also loved music, and we occasionally performed together at various coffee houses around town. Life was good.

Around the time I was to graduate, my girlfriend

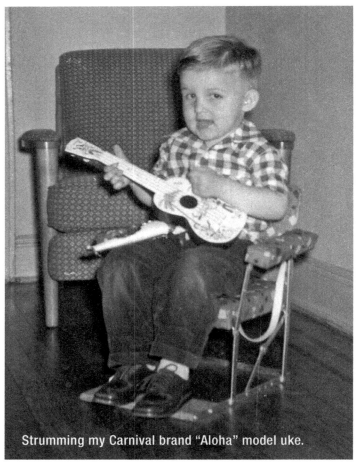

Strumming my Carnival brand "Aloha" model uke.

went home for the weekend to her parent's house somewhere in California's central valley. When she returned a few days later, she announced that she had a surprise for me, and presented me with a lovely little Martin style 0 soprano ukulele.

I was flabbergasted. Aside from my parents, no one had ever given me a gift this nice before. While thanking her profusely, I couldn't stop my mind of thinking "OMG, what must this have cost her?" After all, we were both starving students at the time. But before I could ask about the Martin's price, she said: "You won't believe this, but I found your uke at a thrift store in Modesto and it only cost $1!" Now for those of you who know how pricey Martin ukes are these days (and may be skeptical of my girlfriend's find), I must remind you of how relatively undesirable ukuleles were in the mid 1970s. My personal theory is that Tiny Tim single handedly made the ukulele the un-coolest in-

My Martin Style O Soprano Ukulele

pop culture, there's little doubt that in the 1970s, ukuleles were generally undesirable. I know this because I had the distinct displeasure of experiencing this first hand: With my then-new-to-me Martin ukulele, I attended a party thrown by a college friend. Not knowing many of the folks in attendance, I sequestered myself in a corner and strummed a few of the 20s era novelty songs I'd learned since acquiring the uke. At one point, an attractive young woman came up and asked with a somewhat judgmental tone: "Is that a ukulele?" After I nodded "yes," she said scornfully "My *Grandmother* played the ukulele." If I'd passed out drunk at that party, I probably would have awoken with the word "Geek" scrawled in marker pen on my forehead.

I'm happy to say that that was the worst of what I experienced when playing my little Martin uke. By the early 1980s, I'd joined a mostly-acapella music group called "The JeloTones." In addition to adding my tenor voice to their musical blend, I taught them some of my favorite novelty songs, including "Nagasaki" and "Ain't Misbehavin'" both of which which soon added to the band's repertoire. Whenever we'd perform our regular do-wop songs (we regularly busked in downtown Santa Cruz), I'd have my little Martin uke's neck tucked under my belt behind my back. When it was time to play one of my novelty songs, I'd pull the ukulele out to accompany our singing. When we started playing stage gigs, I decided that it would be a good idea to install a pickup in my Martin, so I could plug it into the PA. I extracted the piezo element from a cheap guitar suction-cup surface pickup and glued it inside the uke under the bridge. Then, I screwed up: I tried drilling a hole though the side of the instrument, only to have the thin-wood side cave in all around the hole. My solution was to craft a diamond-shaped escutcheon plate from a small piece of ebony. It not only covered up the damage around the drilled hole, but it provided a stronger mount for the 1/8" jack I installed. After all that, the pickup sounded pretty bad, so I ended up mic'ing it most of the time.

Now, more than 40 years after I received that $1 Martin uke, I'm still playing it. It's traveled with me all around the country and bears the dings and scratches from decades of happy strumming. Although I've owned and played many ukes that were fancier and definitely more expensive, it'll always hold a special place in my heart, with a sweet sound that never fails brings a smile to my face.

strument on the planet. A regular on NBC's trend-setting TV program "Rowan & Martin's Laugh-In," Tiny, AKA Herbert Khaury, sang tin-pan-alley-era songs like "Tiptoe Through the Tulips" (his signature song) in a high falsetto voice. Although he was an accomplished musician with an encyclopedic knowledge of early songs, his "Laugh-In" persona was decidedly comedic verging on ridiculous.

Regardless of Tiny Tim's actual influence on musical

INTRODUCTION

When I first started collecting vintage ukuleles in the mid-1980s, I had no particular goal in mind. I was regularly traveling around the U.S. on business at a time when ukuleles were extremely unpopular and virtually unwanted. As was my regular habit as an amateur musician and an antiques fancier, I browsed through the music stores, junk shops and flea markets in virtually every small town I visited. I often found an interesting uke or two to purchase for very little money; I rarely spent more than $35. on any single instrument. By the mid-1990s I had filled the walls of my cottage with all manner of vintage four-stringed specimens: early Hawaiians, Martins and Lyon & Healys, Harmonys and Regals, molded plastic Mastros and Carnivals, as well as no-name ukes both plain and fancy. My collection grew further during the early days of Ebay online auctions, when old ukuleles, likely unearthed in cobwebby attics and old steamer trunks, came up for auction (my apologies if I ever bid against you).

When the ukuleles' popularity was on the rise in the early 2000s and instrument prices soared, I switched my collecting pursuits to uke-related ephemera, including instruction books, sheet music, phonograph records, newspaper ads, musical instrument catalog pages, vintage strings and tuners and such. These materials not only provided seminal information about particular ukulele models and makers, they also helped me learn more about the people who played and promoted the instruments and the ukuleles' impact on American music and culture. I soon became obsessed with finding out all I could about the golden age of the ukulele in the 1920s, as well as it's resurgence after WWII and in the 1950s. Thanks to the extensive archive of early newspapers and printed materials found on the internet and in reference libraries, I've dug up a fair number of ukulele-related facts, trivia and interesting stories that, to my knowledge, have not surfaced in modern times.

In 2015, I began sharing my uke-related research and resources by writing both a regular column and feature articles for Ukulele Magazine. After a few years, I had accumulated enough written material and photographs for a book of considerable size and content; the book you now hold in your hands. Much of this book's content is material repurposed from my columns and articles. I've also added a considerable amount of new material and photos of instruments from my own collection of instruments as well as those borrowed from fellow uke collectors.

Although there have been quite a number of books written about vintage ukuleles, in my view, most are basically picture books with only sparse information about the instruments and their makers. My overarching goal was to create a book that explored all aspects of the instrument in greater detail than ever presented before. Of course, the book had to be a visual feast, allowing readers to see these remarkable vintage instruments in all their glory. I've relied on my nearly 40 years of experience as a professional studio photographer to create images that reveal the remarkable beauty of ukuleles, whether they are made of sumptuously fancy woods or adorned with colorful decorative finishes. I've included plentiful close ups of the fine details that grace many instruments: shapely bridges, complex body bindings, fancy inlays, etc.

To supplement the photographs, I've included a wealth of information gleaned from more than a decade of historical research. This not only covers facts about the instruments themselves—brand names, model numbers, features, specifications, etc.—but the histories of some of the more prominent ukulele builders and manufacturers from the late 1800s all the way up to the mid-1960s. I've also delved into the life and legacy of some of the best ukulele players and performers who were popular in the period between the early 1900s and the late 1950s.

By design, this book is episodic rather than linear, meaning you don't have to read it sequentially from first page to last. Instead, the various chapters and sections of this book can be perused at will, in any order. Some chapters explore the ukulele during various time periods, from its earliest origins in Hawaii at the turn of the last century to its golden period in the 1920s to its presence in World War II to its renewed popularity in the 1950s and early 60s. Other chapters examine various aspects of vintage ukes. For example, how inventive minds came up with some notable improvements and also produced some truly unusual instruments in terms of designs and features. The last chapter of this book explores a variety of uke accessories (capos, strings, etc.) and ephemera.

Ultimately, I hope this book will give you a greater appreciation of the "jumping flea" as it's sometimes called, as well as a more comprehensive understanding of how this little instrument has brought joy all across the globe. After perusing this book, I hope you'll agree that, more than being just utilitarian musical instruments, vintage ukuleles were the product of artful creation. That's at least part of the reason they're still bringing joy to folks who are playing them today.

Sandor Nagyszalanczy
June 14, 2023

PHOTO CREDITS

All photos by Sandor Nagyszalanczy, unless otherwise credited.

Pgs. 10, 12 and 14
Courtesy of the San Francisco Museum of Craft and Design

Pg. 13
Photo courtesy of Shawn Yacavone and Ukulele Friend

Pg. 19 and 20
Nunes Radio Tenor uke courtesy of Frank Ford

Pg. 25, bottom
Photos courtesy of Shawn Yacavone and Ukulele Friend

Pg. 26, top
Photo courtesy of Mick Marlar

Pg. 30, top
Photo courtesy of Shawn Yacavone and Ukulele Friend

Pg. 52, top
Gibson UB banjo uke courtesy of Rick McKee

Pg. 52, bottom
Gibson brochure image courtesy of Tom Walsh

Pg. 63, left
Photo by Cartwright Thompson, courtesy of Joel Eckhaus

Pg. 64, bottom right
Photo courtesy of Mick Marlar

Pg. 69, right & pg. 70, top right
Hollywood Style 3 uke courtesy of Rick McKee

Pg. 71, top
Photo courtesy of Gary Schireson

Pg. 95 & pg. 96, bottom
National Style 3 uke courtesy of Rick McKee

Pg. 98, right
Dobro uke courtesy of Gregg Miner

Pg. 153, bottom
Photo courtesy of Mick Marlar

Pg. 163, right and bottom left
Photos by Jim Beloff

Pg. 172
Wendell Hall Master Uke courtesy of Rick McKee

Pg. 208
Altpeter uke courtesy of Gregg Miner

Pg. 231, top
Premier and Bacon banjo ukes courtesy of Rick McKee

Pg. 287, top and bottom
Photos courtesy of Gene Reese

Pg. 310, upper left
Surf-a-le-le and 8-string Treholipee ukes courtesy of Tony Graziano

Pg. 313, bottom & pg. 314, upper left
Photos courtesy of Shawn Yacavone and Ukulele Friend

Back cover, upper photo
Courtesy of Mick Marlar

THE ART OF VINTAGE UKULELES • SANDOR NAGYSZALANCZY

Chapter One
The Hawaiian Ukulele is Born

When you hear a musical performance, have you ever thought about the origins of the instruments the band members are playing? The truth is that practically every type of instrument, from drums and percussion to plucked and hammered strings to horns & woodwinds, was first created hundreds, if not thousands of years ago. Of course, most have evolved considerably: Take, for example, the modern acoustic guitar, which likely evolved from the middle eastern oud and the lute, both of which predate modern history. Now contrast this with the ukulele, an instrument that didn't exist a mere 150 years ago. Not only is the uke one of the world's newest instruments, it's also one of the most popular, in no small part because of how easy it is for a beginner to learn to play.

The story of how the ukulele came into existence is a fascinating one that starts with an island nation (not Hawaii) in turmoil, a long sailing voyage, and a trio of talented craftsmen who helped transform a traditional Portuguese instrument into what we call the ukulele today. As the uke became more and more popular, the first generation of Hawaiian luthiers produced the beautiful looking—and sounding—ukuleles that are still highly coveted today.

1.1 The Uke's Portuguese Origins

"When did the Hawaiians invent the ukulele?" a friend of mine recently asked as I was giving her a tour of my collection of vintage ukes. The belief that Hawaii lays sole claim to the ukulele—the instrument

Three early ukuleles made in Honolulu near the end of the 19th century.

that would seem to have been developed over centuries in relative obscurity among the descendants of the Polynesians—is a widely held misconception, and one that I've often felt obliged to dispel. "In fact," I informed her, "the earliest ukes only date back to the late 1880s." Then, pausing for effect, I added: "And they weren't invented by the Hawaiians." Looking like a six-year-old who has learned that Santa Claus doesn't exist, my confused friend furrowed her brow and considered the ukuleles hanging on my wall anew.

True, the actual history of the ukulele begins on an island, but not one in the Hawaiian chain, nor one in the Pacific Ocean, for that matter. Madeira, a small mountainous speck of land in the Atlantic southeast of Portugal, about a 350-mile swim from the coast of North Africa, is the actual birthplace of the beloved uke.

Rich volcanic soil and palm trees on the big island of Hawaii.

Not unlike the Hawaiian Islands, Madeira has a tropical climate and is part of a volcanic archipelago. The heavily forested island (Madeira means "wood" in Portuguese) once had a thriving timber industry and a long history of furniture making. But it's probably best known for Madeira wine, the fortified, sherry-like beverage that became popular, in part, because it didn't spoil on long sea voyages. Grape growing and winemaking have been a staple industry there since the 16th century. Two centuries ago, Madeira was also a popular tourist spot for European visitors who were drawn to its picturesque landscapes and exotic flora. Visitors were often entertained by music played in the streets of Funchal, the island's bustling port city. Because there were no closeable windows on the houses in this hot climate, it must have been difficult to not hear strains of music, both day and night. Local musicians strummed waltzes, mazurkas and folk tunes on the Spanish guitar and a small, guitar-like, four-string instrument called the machête (pronounced "ma-CHET"), also known as the braguinha or the "machête de Braga" after the city in northern Portugal where the instrument originated.

Unfortunately, by the mid 1800s, Madeira wasn't such a great place to be. Poverty, famine, and a series of natural disasters that led to the collapse of the wine industry made the island a better place to escape from than to. Scores of unemployed Madeirans sought to leave their overcrowded homeland and launch a new

THE ART OF VINTAGE UKULELES • SANDOR NAGYSZALANCZY

An old postcard depicting the capitol city of Funchal on the Portugues Island of Madeira.

life elsewhere. It just so happened that as things were going wrong in Madeira, life was flourishing a half a world away, in the Sandwich Islands—Hawaii as it was commonly known then—where the sugar industry was booming.

In 1874, Hawaiian planters shipped over 25 tons of sugar to the mainland alone. But there was a problem: After decades of European colonization and introduced diseases, the native population was in decline, so there weren't enough workers to man the plantations and factories. Desperation led planters on a world-wide search for labor, a search that eventually reached the Portuguese islands. Madeiran officials had no trouble finding men and women who were willing to sign three-year contracts to work in the sugar cane fields. In addition to wages of $6 to $10 a month, indentured emigrants would be provided with room and board, as well as sailing passage to their new Pacific promised land.

Among the more than 25,000 Madeirans who came to Hawaii in the late 1800s were three simple woodworkers from Funchal: 40-year-old Manuel Nunes, 37-year-old Augusto Dias, and 28-year-old Jose do Espirito Santo. Joined by their families, the men packed aboard the 220-foot-long British clipper ship SS Ravenscrag, and embarked on the arduous 4-month-long, 12,000 mile journey to Oahu. Little did they know that this new adventure would not only bring them prosperity, but would lead to the creation of a new instrument.

The poor, sea-weary immigrants finally arrived in Honolulu Harbor on a quiet Saturday in August

The British clipper ship SS Ravenscrag.

An early ukulele made by Augusto Dias.

A Portuguese machête made by
Octavianno Joao Nunes da Paixao.

THE ART OF VINTAGE UKULELES • SANDOR NAGYSZALANCZY

1879. No sooner had they docked, when one of the passengers, an accomplished musician named Joao Fernandes, launched into a joyous song and dance to celebrate the ship's safe arrival. Fernandes, a talented player who could play any song he'd heard only once, performed on a machête borrowed from a fellow passenger. He had also entertained the passengers during the long sea voyage, plucking out each song's melody while the strumming the chords. Evidently, he wasn't the only one who could play the instrument. Just a couple of weeks after the Ravenscrag's arrival, the following item ran in the September 3, 1879 edition of Honolulu's Hawaiian Gazette newspaper: "…Madeira Islanders recently arrived here have been delighting the people with nightly street concerts. The Musicians are fine performers on their strange instruments which are a kind of cross between a guitar and a banjo, but which produce very sweet music in the hands of the Portuguese minstrels."

Nunes, Dias and Santo went to work on sugar plantations on Hawaii, Maui and Kauai. After they'd fulfilled their contractual obligations, all three headed straight for Honolulu, the Kingdom's capital and center of commerce, with the ambition of returning to their former professions in woodworking. Fortunately for them, Honolulu had a flourishing furniture trade at the time, with more than a dozen local woodwork-

ing businesses. Nunes and Santo got jobs at Hawaii's largest furniture store, The Pioneer Furniture House. Dias set up his own small woodworking shop in 1884, settling in Honolulu's seedy, low-rent Chinatown district. He made not only furniture, but also musical instruments. Within a year, Manuel Nunes had opened his own shop just three blocks away and both Diaz and Nunes were advertising their businesses in the local newspapers. Dias described himself as a "maker of guitars, machêtes, and all stringed instruments." Santo soon followed suit, opening his shop just a few doors down from Nunes. In addition to building instruments, all three eked out a living by reselling commercially-made instruments, doing repair work, selling strings, etc. Dias even gave music lessons. The trio of luthiers endured many years of struggle, surviving several devastating neighborhood fires.

How did these three simple Madeiran woodworkers suddenly become luthiers? It's unclear whether any of them had ever even built an instrument before coming to Hawaii. There's some speculation (but no evidence) that Manuel Nunes may have been related to Octavianno Joao Nunes da Paixao (1812-1874), one of Madeira's most accomplished instrument makers. The most likely explanation is that Nunes, Dias and Santo all started building instruments while still pursuing general woodworking jobs, probably as a side business

A 5-string Portuguese rajão made by Manuel Nunes.

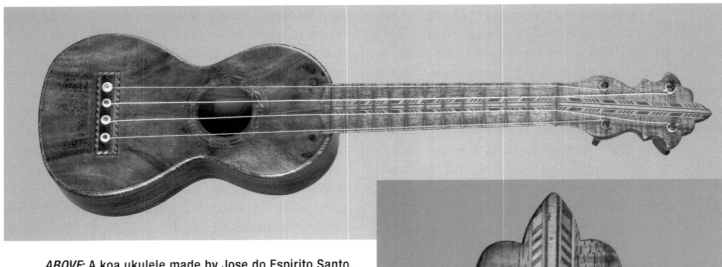

ABOVE: A koa ukulele made by Jose do Espirito Santo.

RIGHT: Fancy headstock of Jose do Espirito Santo's uke.

to earn extra money. Despite their lack of formal lutherie training, it's clear from the quality of the instruments they built that these Madeirans knew what they
were doing.

The first printed mention of an instrument clearly
identified as a ukulele came just a decade after the Ravenscrag's arrival. So who actually built the first one?
The honest answer is…no one really knows! All three
built machêtes that looked a lot like ukuleles, and Santo advertised that he could "make guitars of all sizes."
Manuel Nunes claimed that he had invented the ukulele, boldly announcing this in newspaper ads and on
his instrument labels (see section 1.2).

Whatever part Nunes or Dias or Santo may have had
on the creation of the uke, it's most likely that the first
true ukuleles were hybrid instruments; a mash up of
the machêtes and another smallish Portuguese instrument, the 5-string rajão (pronounced rah-ZHOW).
The petite size and body outline of the machêtes, as
well as its 17-fret fingerboard provided the basis for
the ukuleles' overall shape and configuration. But the
machete's D-G-B-D tuning wasn't used. Instead, the
ukulele employed the tuning of the rajão's top four
strings: G-C-E-A, minus its fifth string (a low D).
Why use this tuning? "When and why it (the tuning)
was changed to my-dog-has-fleas is one of those little
mysteries that always leads to more questions than an-
swers," the late-great musical historian John King said
in "The Ukulele A History", a book he co-authored
with Jim Tranquada.

Another important element that distinguishes Hawaiian ukuleles from their Portuguese brethren is the
material they're made from. Machêtes and rajáos are

typically built with spruce tops and bodies made of ju-
niper and other light woods. Virtually all early ukuleles
were made entirely from koa, a golden honey-brown
wood prized by the Hawaiians and traditionally used
for furniture and all manner of quality goods. Ukuleles,
such as the one made by Jose do Espirito Santo (shown
above) were, by and large, crafted from highly figured
koa, and often had the same kinds of ornate decorations found on machêtes. Their tops and bodies are so
eggshell-thin that these ukes are incredibly light and
produce a great deal of sound for their diminutive size.

Having a unique name is something else that helps
distinguish early ukuleles from other instruments, but
exactly how the uke got its name is another mystery.
There are many stories out there, but here's one sensi-

Portrait of Hawaii's last king, David Kalakaua.

found its way to the islands decades earlier.

Around 1900, novelist Jack London wrote that the ukulele was "...the Hawaiian (word) for jumping flea as it is also a certain musical instrument that may be likened to a young guitar." Six years later, the virtuoso uke player and teacher Ernest Kaai wrote in his ukulele instruction book that "the Hawaiians have a way of playing all over the strings... hence the name ukulele.

Whatever the exact etymology of the word, the appeal for the instrument spread quickly, in part thanks in part to one of its earliest champions: David Kalākaua, Hawaii's last king. Kalākaua, his Queen Emma, and the future queen Lili'uokalani (who composed that most sacred of Hawaiian songs, "Aloha Oe") were all accomplished musicians and patrons of the arts. Their support and promotion of the ukulele encouraged other Hawaiians to take up the instrument and develop their own music and styles. In addition to featuring the ukulele at Royal events, Kalākaua learned to play the uke himself and often included ukulele performances at his own informal gatherings. In the January 1922 issue of "Paradise of the Pacific" magazine, musician Joao Fernandes said of Kalākaua's parties: "We would go to the King's bungalow. Lots of people came. Plenty kanakas (native Hawaiians). Much music, much hula, much kaukau (slang for "food"), much drink. All time plenty drink. And King Kalākaua, he pay for all!"

ble explanation: Hawaii actually had the word "ukulele" before they had the instrument. An 1865 dictionary defined the word as "a cat flea;" a pest that had

Postcard image of a Hawaiian band playing for the Pineapple Packers Association at the 1915 Pan Pacific International Exhibition in San Francisco.

Clearly King David earned the nickname by which he's still celebrated today: "The Merrie Monarch."

As a new generation of Hawaiian ukulele makers set up shop—including Jonas Kumalae, (see section 1.3) who would bring the uke to the attention of mainlanders at San Francisco's 1915 Pan Pacific International Exhibition and spark the world's first uke craze—the original luthiers slowly faded into obscurity. By 1900, Santo had closed his shop, but continued to work at home for a few more years before he died. Dias lost his shop in a devastating fire that destroyed much of Honolulu's Chinatown that

same year. Manuel Nunes, the most prolific luthier of the three, continued building instruments for many years. He taught the art of ukulele making to numerous craftsmen, including his son Leonardo, who ran the Nunes factory in Los Angeles until 1930. Another of Manuel's apprentices, Samuel Kamaka, started his own one-man shop in 1916 (see section 1.4). Now, more than 100 years later, the Kamaka 'Ukulele and Guitar Works on South Street in Honolulu carries on the legacy of three Portuguese emigrants who forever changed Hawaiian music and gave the world the gift of the "jumping flea."

Early ukuleles often sported attractive labels or decals implying their Hawaiian origins, even when they weren't actually made in Hawaii.

A special "tabu" emblem trademarked in 1916 was created as a means to verify that any ukulele bearing the mark was actually made in Hawaii.

SIDEBAR: The Tabu Mark

As the first great surge of interest in the ukulele was sweeping across America, Hawaiian makers were faced with a dilemma: Some less-than-scrupulous mainland manufacturers were making cheap ukes and passing them off as if they were made in Hawaii. Such instruments often had attractive labels or decals implying their Hawaiian origins. In an attempt to stem the tide of fake Hawaiian ukes, the Honolulu Advertising Club trademarked a "Made in Hawaii" emblem in 1916. Their "tabu" trademark verified that the ukulele bearing it was actually made in Hawaii. The mark was typically stamped inside a uke's body, visible through its sound hole, or on the back of its headstock. The emblem featured a pair of crossed kapu sticks (traditional symbols of Hawaiian authority) under a crescent or "hoaka," a symbol closely associated with alii (Hawaiian royalty) surmounted by the Hawaiian crown. The tabu trademark was quickly adopted by M. Nunes & Sons as well as some of his competitors, including James Anahu and the Paradise Ukulele and Guitar Works. Despite the attempt to designate instruments as island made, the tabu mark was also used by Leonardo Nunes, who built his ukuleles in Los Angeles.

1.2 Manuel Nunes, Inventor of the Ukulele?

I wonder if Manuel Nunes had any clue of what lay ahead when he and his family boarded the British sailing ship Ravenscrag in 1879 and left their home in Madeira to journey to a small island in the middle of the Pacific? I doubt that neither he nor his shipmates Augusto Dias and Jose do Espirito Santo could have guessed that they would have a hand in the development of a brand new stringed musical instrument: the ukulele.

Like Dias and Santo, Nunes secured his journey by agreeing to work as a laborer on a Hawaiian sugar plantation. Nunes, who had been trained as a marceneiro (cabinetmaker), moved to Honolulu after fulfilling his labor contract and set up shop in the city's worst slum, where rents were low and crime was high. To make ends meet, Nunes built furniture and cabinets,

A portrait of Manuel Nunes in his later years.

repaired instruments and sold used instruments and supplies (strings, pegs, etc.). He also built some new instruments, including guitars and traditional Portuguese machetes and rajãos. Nunes announced his business as a "cabinetmaker's shop of stringed instruments, guitars and machêtes." By 1889, Nunes was listed in Honolulu's city directory as a "guitar maker" and, along with Dias and Santo, was one of the first persons to build stringed instruments of any kind in Hawaii.

By the time Manuel and sons Leonardo and Julius formed M. Nunes & Sons in 1909, Santo had died an untimely death from blood poisoning and Dias had retired due to tuberculosis. Although no photos exist of the Nunes business, its likely to have been a relatively small workshop with few machines, were ukes were built one at a time by a small number of craftsmen. In addition to selling locally, the majority of Nunes instruments were sold through the Southern California Music Company in Los Angeles.

Most Nunes' ukes bear the headstock decal "M. Nunes Inventor 1879" as well as a paper label inside

LEFT: Two ukuleles built by members of the Nunes family: The one at right was made by family patriarch Manuel Nunes, while the uke at left was made by his son Julius.

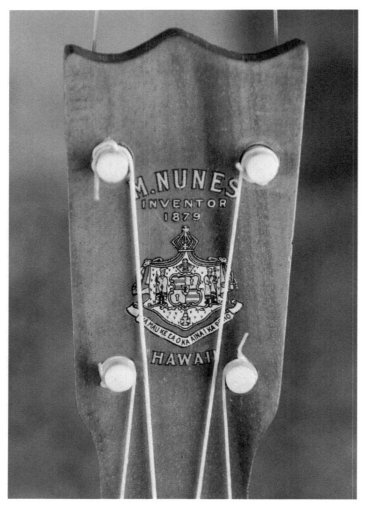

The headstock of this M. Nunes ukulele claims Manuel as the "inventor" of the ukulele in 1879.

This newspaper ad for M. Nunes and Sons ukuleles, taro-patch fiddles and steel guitars was created by the Southern California Music Company, which sold Nunes ukes by mail order.

that body proclaiming "M. Nunes & Sons Inventor of the Ukulele and Taro Patch Fiddles in Honolulu in 1879." While Nunes' claim is doubtful—modern scholars say that's it's much more likely that Nunes, Dias and Santos all contributed to the adaptation of traditional Portuguese instruments into what became the Hawaiian ukulele—it's clear that Nunes staged the most successful marketing campaign: A 1909 Hawaiian newspaper ad stated that "The inventor of the ukulele is M. Nunes, and he had been making ukuleles for the trade almost continuously since he invented it in 1879." In a Honolulu business directory, M. Nunes and Sons listed themselves as "Manufacturers of the only genuine ukulele, Hawaii's sweetest toned instrument." Even Manuel's daughter Angeline stated in a 1915 Ukulele Method book that her father was "the first to use Hawaiian wood in its (the uke's) construction."

Little is known about the full range of instruments that M. Nunes & Sons built, but from existing examples we know that they built koa wood soprano ukes and taro patches (8-string ukes) in several styles, including style 1 (rope soundhole rosette, no bindings, as shown here), style 2 (rope binding on top & sound

The body of this koa wood style 3 Nunes taro-patch ukulele features rope binding and a "parend" moustache-like inlay.

hole rosette) and style 3, which was the same as the style 2, but with a "parend," A.K.A moustache inlay. Construction of Nunes ukes was very similar to his contemporary rivals: bodies were constructed from very thin (5/64 in. thick) koa, with the back braced to form a slight arch; a traditional method for adding strength to a relatively fragile instrument. Metal frets set were directly into the neck—no applied fretboards were used. The majority of Nunes ukes came with violin-style friction tuning pegs made of white plastic.

Manuel's son Leonardo left the family business around 1913 and moved to Los Angeles where he set up his own ukulele building business, producing "Ukulele O Hawaii" brand instruments for a number of Californian music shops (and possibly for Gretsch as well; see section 2.3). This included the Southern California Music Company where, curiously, his ukes sold in direct competition with his fathers! Leonardo produced primarily soprano ukes in several styles, but also built taro patches, tiples, concert-scale "minis" and a 6-string ukulele variant called a "Lili'u." In 1925-26 Leonardo trademarked a new line of "Radio Tenor" ukuleles, which included both 4-string and 8-string models. Of all the Nunes family instruments, these concert-scale instruments are highly coveted for their playability and superior tone.

RIGHT: Sometime after Manuel's son Leonardo Nunes left the family business, he built this "Radio Tenor" model ukulele at his shop in Los Angeles.

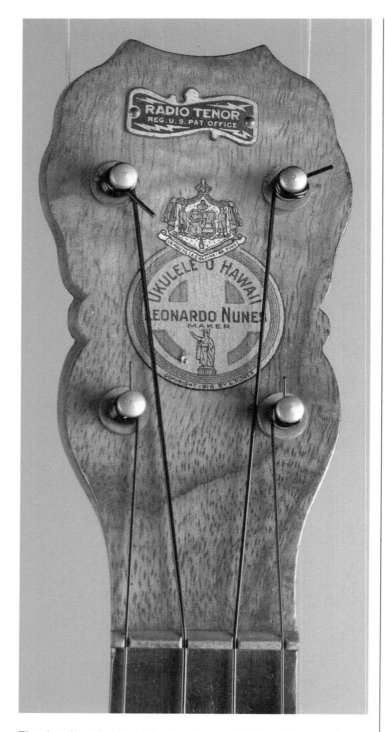

The decal on the headstock of Leonardo Nunes' Radio Tenor ukulele includes the brand name "Ukulele O Hawaii," which he copyrighted in 1916.

Manuel Nune's gravestone, proclaiming him as the inventor of the ukulele.

As the demand for ukuleles rose on both the islands and in the mainland, second son Julius did a brief stint as an independent ukulele builder, producing instruments simply labeled "Nunes" (the uke at right on pg. 17) In 1915, 72-year-old papa Manuel handed over the reins of the business to Julius who served as general manager of the family company. Manuel retired just 2 years later and died in 1922 from heart failure. Al-though M. Nunes & Sons had been the most successful of the original trio of ukulele builders, they went out of business in 1918; unfortunate timing, as the first big ukulele craze was just sweeping across the mainland. Leonardo's company continued building instruments until it ceased operations sometime in the 1930s.

Manuel Nunes may not have single-handedly invented the ukulele, but his legacy is written in stone in at least one location: "Inventor of the Ukulele" is engraved on his granite headstone at the King Street cemetery in Honolulu.

A circa 1920s photograph of Jonah Kumalae, his wife and eight children standing in front of their stately home in Honolulu.

1.3 The Prolific Jonah Kumalae

When I was doing the research for this book, I had a lot of questions about Kumalae ukuleles: When and where were they made, what models they produced, etc. But after learning more about the man who created the company that bore his name, I was left wondering if Jonah Kumalae ever slept! Not only was he a luthier and businessman who founded one of the most prolific uke manufacturing companies in the islands, but he was also a family man with eight children a talented musician, publisher of a democratic newspaper, and a politician who served at various times as Hawaii's Food Commissioner, director of the Hawaii Land Company, and as a member of Hawaii's Territorial Legislature. He even ran for Mayor of Honolulu in 1923.

Little is known of Jonah Kumalae's early life, except that he worked for a time as a school teacher and as a farmer and poi manufacturer. Although Kumalae may have started building ukuleles as early as 1895 (how he got into lutherie is anybody's guess), his company didn't become prolific until the early 1910s, when they began mass producing anywhere from 300 to 600 ukuleles per month. Working out of a 20,000 square foot

RIGHT: Two koa wood ukuleles made by Jonah Kumalae stand upright in this photo, the one at right being the fancier model with rope-style binding around the top of its body.

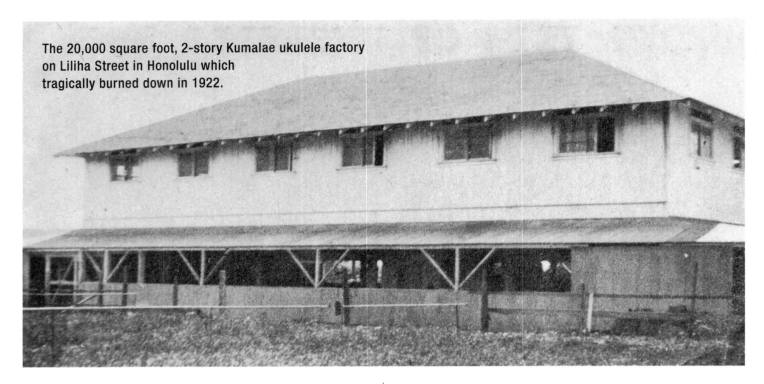

The 20,000 square foot, 2-story Kumalae ukulele factory on Liliha Street in Honolulu which tragically burned down in 1922.

2-story factory building on Liliha Street in Honolulu, all the ukuleles and taro patches (8-string ukes) Kumalae built were made of koa wood sourced from trees logged on the Big Island of Hawaii.

The first big windfall for Jonah Kumalae's ukulele business came in 1915, when he won a bid to display ukuleles in the Hawaiian Building at the Panama-Pacific International Exposition in San Francisco. His ukes won Kumalae a Gold Award, which he touted on the decals adorning the headstocks of all instruments he subsequently produced. The public's exposure to Hawaiian music at the Exposition not only helped

This hand-colored postcard shows the Hawaiian Building at the 1915 Pan Pacific International Expo in San Francisco where Kumalae first presented his ukuleles on the mainland.

All Kumalae ukuleles built after 1915 have a headstock decals that proclaims the company's gold medal won at the Pan Pacific International Expo.

models featured rope binding around both tops and sound holes (the uke at right on page 21). The style 25 also had rope-style wood stripes down the center and edges of the fingerboard. It's unclear what models of taro patch they produced as these are exceedingly rare; I've never even seen a photo of one. There's also evidence that Kumalae made a small number of banjo ukes and mini sized "sopranino" ukuleles.

Like most Hawaiian ukes made during this period, the bodies of Kumalae's ukuleles were egg-shell thin and had a slightly arched back. Because they were individually hand-made, no two bodies are exactly alike. Metal frets were set directly into the necks; no applied fingerboards. All instruments were finished in French polished shellac. Friction wood pegs came standard, but celluloid or mechanical tuners could be fitted for an additional cost.

Unfortunately, Kumalae experienced a devastating setback in October of 1922 when a fire destroyed the Liliha Street factory, burning up more than four thousand instruments and causing at least $10K in damage. But thanks to Jonah's tenacity, Kumalae regrouped and resumed ukulele production, being one the few uke manufacturers who stayed in business during the Great Depression which spanned most of the 1930s. It was only after Jonah's death in 1940 that his ukulele company closed its doors.

boost the popularity of the uke in America, but enabled Kumalae to do a brisk business selling instruments labeled "Ukulele o Hawaii," an odd choice since Leonardo Nunes also built ukes with the same brand name. Kumalae's Mainland dealers included Lyon & Healy, Oliver Ditson, C. Bruno & Son, the Bergstrom Music Company and Sherman, Clay & Co..

Back in the islands, Kumalae ukuleles were sold at local tourist shops and hotels, including the Royal Hawaiian Hotel on Waikiki beach in Honolulu. It's also believed that Kumalae ukes were given to first-class passengers aboard steam ships bound for the Hawaii islands in the 1920s.

At their peak, Kumalae was producing six different models of soprano-sized ukuleles, numbered 20 through 25 (sometimes numbered as styles 0 – 5). Their cheapest model was the Style 20 uke with a body made from plain, straight-grained koa and just one narrow ring inlaid around the sound hole. More expensive models were made from more attractive figured koa and sported fancier appointments: Their top

The paper label inside a Kumalae ukulele showing the brand name "Ukulele o Hawaii."

The two pineapple ukes at center and left are Kamakas, while the uke at right was made by Kamaka for the Aloha Mfg. Co.

1.4 The Kamaka Pineapple

Several decades ago, I bought my first Kamaka ukulele (the one at far left in the photo above). Featuring some really cool artwork its owner added, it was, and still is, a great playing and sounding instrument. But when my mother saw it, she asked me why it was shaped like a canned ham? Of course, I explained that it was actually shaped like a pineapple. Little did I know at the time of how this uke body shape came about, or how it was significant to the success of Kamaka.

It all began more than a century ago, when Samuel Kaialiilii Kamaka (Senior) started a one-man shop in the basement of his Kaimuki, Hawaii home. Kamaka learned his trade when he was apprenticed to luthier

Manuel Nunes in the early 1910s. Nunes was one of the original creators and builders of ukuleles as uniquely Hawaiian instruments. In 1916, Sam Sr. opened the "Kamaka Ukulele and Guitar Works" on South Street in Honolulu where he produced high-quality guitars and ukuleles made primarily from beautiful native koa wood.

After building ukes with traditional Spanish "figure eight" shaped bodies for many years, sometime around 1927, Sam Kamaka experimented with a new body shape, one which he hoped would produce a more mellow sound. Friends remarked that his new oval-shaped ukulele looked like a pineapple, so Sam commissioned one of his artist friends to paint the instrument to resemble the fruit (pineapple plantations abounded on the island of Oahu). Legend maintains that only the

THE ART OF VINTAGE UKULELES • SANDOR NAGYSZALANCZY

A vintage photo of Sam Kamaka senior in his workshop holding one of his hand-painted pineapple ukes.

As a bonus, they were also somewhat easier to manufacture than traditional figure-eight-shape ukes. Recognizing the value of his creation, Sam Sr. applied for a U.S. design patent, which he was granted in 1928 (see pg. 191 in Section 5.1). At a time when competition was high due to the uke's ever increasing popularity, the patent gave Kamaka an edge, as his was the only company allowed to produce pineapple ukes; by the time his patent ran out in 1940, Kamaka was the only Hawaiian ukulele maker still in business.

All early Kamaka pineapple ukes were constructed with one-piece koa tops and backs, two-piece bent sides and koa necks with frets set directly into them; no applied finger boards. The non-painted ukes received a large pineapple decal on the top between the sound hole and bridge. A blue "Kamaka Special Pineapple" label inside the body visible through the sound hole has Kamaka's patent and "strictly hand made by S. K. Kamaka" printed on them. Each label also shows an individual serial number hand written at the bottom. Pineapple headstock decals typically featured the Hawaiian coat of arms and state motto: "Ua Mau Ke Ea O Ka Aina I Ka Pono." (The life of the land is perpetuated in righteousness), although some uke headstocks, such as the one shown on page 27, have a decal with a smaller pineapple below the Kamaka name.

Kamaka's pineapples came in several styles, the fanciest of which had rope binding and mother of pearl purfling around the top of the body, sound hole and along the edges of the fingerboard. The majority of vintage pineapples feature the same rope bindings sans the pearl, sometimes with a rope stripe down the center of

first 50 pineapple ukes were hand painted, some only on the front, some only on the back, making these special ukes some of the rarest and most desirable of all Kamaka ukuleles.

Not only did Kamaka's pineapple ukes have distinctive looks, but they had a fuller, more resonant sound.

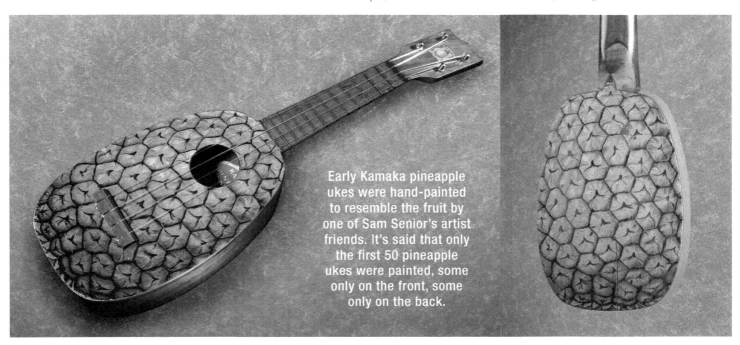

Early Kamaka pineapple ukes were hand-painted to resemble the fruit by one of Sam Senior's artist friends. It's said that only the first 50 pineapple ukes were painted, some only on the front, some only on the back.

The ladies in this Hawaiian ukulele ensemble are all playing Kamaka pineapple ukes in this circa 1930s photo.

the fingerboard. Kamaka also produced an unknown number of Pineapple ukes for the Aloha Manufacturing Company. These have an Aloha decal on the headstock that says "Souvenir of Hawaii" (see the uke at far right in the photo on page 20.

In the 1930s, Kamaka did a run of pineapple ukes made from Philippine mahogany stained in a reddish color. These had the same Hawaiian coat of arms Kamaka as earlier pineapples, but had a yellow label inside. In the late 1930s, Sam Kamaka gave his friend and fellow uke builder Johnny Lai permission to build pineapple ukes, allowing him to work at the Kamaka factory when it was closed evenings and weekends. Lai built his pineapples from monkeypod wood, which was less expensive than koa. Initially, he used the name "Ka-Lai," combining "Kamaka" and "Lai," but later changed it to "Ka-Lae" as he thought it sounded more Hawaiian.

During the Korean War (1950-1953), Sam Sr.'s son Frederick carried a pineapple uke made by his father while serving in the U.S. Army. Fredrick said the uke symbolized home for him, and gave him hope amidst

LEFT: Pre-1950s non-painted ukes have a large pineapple decal on the top and a blue "Kamaka Special Pineapple" label inside the body.

THE ART OF VINTAGE UKULELES • SANDOR NAGYSZALANCZY

the chaos and uncertainty of war.

Starting around 1950, Kamaka pineapples were built with plastic tortoise shell bindings around the top of their koa bodies and were fitted with rosewood bridges and extended fingerboards. These have a gold Kamaka label inside the body, and a gold double "K" decal on the headstock. The top of the example shown below, was decorated by its owner who used colored ball-point pens to draw hibiscus flowers and a Hawaiian chief (ali'i) as well as the words "My Beautiful Hawaii."

Kamaka is still building pineapple ukes today, as well as many other shapes and styles of ukuleles. The company is still family owned and run, following sensible advice once given by Sam Sr. to his sons: "If you make instruments and use the family name, don't make junk."

This vintage Kamaka pineapple uke has a fancy rope-bound fingerboard and center stripe.

Fifties-era Kamaka pineapple ukes feature fake tortoise shell body bindings and rosewood fingerboards. This example was hand decorated by its owner.

Honolulu luthier David Mahelona's signature violin uke with a body shape that's based on a traditional violin.

1.5 David Mahelona Violin Uke

Some of the most magnificent vintage ukuleles to come out of the Hawaiian Islands are the violin ukes made by luthier David Mahelona in the 1920s and/or 30s. There are few other ukuleles that can compare, in terms of unique appearance, collectability, and even tone.

To say that these violin ukes are rare is an understatement; only a handful are known to exist. Appropriately enough, one example is in the collection of the Bernice Pauahi Bishop Museum in Honolulu, Hawaii's premier natural and cultural history museum.

Relatively little is known about David Mahelona, the craftsman whose signature instruments were violin-shaped soprano ukuleles. I've read (but not been able to confirm) that Mahelona was born in Hawaii in 1899 and that he worked as a manager for prolific ukulele maker Jonah Kumalae prior to setting up on his own shop in the 1920's. It has also been postulated that Mahelona made a violin uke for "Merrie Monarch" David Kalākaua, the last Hawaiian King. But as Kalakaua died in 1891, this is virtually impossible.

One thing we definitely know about David Mahelona is that he was one heck of a good ukulele craftsman. The build quality of the violin uke he built, shown here, is stellar. It's body and neck are made entirely from Hawaiian koa wood. Grain figure wise, the wood is relatively plain, but still lends the uke a rich sound even 100+ years after it was made. The body is a sort of hybrid of a regular soprano uke and a traditional violin, with the violin's characteristic hour-glass

Rope binding and pearl purfling surround the top of the violin uke's characteristic hour-glass shaped body.

The uke's thin koa back is slightly arched, with a small protrusion that extends over the neck's heel.

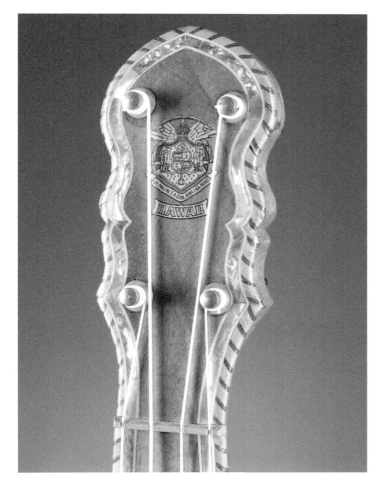

Rope binding and pearl also surround the violin uke's fingerboard and shapely headstock.

The uke's headstock decal features the coat of arms of the Kingdom of Hawaii.

Another example of Mahelona's violin ukes, this one with an extended fingerboard and a fancy scalloped parend pearl inlay.

shape. Unlike a violin, the top of this uke is flat, but like other early Hawaiian ukes, the back of the uke is slightly convex. The top end of the back runs over the end of the neck's heel, and the uke's frets are set directly into the neck—no separate fingerboard. Both of these features are also commonly found on vintage Hawaiian ukuleles.

Decoration wise, this is definitely one of the fanciest ukes I've ever seen. The entire top, neck and headstock are rimmed with an attractive rope-style binding and flashy mother-of-pearl purfling. Pearl was also used for the uke's sound hole rosette and fret marker dots. The uke's uniquely shaped headstock bears a decal showing the coat of arms of the King-

dom of Hawaii above the words "ua mau ke ea o ka aina i ka pono" which is most commonly translated as "The life of the land is perpetuated in righteousness." The "chess piece" style Bakelite tuners on this violin uke are not original.

The other Mahelona violin ukes still in existence show some variations to the one seen here. The one in the Bishop Museum's collection is very similar to this one, but has a body made from fancier koa wood. The fanciest example I've seen, which is part of Shawn Yacavone's museum collection, is not only made from highly figured koa, but features an extended fingerboard as well as a fancy scalloped parend (AKA "moustache") pearl inlay at the base of the body.

1.6 Echo Uke: A Hawaiian Oddball

To the untrained eye, vintage Hawaiian ukuleles look fairly alike: Practically all of them are soprano sized and most have thin-waisted, Spanish-guitar-shaped bodies and are made of koa wood. They differ primarily in their headstock shapes and decorative elements, (rosettes, purflings, etc.).

Echo brand ukuleles look just like other 1920's era Hawaiian ukes, but some of their instruments have a small and rather curious difference: On the underside of the top, directly beneath the bridge, there's a small block of wood holding two thin metal prongs, each bent into a shape that's like the handlebars of a bike (see the photo below). These prongs are designed to respond to the vibration of the soundboard when the uke is played and resonate, sort of like the sympathetic strings on an Indian sitar, thus producing an "echo-ey" sound.

Unfortunately, the vibrating prongs don't actually create any sort of sound you can hear, even if you put your ear right up to the sound hole. Despite its lack of performance, the echo device was supposedly patented, as claimed on labels found inside some Echo ukes—not all of them featured the device (I say "supposedly" because I'm not sure anyone has ever seen the actual patent). One build feature that does contribute to the sound of an Echo uke is its greater body depth, which, at 2 3/4 inches, gives these ukes a fuller and slightly louder sound than most other Hawaiian ukuleles I've played (see the bottom photo on page 32).

Echo ukes were made by the Hawaiian Mahogany Company (HMC), which started in 1921 as a timber business that cut, milled and sold koa, ohia, and other hardwood lumber (Hawaiian mahogany was then a commonly used name for koa wood). HMC also ran workshops that used the lumber for manufacturing furniture, flooring, souvenir curios—and Echo brand ukuleles. The company's principal owner was the Honolulu-based C.Q. Yee Hop & Co., Ltd., primarily a food business that owned supermarkets, a brewery, and a large cattle operation on Hawaii's Big Island. In the mid 1920's, Yee Hop expanded HMC's operations by

LEFT ABOVE: Echo ukes made by the Hawaiian Mahogany Company came in several models, ranging from the plainest (right) to the fanciest (left) which featured multi-colored wood purfling, rosette and center stripe.

LEFT BELOW: A small mirror placed inside the uke reveals the pronged "echo device" on the underside of the top.

A bright yellow paper label inside the body identifies this ukulele as an Echo with a "patented" Echo device.

building a sawmill in Kona to process trees cut from the local hardwood forests. The operation not only yielded valuable koa lumber for HMC's manufacturing endeavors, but also created more open grazing land that helped Yee Hop's beef business thrive.

HMC Echo ukes came in several models, ranging from the plainest which sported three narrow sound hole rings (the right-hand uke in the top photo on page 31), to models with rope binding and extended fretboards. Their fanciest model, shown at left in the photo on pg. 31, featured multi-colored wood purfling around the top and sound hole, as well as a stripe running down the center of the fingerboard.

Many vintage Hawaiian ukes didn't feature the name of their actual manufacturer and often, the same instrument made by the same company was sold under different brand names. HMC's Echo ukes sold in Hawaii were sometimes branded as "Pele," while Echos sold on the mainland were often re-branded by music retailers: San Francisco dealer Jules M. Sahlein sold them under his trademarked "Y'Ke Ke" brand name, while Schireson Brothers of Los Angeles offered them as "Mai Kai" ukuleles.

In 1929, HMC reincorporated as C.Q. Yee Hop

The Echo ukulele, at left, has a deeper body than a typical Hawaiian uke (right). The deeper body gives Echo ukes a pleasing tone and greater volume.

This period photo shows the rather disorganized interior of the Hawaiian Mahogany Company factory where Echo ukes were built.

& Co. and expanded their instrument line to include "Malolo" and "Royal Hawaiian" ukuleles. These were produced for The Matson Shipping Co., as Yee Hop was a shareholder in Matson, and Matson a shareholder in Waikiki's Royal Hawaiian Hotel which opened in 1927. It's rumored that Matson gave these ukes away to some first class passengers aboard their cruise liners. Their flagship, S.S. Malolo, was the first luxury steamship to transport paradise-seeking tourists from the U.S. mainland to Honolulu.

San Francisco dealer Jules M. Sahlein sold Echo ukes under his own trademarked "Y'Ke Ke" brand name.

The Hawaiian Mahogany Company, reincorporated as C.Q. Yee Hop & Co. in 1929, expanded their instrument line to include "Malolo" (top) and "Royal Hawaiian" (bottom) ukuleles.

Chapter Two
The Mainland Gets into the Act

Ukes built on the U.S. mainland by (left to right): Martin, Lyon & Healy, Gibson and Harmony.

By the time the first big ukulele craze got underway in the late 1910s and early 1920s, Hawaii wasn't the only place that ukuleles were being produced in large numbers. Big-time musical instrument manufacturers including Martin, Gibson, Lyon & Healy, Harmony and Regal got into the ukulele game as soon as they realized the huge monetary potential of that small four-stringed instrument. Most of these manufacturers staked their share building instruments including guitars, mandolins and banjos during the periods of their popularity. But as public interest in those instruments waned in the first couple of decades of the 20th century, the popularity of the ukulele increased almost exponentially. This new craze was fueled, at least in part, by the introduction of Hawaiian music at the 1915 San Francisco Pan Pacific Exhibition and in Broadway's "Bird of Paradise" musical play, as well as uke's frequent appearance on vaudeville stages across the country. In the case of companies like Martin, who had previously anchored their success by producing only one or two types of instruments (prior to 1916, Martin built mostly guitars and some mandolins), making ukuleles became essential to maintaining their livelihood.

This chapter focuses on eight mainland companies that were building ukes in the early 20th century. In reality, there were dozens of ukulele producers in the continental U.S., including Oscar Schmidt, Favilla,

THE ART OF VINTAGE UKULELES • SANDOR NAGYSZALANCZY

Among the many musical instrument companies that built ukuleles in the early 1900s were (left to right): S.S. Stewart, B&J (Buegeleisen and Jacobson), Oscar Schmidt and Favilla.

Like many other companies, Oscar Schmidt not only built ukuleles under their own brand (the lower uke), but also produced similar models for other companies, in this case Wurlitzer (the upper uke).

THE ART OF VINTAGE UKULELES • SANDOR NAGYSZALANCZY

S.S. Stewart, and Buegeleisen and Jacobson (B&J), to name but a few. Some of these, such as the Schireson Brothers (makers of Hollywood brand ukes; see Section 2.5), produced ukuleles in relatively small numbers. Others, including Harmony and Regal, cranked out inexpensive ukuleles by the hundreds of thousands, thus helping to increase the instrument's popularity by putting affordable ukes in the hands of the general public.

One rather frustrating aspect of discussing vintage ukuleles is that it can be quite difficult to keep track of who made what and when. This is because instrument companies typically produced many different brands of ukuleles, often ordered by wholesalers who sold them to music stores. Subsequently, ukes with the same brand name may, over time, have been produced by two or more different manufacturers. For example, the Wurlitzer-branded soprano was actually produced by Oscar Schmidt, who had their own fancier version of the same uke. The unique looking "peanut" uke, invented and initially manufactured by Nichola Turturro (see Section 5.4), was later produced by S. S. Stewart and Regal's "Mapeliene" line of stenciled ukes were also sold under the Sterling and Norwood brands.

2.1 C.F. Martin: The Uke's Gold Standard

If there's a single company in the continental United States that set the gold standard for quality ukuleles, it's certainly C.F. Martin & Company of Nazareth Pennsylvania. Not only were they the first American company to manufacturer and sell ukes beginning in 1917, when Hawaii was still just a US territory, but, arguably, they've produced more high-quality instruments in the last 100 years than any other mainland producer.

In the first 75 years after their founding in 1833 by German immigrant Christian Frederick Martin Sr., the company produced flat-top guitars, adding mandolins to the line in 1895. Around 1907, James W. Bergstrom, a music retailer with a store on Fort Street in Honolulu that sold Martin guitars, introduced Frank Henry Martin (C.F. Sr.'s son who took over the company in 1880) to a relatively-new Hawaiian instrument: the ukulele. Evidently, Bergstrom placed an order for six ukes, which Frank Henry built in similar fashion to Martin guitars, fitting them with spruce tops and, likely, mahogany bodies and necks. Unfor-

An assortment of different ukulele models and sizes, all built by C.F. Martin in Nazareth Pennsylvania.

Early Martin soprano ukes came in three styles (left to right): Style 1, Style 2 and Style 3, all made of mahogany.

tunately, these first sample instruments didn't produce the right "Hawaiian-ish" tone that Bergstrom expected. Plus, at $6.50 each (the equivalent of $217 in 2023 dollars), they were too expensive compared to the Hawaiian-made ukes Bergstrom carried. Unfortunately, no one knows what became of these first six Martin ukuleles, and some consider these to be the "holy grail" of vintage ukuleles.

Flash forward nine years: The Hawaiian music craze was spreading like wildfire across America and the demand for ukuleles was growing exponentially. In response, F.H. Martin began building ukuleles in earnest in 1916, initially to supply their New York dealers. By 1917, the first year that Martin listed ukuleles in their catalog, they had developed three models that became mainstays in Martin's line: Style 1, Style 2 and Style 3. Each model was available as a four-string soprano-sized instrument or as an 8-string concert-sized "taropatch" model (see the sidebar page 46) . All of these early instruments had bodies and necks made from mahogany,

RIGHT: Martin produced ukuleles for other companies, including this Style 0 soprano for Chas. H. Ditson of New York.

which gave them the right sound. All three styles were fitted with violin-like ebony tuning pegs. Early Style 3 ukes have a kite-shaped ivoroid inlay on the headstock.

In addition to standard Martin-branded instruments, they also produced lines of so-called "customer" ukuleles for various music stores and other instrument companies, including Wurlitzer. One of these customers was Chas. H. Ditson, who had one of New York City's largest music stores. Martin's Ditson-branded ukes came in the same styles with the same features as regular Martin ukes, but had wider waisted bodies, making them look somewhat like small dreadnought style guitars (the dreadnought guitar body was developed by F.H. Martin). Wizard of the Strings Roy Smeck owed and played a Ditson Style 5 uke, which you can see at the bottom of the upper left photo on pg. 182.

By 1919, Martin expanded their ukuleles offerings with new models featuring bodies made of Hawaiian koa wood. These were distinguished from regular mahogany ukes by a "K" added to their model numbers: Style 1K, Style 2K, and Style 3K. Martin also began building tiples for New York's William J. Smith Co. The tiple (pronounced "TEE-play") is a 10-string instrument of Spanish origin that was quite popular with ukulele players in the 1920s through the 1940s. It is close in length to a tenor ukulele, but with a deeper body which gave it greater volume than regular ukes.

As Martin's ukulele production and sales continued to soar through the 1920s, they continued to introduce new models: The intro-level mahogany-only Style

A pair of Style 3 Martin ukes, with a koa Style 3K on the left and a mahogany Style 3M on the right.

Besides ukuleles, Martin also produced tiples, 10-string instruments of Spanish origin, including the T28 model which features a spruce top and Indian rosewood back and sides.

The relatively plain Style 0 uke joined Martin's line of soprano ukuleles in 1922 as their most affordable ukulele.

Also joining Martin's uke line in 1922 was the top-of-the-line Style 5K. Built from highly figured koa wood and featuring extensive pearl and abalone inlays and bindings, it's one of the fancy ukes ever produced.

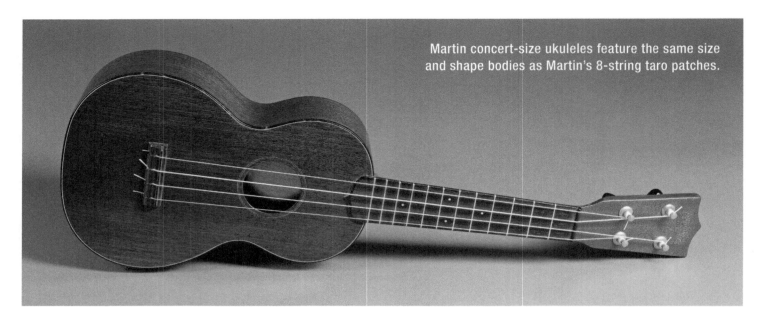

Martin concert-size ukuleles feature the same size and shape bodies as Martin's 8-string taro patches.

O and the koa-only top-of-the-line 5K in 1922; The concert-size four-string mahogany 1C in 1925; and the mahogany tenor-size 1T in 1928. The baritone B51 model wasn't added to the line until 1960.

Predictably, the higher the model number of a Martin ukulele, the fancier—and more expensive—it was. The lowly Style 0 has a simple mahogany body with no bindings at all, just a simple ring around the sound hole and three small marker dots on its 12-fret rosewood fretboard. Style 1 and 1K ukes feature a simple binding around the top, while Style 2 and 2K ukes have fancier celluloid bindings on both the top and back of the body. (Both Styles 1 and 2 also have rosewood fingerboards, most with fret marker dots at the 5th and 10th frets and a pair of dots at the 7th fret.) Style 3 and 3K Martin ukuleles are fancier still, with an elaborate 7-ply black and white celluloid binding around the top and sound hole, with a 3-ply version of the same binding around

With a mahogany body that's one size up from a concert uke, Martin's 1T model tenor joined the line in 1928.

THE ART OF VINTAGE UKULELES • SANDOR NAGYSZALANCZY

Martin's largest ukulele, the baritone B51 model was first produced in 1960. It looks huge compared to the Style 1 soprano next to it.

the back of the body. Style 3 fingerboards are made of ebony with large pearl fret position markers and (on most) a multi-ply celluloid center stripe. These fingerboards have 17 frets and extend over the body all the way to the sound hole. Most Style 3 ukes also had an inlaid celluloid "parend" ornament on the top at the bottom of the body. The top-of-the-line Martin 5K is one of the poshest ukuleles ever produced. Its body is made from highly-figured Hawaiian koa wood with celluloid binding and abalone pearl purfling around the top, back and sound hole. Its mahogany neck is topped with a 17-fret ivoroid-bound ebony extended fingerboard featuring fancy pearl inlays at the 3rd, 5th, 7th, 10th, 12th and 15th frets. The uke's koa-veneered headstock boasts a fanciful pearl arabesque scroll inlay. On the whole, the 5K is elegant and gorgeous; a piece of ukulele jewelry.

Far from staying constant, the specific features of Martin ukes were subject to substantial changes over their many years of production. For example, early Style 1 and 1K ukes featured bindings made from rosewood; in 1936 bindings were changed to celluloid tortoise shell. Fingerboards on Style 3 and 3K ukes had center stripes until around 1955, when they were eliminated; the parend inlay was discontinued in 1950. All styles saw changes in either the number and style of fingerboard dots, type of tuning pegs, style of the nut or bridge, headstock ornamentation and more. Even the Martin logo changed in the early 1930s from a stamp

The body binding and sound hole rosettes found on Martin ukes range from relatively plain to fancy. Shown here are (from left to right) Style 1, 2, 3 and 5K soprano ukuleles.

The bindings found on the backs of soprano ukes, ranging from (left to right) Styles 1, 2, 3 and 5K.

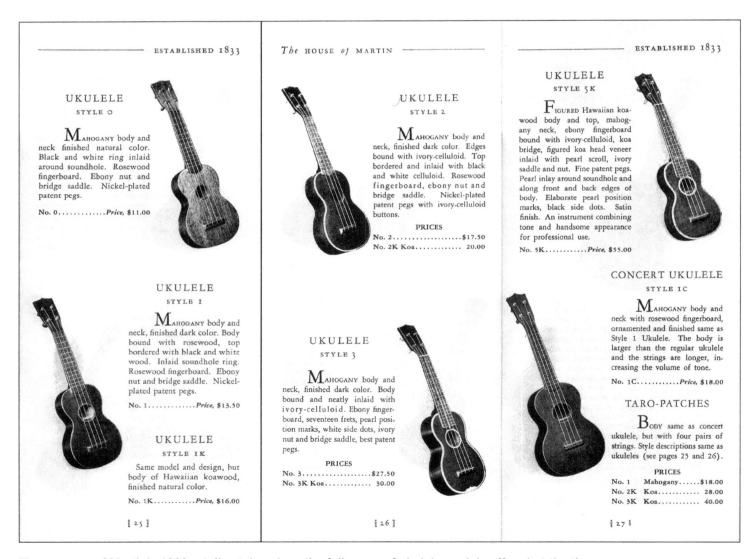

ESTABLISHED 1833

The HOUSE *of* MARTIN

ESTABLISHED 1833

UKULELE
STYLE O

Mahogany body and neck finished natural color. Black and white ring inlaid around soundhole. Rosewood fingerboard. Ebony nut and bridge saddle. Nickel-plated patent pegs.

No. 0............*Price, $11.00*

UKULELE
STYLE 1

Mahogany body and neck, finished dark color. Body bound with rosewood, top bordered with black and white wood. Inlaid soundhole ring. Rosewood fingerboard. Ebony nut and bridge saddle. Nickel-plated patent pegs.

No. 1............*Price, $13.50*

UKULELE
STYLE 1K

Same model and design, but body of Hawaiian koawood, finished natural color.

No. 1K............*Price, $16.00*

[25]

UKULELE
STYLE 2

Mahogany body and neck, finished dark color. Edges bound with ivory-celluloid. Top bordered and inlaid with black and white celluloid. Rosewood fingerboard, ebony nut and bridge saddle. Nickel-plated patent pegs with ivory-celluloid buttons.

PRICES

No. 2...................$17.50
No. 2K Koa............. 20.00

UKULELE
STYLE 3

Mahogany body and neck, finished dark color. Body bound and neatly inlaid with ivory-celluloid. Ebony fingerboard, seventeen frets, pearl position marks, white side dots, ivory nut and bridge saddle, best patent pegs.

PRICES

No. 3...................$27.50
No. 3K Koa............. 30.00

[26]

UKULELE
STYLE 5K

Figured Hawaiian koawood body and top, mahogany neck, ebony fingerboard bound with ivory-celluloid, koa bridge, figured koa head veneer inlaid with pearl scroll, ivory saddle and nut. Fine patent pegs. Pearl inlay around soundhole and along front and back edges of body. Elaborate pearl position marks, black side dots. Satin finish. An instrument combining tone and handsome appearance for professional use.

No. 5K............*Price, $55.00*

CONCERT UKULELE
STYLE 1C

Mahogany body and neck with rosewood fingerboard, ornamented and finished same as Style 1 Ukulele. The body is larger than the regular ukulele and the strings are longer, increasing the volume of tone.

No. 1C............*Price, $18.00*

TARO-PATCHES

Body same as concert ukulele, but with four pairs of strings. Style descriptions same as ukuleles (see pages 25 and 26).

PRICES

No. 1   Mahogany......$18.00
No. 2K   Koa........... 28.00
No. 3K   Koa........... 40.00

[27]

These pages of Martin's 1930 retail catalog show the full range of ukulele models offered at the time.

Style 3 Martin soprano ukes feature 7-ply black and white celluloid binding around the top and sound hole, an extended ebony fingerboard with a center stripe, and a celluloid "par-end" ornament inlay at the bottom of the body.

Martin reserved the most highly figured Hawaiian koa wood for their flagship Style 5k ukes.

on the back of the headstock to a decal on the front. As only a very few early Martin ukes were given serial numbers, production variations are the best indication we have of when a particular uke was manufactured.

Speaking of manufacturing, it's an oft-told tale of how ukuleles saved the Martin Guitar company. Between 1916 and 1926, Martin built fewer than 17,000 guitars…and nearly 57,000 ukes: more ukuleles than guitars built in the company's entire 93-year existence! Their peak uke-production years were 1925 and '26 during which they produced more than 25,000 soprano- and concert-size ukes and taropatches. To meet demand, Martin added a new two-story wing to their North Street factory building

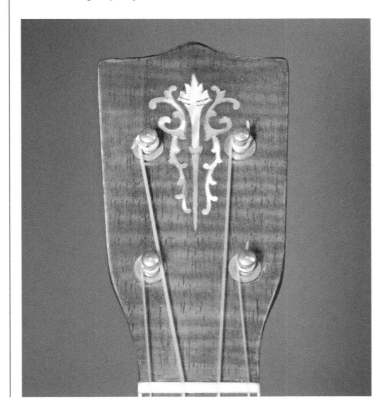

RIGHT: The Style 5K's koa-veneered headstock features a fancy pearl scroll inlay.

Martin's Style 3 soprano ukes underwent some changes sometime around 1955, losing its fingerboard center stripe, diamond fret markers and celluloid parend body inlay.

In the early 1930s, Martin changed its logo from a stamp on the back of the headstock to a decal on the front.

To help increase ukulele production, Martin added a two-story wing to their North Street factory in 1925.

in Nazareth, PA, which is sometimes referred to as "the house that ukes built." As ukulele sales decreased in the late 1920s, their building expansion gave them room to increase guitar production. That, and the profits garnered during the peak uke production years helped Martin get through the Great Depression of the 1930s, when so many instrument manufacturers went out of business. In 2018, that building was designated as a National Historic Landmark.

As uke sales dropped and guitar sales grew in the 1930s and 40s, Martin continued to build many styles of ukuleles. taropatches were discontinued around 1930, due to a drop in their popularity. As high-quality Hawaiian koa wood was in short supply in the late 1930s, Martin phased out koa ukes, including their flagship Style 5K (Martin did then produce a small number Style 5s with figured mahogany bodies). By the late 1940s, Martin offered just six models of mahogany ukuleles: four sopranos, one concert and one tenor. Despite a small revival of interest in the uke in the late 1940s and early 50s, by the time the guitar craze of the 1960s was in full swing, Martin was only producing relatively small numbers of ukuleles, mostly tenors and baritones. By 1977, Martin was only building ukes on special order. They officially discontinued making ukuleles in 1995, only to resume pro-

duction in 2006 starting with the re-release of their iconic Style 5k model. As of this writing, Martin is still manufacturing an extensive line of soprano, concert and tenor ukuleles.

RIGHT: By 1977, Martin was only building ukes on special order, which resulted in some less than conventional instruments, such as this Style 2 soprano which has a parend inlay normally only seen on pre-1955 Style 3 models.

SIDEBAR: The Taropatch Ukulele

An early ukulele cousin, the taro patch is an instrument with eight strings set in four courses of two strings each, tuned to the standard "my-dog-has-fleas." Taro patches evolved from the 5-string Portuguese Rajao, are a bit louder than regular soprano ukes due to their slightly larger body size, and offer a more sonorous sound, thanks to their doubled strings. Sometimes referred to as "taro patch fiddles" (though they look nothing like violins) the taro patch allegedly got its name from being played in taro fields by native Hawaiians. But scholars suggest that the term was more likely a derogatory slur coined by haoles (white Islanders), who viewed native workers as ignorant and lazy. Mark Twain, who visited the islands in 1866, once referred to indolent native Hawaiian State Legislature delegates as "taro patch members."

First produced in the Hawaiian Islands in the late 1800s, taro patches were soon being made on the mainland by legendary guitar manufacturer C.F. Martin & Co. Martin started building taro patches in August of 1916, mere months after the introduction of their first line of soprano ukuleles. Featuring mahogany bodies and necks, three models were initially offered: Style 1, Style 2 and Style 3, plain to fancy. Each had the same bindings & decorations as the same-style soprano ukulele. By 1919, taro patches appeared in Martin's instrument catalog right alongside other ukes. In 1924 the line expanded to include koa-bodied taro patches in styles 1K, 2K and 3K. The earliest koa wood taro patches sold for $.75 more than the same model in mahogany (koa only cost around $.30 a board foot back then). The Style 1 taro patch seen here was built circa 1918, this mahogany-bodied instrument features a 15-inch scale, rosewood fretboard and body bindings, and violin-style friction tuning pegs made of ebonized bulletwood.

Early stars of vaudeville and cinema often played Martin ukuleles, but few adopted the taro patch. One who did was screen legend Buster Keaton. In 1924, Keaton ordered a custom Style 3 taro patch complete with his name inlaid in pearl letters on the headstock. You can see and hear Keaton and uke virtuoso Cliff

RIGHT: Evolved from the 5-string Portuguese Rajao, Martin's taro patch ukuleles have a larger body size and offer a more sonorous sound, thanks to their doubled strings.

Edwards (AKA "Ukulele Ike") play this very instrument in the 1930 movie Doughboys. It's a most unorthodox duet: Keaton frets the chords as Edwards rhythmically taps the strings with a pair of drum sticks! (See the bottom photo on pg. 170.)

Even though Martin continued to promote and produce taro patches throughout the "uke crazed" 1920s, it remained the least popular of their ukulele line. This was likely because it took more time and trouble to tune the twice as many strings, and it cost about 25% more than a regular uke. Martin stopped making taro patches in 1930, but it remained available as a special order instrument until 1935.

Despite its demise, the taro patch fostered the birth of an instrument that's still popular today. Four-string taro patches were available on special order as early as 1919, but in 1925, Martin created a new model: the 1C "concert ukulele." This version mated the taro patch's scale length and larger-than-soprano-sized body with four strings and a narrower neck. Although it was only offered in Style 1, the public loved it and sales quickly grew. Martin's catalog described their concert uke as: "A large ukulele with a tone of great carrying power."

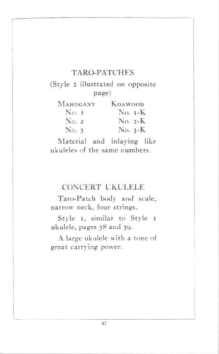

ABOVE LEFT: This circa-19-teens Martin taro patch uke features friction pegs made of ebonized bulletwood.

ABOVE RIGHT: The larger-than-soprano body of the taro patch was used to built Martin's concert-sized 4-string ukes.

LEFT: By 1924, Martin was producing six different taro patches models, including Styles 1, 2 and 3 in both mahogany and koa wood.

Gibson's fancy Uke-3 model has 5-ply bindings on top and 3-ply binding on the back, much like Martin's Style 3 sopranos.

2.2 Gibson Gets a Late Start

Unlike many of their competitors, the Gibson Company got a relative late start in the ukulele business: They'd been building mandolins and guitars since the company's founding in 1902, but didn't begin producing ukes until 1926-27 (with the exception of their banjo ukes), about a decade after the C.F. Martin Company had begun manufacturing ukuleles in earnest. Likely patterning their models after Martins, Gibson's first line of ukes included three styles of soprano and one tenor: The style "Uke-1" had no bindings, a marquetry sound hole rosette and dot fretboard markers at the 5th, 7th and 10th frets. The style "Uke-2" had 3-ply ivoroid bindings front and back, a marquetry

"Paderewski of the uke" performer Ray Canfield was an early endorsers of Gibson ukes.

Gibson's 1929 instrument catalog describes their three soprano models and one tenor model.

sound hole rosette and pearl dot fretboard markers at the 3rd, 5th, 7th and 10th frets. The first production style "Uke-3" (which was notably similar to Martin's Style 3 ukes) had 5-ply bindings on top (white-black-white-black-white) and 3-ply binding on the back, a multi-colored-wood marquetry sound hole rosette, an ivoroid-bound extended fretboard with fancy pearl inlays on the 3rd, 5th, 7th, 10th, 12th and 15th frets, and an inlayed pearl torch-like decoration on the headstock. The style "TU" tenor ukes (which they called "grand concert size") had the same appointments as Uke-2 sopranos, but with pin-style bridges. All models featured dark-stained mahogany bodies, bridges and necks, rosewood fretboards with nickel silver frets, high-quality "Patent" tuners with ivoroid buttons, and headstocks with "The Gibson" silk screened in silver ink. Unlike Martin, Gibson didn't produce any koa models, possibly because mahogany was less expensive and easier to source than Hawaiian koa wood.

By the late 1920s, Gibson's uke production was in full swing building instruments that were on par with other quality brands, including Martin and Lyon & Healy. Professional players of the period, including Vaudevillian Doc Morris and popular song composer Ray Canfield, called the "Paderewski of the uke" (see Section 4.2), were early endorsers of Gibson ukes. Both were known to perform on Style Uke-3 and custom soprano Gibsons. The introductory text in the ukulele section of Gibson's 1929 instrument catalog gleefully announced: "Like the Pipes of Pan, the Ukulele has drawn thousands of men, women, boys and girls into the land of musical joy and happiness." Gibson's price of happiness at that time was $10., $15. and $20 for styles 1, 2 and 3 soprano ukes respectively. Their TU tenor, referred to as "Grand Concert Size," sold for $30 (they later expanded the tenor line to include style 1 and style 3 models).

Despite the straight-forward style specifications of the ukes described in Gibson's catalogs, numerous feature changes occurred to each model as ukulele production continued in the 1930s and 40. One of the only consistent changes was that the headstock

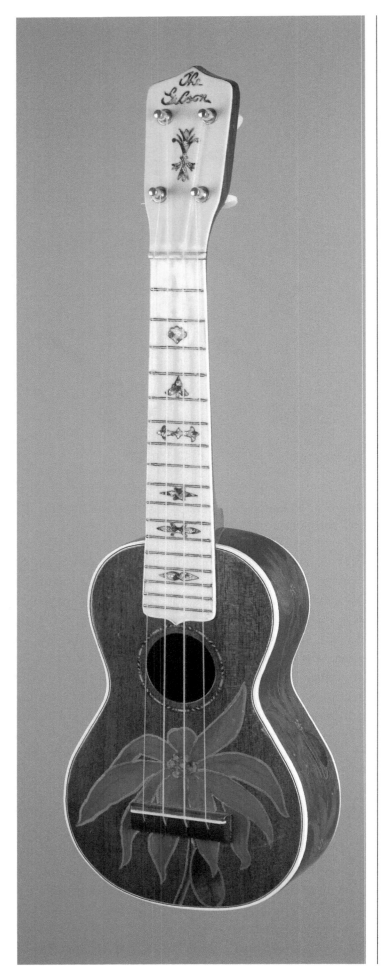

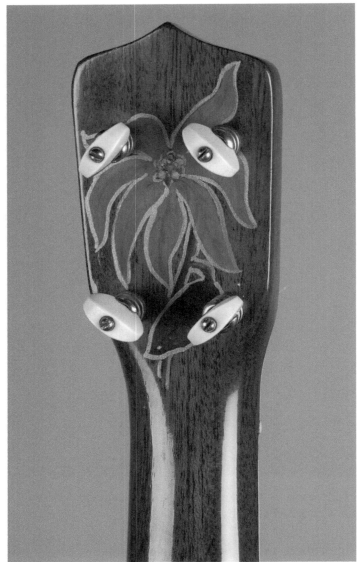

LEFT: The Gibson custom Poinsettia model features hand-painted poinsettia flowers on the top, back and sides of its mahogany body.

ABOVE: Even the back of the Poinsettia model's headstock sports a painted flower.

logo "The Gibson" was changed after 1937 to simply read "Gibson." Beyond that, there's practically no end to the number of variations for each style of Gibson uke that was built. While Martin made relatively minor feature changes to their various uke models over many decades, Gibson seemed to change model specifications almost randomly. This may be due to the fact that Gibson typically built ukes in small batches at a time, as well as readily building custom ukes to order. According to Australian ukulele Guru Chuck Fayne: "Regardless of what anyone—including Gibson—says, they made whatever they felt like making, including a ton of custom instruments." Among

ABOVE: The Poinsettia's ivo-roid-plastic-overlayed neck and headstock feature decorative inlays done in multi-colored pearloid.

RIGHT: Extensive pearloid, sparkly inlays and rhinestones applied to the uke's fretboards, headstocks and bodies are hallmarks of Gibson's highly ornate "Florentine" ukes produced on special order.

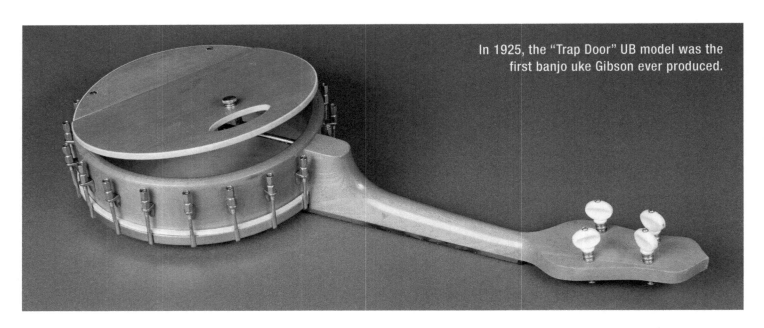

In 1925, the "Trap Door" UB model was the first banjo uke Gibson ever produced.

STYLE UB-4

STYLE UB-3

STYLE UB-5
The highest peak of Uku-lele-Banjo construction. Of black walnut with profes-sional resonator. All metal parts gold plated. 8 inch rim.

STYLE UB-4
Same as UB-5 but all metal parts highly nickeled and polished.

STYLE UB-3
Finished in deep, rich brown walnut with sun-burst effect on the exclusive Gibson resonating back. 8 inch rim. Absolutely accurate, a very exceptional instrument.

STYLE UB-2
Same as UB-3 but without some of the re-finements in finish. A very popular model.

STYLE UB-2

STYLE UB-1

STYLE UB-1
Priced within reach of every purse—yet meas-uring up to every Gib-son standard. 6 inch rim. Finished in light natural mahogany.

You'll be proud to play a

Gibson

EASILY mastered — yet capable of the truest musical interpretation—you need never have a dull moment when you play a GIBSON Ukulele-Banjo. They are the friendly, companionable instruments of modern music, making it possible for everyone to assert in some measure that natural craving for musical expression.

The key to unlimited good times for the player. Rich harmony... sweet melody... fun... joy... laughter—all are yours with the GIBSON.

Wherever you are—at home—at parties or on the beach you can liven things up with one of these snappy, jazzy, yet mellow voiced GIBSONS. You will never be lonesome—even when alone.

Whether artist or amateur you will find the GIBSON Ukulele-Banjo a source of pride and keen musical delight. Low priced—within the reach of all—but built with true GIBSON precision throughout.

In the mid 1920s, Gibson expanded its line of banjo ukes to include five models, ranging from the plain UB-1 to the very fancy UB-5.

THE ART OF VINTAGE UKULELES • SANDOR NAGYSZALANCZY

The Gibson UB-3 banjo uke features the same fretboard and headstock inlays as their style Uke-3 soprano uke.

those was a highly decorative custom model known as the "Poinsettia." This all-mahogany uke featured hand-painted poinsettia flowers on the top, back and sides of the body as well as the back of the headstock (and, on some ukes, the front of the headstock as well). The Poinsettia's fretboard and headstock was capped in rich-looking ivoroid plastic; both had elegant inlays done in multi-colored pearloid, which was also used for the "Gibson" inlay atop the headstock. The Poinsettia was available as a special order from Gibson from 1926 to around 1935 or so (Ray Canfield's holding one on the cover of his Instruction Booklet, pg. 162).

Even rarer than Gibson's Poinsettia ukes were a handful of highly ornate "Florentine" custom ukuleles, likely produced on special order. Considering the extensive pearloid, sparkly inlays and rhinestones applied to the uke's fretboards, headstocks and even bodies, calling these instrument "over the top" is definitely an understatement! The inspiration for these ultra-fancy ukes likely sprang from the super fancy Florentine plectrum and tenor banjos Gibson produced in the late 1920s.

Speaking of banjos, Gibson produced some really terrific banjo ukes—not too surprising, considering that they had been manufacturing banjos since 1918. Their first ukulele banjo was the UB model, first produced around 1925. Commonly known as the "Trap Door" banjo uke, this model's defining feature was its unique two-piece, hinged rear resonator, which could be left closed or it could be opened, which directed more of the instrument's sound towards the player. Some time in the mid 1920s, Gibson expanded its line of banjo ukes to five models, ranging from the plain UB-1 through the much fancier UB-5. Their UB-3 model featured the same fretboard and headstock inlays as their Style Uke-3 soprano uke. The backs of their high-end UB-4 and UB-5 models were both fitted with decorative walnut resonators, and only differed in that the UB-4's metal hardware was nickel plated; the UB-5's was gold plated.

Gibson was well known for the many variations they introduced in their standard instrument models. For example, with their Style Uke-3 ukulele: After the initial run of "torch headstock" Uke-3s, Gibson quickly came up with a less fancy version that was, no doubt less, costly to produce: They replaced the headstock torch inlay and fancy floral fretboard decorations with easier-to-inlay diamonds and snowflakes, also elimi-

After the early run of Style Uke-3 ukes, Gibson replaced the headstock torch inlay and fancy floral fretboard decorations with simple diamonds and snowflakes.

nating the marker at the 15th fret (see the photo p.53). In later years, Gibson fitted Uke-3s with shorter 13-frets fretboards and reduced the number of top binding plys to three. Some sported spruce tops, stained dark to match the rest of the uke, reinforced with guitar-style "X" braces instead of simple traditional cross braces. The majority of Uke-3s have silk screened logos, but some examples have the Gibson headstock logo inlayed in pearl. And although the great majority of their TU model tenors had a dark-stained mahogany finish, they did produce some with a honey-to-brown shaded finish on the top, sides and back. They even produced a small number of "electrified" tenors (see Section 7.6, pg. 313).

As the world's hunger for ukuleles diminished in the 1940s and 50s, Gibson's uke production slowed to a crawl, although they did introduce a style 1 baritone model in the early 1960s. As Gibson kept no comprehensive records of the ukes they produced, it's unclear exactly when regular production of ukuleles ceased.

LEFT: Although most Gibson TU model tenor ukes had a dark-stained mahogany finish, some were produced with a honey-to-brown shaded finish.

2.3 Gretsch: From Banjos and Guitars to Ukuleles

When most string-instrument-playing musicians hear the Gretsch brand name, they usually think of the slick looking semi-hollow-body electric guitars played by pop stars, such as rockabilly notable Duane Eddy, Beatle George Harrison or Brian Setzer of the Stray Cats. But the Gretsch Company did a lot more than just make guitars. Founded in 1883 in Brooklyn, New York by 27-year-old German immigrant Friedrich Gretsch, his company initially manufactured a line of banjos, tambourines, and drums. By 1916, under the leadership of Friedrich's son Fred, Gretsch moved to a larger factory and soon expanded its production to include guitars. Gretsch eventually became one of the largest manufacturers of musical instruments in the US.

By the early 1920s, Hawaiian ukes had become very popular in America, providing serious competition for mainland instrument manufacturers. Instead of jumping directly into uke building, Gretsch's first foray into this market was to distribute "Ukuleles O Hawaii" brand soprano ukes, which, at one time, were actually made by Jonah Kumalae and, later, made in Los Angeles by Leonardo Nunes, son of ukulele pioneer Manuel Nunes. At some point, Gretsch rebranded these as "Kaholas" ukes. The boxes that these ukes came in, as well as the paper labels found inside the uke's bodies

Although best known for their semi-hollow-body electric guitars, Gretsch also produced a number of different ukulele models.

ABOVE: The first ukuleles sold by Gretsch were "Ukuleles O Hawaii" brand soprano ukes, which were actually made either by Kumalae or Leonardo Nunes.

RIGHT: "Eagle Brand" gut uke strings were manufactured for Gretsch in Germany.

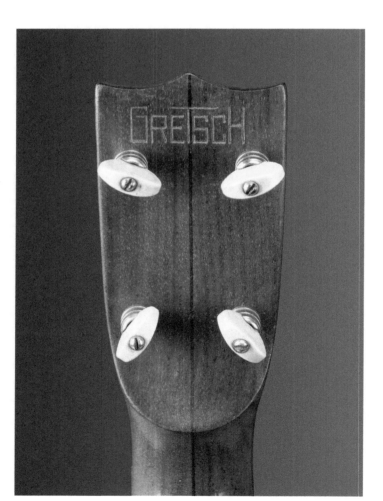

often included the phrase "Ukuleles O Hawaii," which L. Nunes evidently continued to use as well. Gretsch also had their own "Eagle Brand" of gut uke strings which were manufactured for them in Germany.

Gretsch eventually went on to manufacture its own ukuleles at their 10-story-tall factory in Brooklyn. Their most popular model was a mahogany soprano with an applied rosewood fingerboard, no body bindings and a black-white- black-white-black ring around the sound hole. The earliest examples bear a "Gretsch American" stamp on the back of the headstock, which at some point was simplified to simply read "Gretsch" in a bold font. Later-made sopranos have Gretsch decals on the front of their headstocks. They also produced an almost identical uke under the "Sherwood" brand name. The Sherwood, shown at the far right in the photo on pg. 55, has a slightly wider neck and fretboard and is slightly fancier, with the addition of white and black binding around the top. When and why Gretsch launched the Sherwood brand is probably lost to the sands of time—like so many other musical

LEFT: Early production Gretsch ukes are stamped with the company name on the back of the headstock.

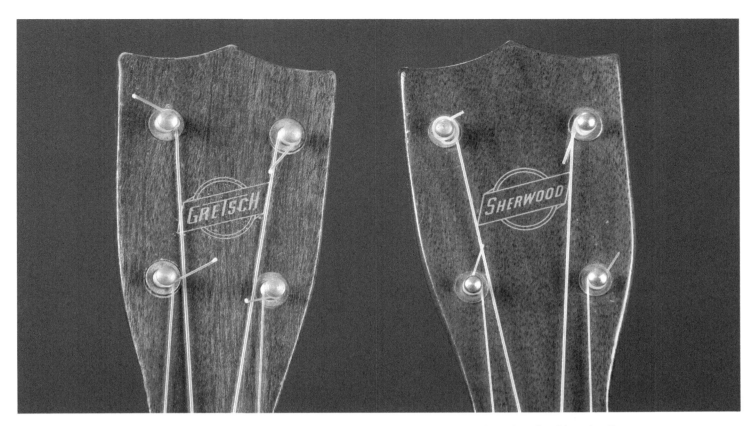

Gretsch's most popular model, a relatively plain mahogany soprano was also produced and sold under the "Sherwood" brand name.

instrument manufacturers of the era, Gretsch kept very poor records of the ukes they produced. Quality wise, both Gretsch and Sherwood brand ukes were made to a slightly lower standard than the Martin, Gibson and Lyon & Healy ukes of the time; their fit and finish is more on par with the higher-end instruments made by Harmony and Regal.

Besides their basic models, Gretsch also produced small numbers of fancier ukuleles, such as the one shown at right. This instrument shares the same construction as their base model ukes, but is made from fancier figured mahogany with top body binding and a Brazilian rosewood fingerboard inlayed with square pearl position markers. Its headstock features a rosewood overlay, fancy pearl inlays, and high-quality mechanical tuners. I've seen an even fancier Gretsch uke, which sported white and black body bindings front and back and a bound ebony fingerboard with fancy pearl inlays very similar to a Martin 5K. Its headstock featured an elaborate floral inlay done in colorful abalone. Unfortunately, it's impossible to know whether this was a one-off custom instrument or a standard

RIGHT: One of Gretsch's fancier models features a figured mahogany body, a Brazilian rosewood fingerboard and a headstock with fancy pearl inlays.

THE ART OF VINTAGE UKULELES • SANDOR NAGYSZALANCZY

GRETSCH BANJO UKULELES

  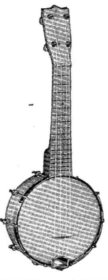 

No. 20—A good, minimum priced banjo-ukulele, made with hardwood neck and 7-inch narrow rim (1¼" wide); lacquer finished in light, natural maple color. Fitted with nickel-plated straining hoop; real calfskin head; natural cedar pegs............Each, $2.20

No. 23—Inexpensive, better quality hardwood ukulele in mahogany shaded lacquer finish, with heavy 7-inch rim, 1¾ inches wide. Has real calfskin head tensioned by a nickel-plated straining hoop; natural cedar pegs.............Each, $3.00

No. 26—Mahogany finished banjo-ukulele with 7-inch rim. Real calf head tensioned in regular banjo style by 10 nickel-plated brackets. Quality patent pegs with ivory-celluloid buttons, pearl position markers. Superior tone.............Each, $6.00

Banjo-ukulele. Nickel-plated rim with 7-inch wood extension resonator; 10 tension hooks; calf head. Superior patent pegs.
No. 28—In crystallized lacquer finish............Each, $7.50
No. 29—In hand-rubbed dark walnut finish......Each, $8.00

"CLAROPHONE" BANJO-UKULELE

No. 43—The old favorite "CLAROPHONE" banjo-ukulele with 7-inch rim and built-in resonator back. Made of rock-maple in a choice of natural or dark walnut lacquer finish. Has 10 nickel-plated tensioning brackets. Real calf-head. Extra quality patent pegs with ivory-celluloid buttons. Sound-holes in the rim give extra tone..............Each, $9.00

GRETSCH SOLO BANJO UKULELE

GRETSCH-built solo banjo-ukulele with unusual tonal power and richness. 8-inch rim and 10-inch extension resonator with nickel-plated metal resonator flange. Choice American walnut, satin finished by hand. Has 12 professional shoe-brackets; heavy counter-hoop, notched for each bracket; 3-piece, built-up, warp-proof neck; ebony fingerboard, ivory celluloid bound; 5-ply rim; detachable resonator, bound in black-and-ivory; quality patent pegs. Rogers calf-skin head; metal parts nickel-plated.
No. 56—Solo Banjo-Ukulele........................Each, $25.00

RESONATOR BANJO-UKULELE

No. 27—A new and very attractive resonator banjo-ukulele with 10-nickel-plated tension brackets. Fine maple construction, finished in golden brown shaded lacquer; 7-inch rim; real calfskin head; detachable, extension resonator; extra quality patent pegs with ivory celluloid buttons............Each, $9.00

125

Long-time producer of regular 4- and 5-string banjos, Gresch also developed a full line of banjo ukuleles.

production model.

From its earliest days as company, Gretsch had built 5-string banjos, and later, tenor banjos. In September of 1928, Frederick Gretsch obtained U.S. patent #1,685,706 for the construction of a banjo ukulele featuring a round metal rim supported by brackets inside of the instrument's wooden body. This rim supposedly improved the resonance of the uke's skin head and increased the forward projection of the sound it produced. Their banjo ukes were sold under both the Gresch and "Clarophone" brand names, the later being same one Gretsch used for their line of regular tenor banjos. A fancier model Gretsch banjo uke is shown at left.

Between 1939 And 1945, Gretsch's then-president Fred Gretsch Jr. served as a Navy commander in WWII, leaving his brother Bill to run the company. As a way of supporting the war effort, Gretsch manufactured a special model: an "Army Uke" given or sold to soldiers going off to fight in the war. (See Section 6.1) These instruments had round bodies made from plywood and were painted green-grey and blue, colors chosen to honor both the army and navy branches of service.

It's likely that Gretsch ended their ukulele production sometime in the late 1950s or early 1960s (again, no reliable records are available). After being acquired by Fender in 2002, Gretsch started building ukes again. They currently offer inexpensive soprano, concert, tenor and resonator ukuleles as part of their "Folk and Bluegrass" line.

LEFT: Gretsch's top-of-the-line "Solo" banjo ukulele was made of American walnut and featured fancy pearl fingerboard and headstock inlays and a large wood resonator.

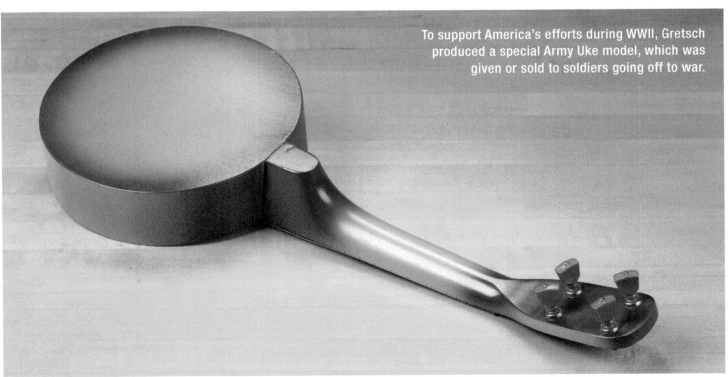

To support America's efforts during WWII, Gretsch produced a special Army Uke model, which was given or sold to soldiers going off to war.

Chicago-based Lyon & Healy produced excellent quality ukuleles during America's uke craze in the 1920s.

2.4 Lyon & Healy's Stylish Ukuleles

When you think of ukuleles made on the American mainland during the 1920s, brands like Martin and Gibson likely first to come to mind. But there's another company which produced excellent quality ukuleles during this period: Founded in 1864, the Lyon & Healy Company, once the largest manufacturer of musical instruments in the U.S., was well known for their wide range of stringed instruments which included guitars, banjos, mandolins and harps. The Chicago-based company produced their first ukuleles in 1915 and then expanded their line in the 1920s to more than a dozen models, most labeled with the "Washburn" brand name—the middle name of founder George W. Lyon.

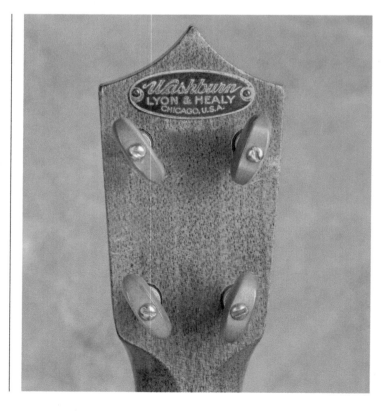

RIGHT: The majority of Lyon & Healy ukuleles labeled are with the "Washburn" brand name—the middle name of company founder Charles W. Lyon.

THE ART OF VINTAGE UKULELES • SANDOR NAGYSZALANCZY

The line included soprano-, concert- and tenor-sized ukuleles, taro patches, banjo ukes and tiples. Models ranged from inexpensive, unadorned ukes made from plain woods to fancy models crafted from figured mahogany or koa and adorned with body bindings, inlays and decorative decals.

The majority of Lyon & Healy's Washburn ukuleles were built with typical figure-of-eight shaped Spanish style bodies, but included some unique details that distinguished them from the instruments made by their competitors. Two of their top models, the mahogany model 5317 "Solo" and the koa wood model 5318 "Superb" ukes feature celluloid bindings, kite-shaped headstock inlays and raised rings around their sound holes. Those two models, as well as the plainer ma-

hogany model 5316 "Collegian" are fitted with shapely "smile-style" bridges (some stamped "PAT. APLD FOR") that are much more elegant than the simple rectangular bridges found on the majority of ukuleles. The Superb's bridge uses ivoroid pins to secure the strings. The Solo's bottom body bout has an attractive gold-colored floral decal. Their top-of-the-line model 5320 "Super Deluxe" koa uke pulled out all the stops: The instrument's entire top, back and sound hole ring all feature ivorine bindings and "Oriental pearl" purfling. Its bridge, headstock overlay and fingerboard are ebony; the latter two feature elaborate pearl inlays.

Unlike most of their competitors, Lyon & Healy produced a wide variety of models with unconventional body shapes. One of their most popular models was

Following the basic "Spanish body" shape most instrument makers gave their soprano ukes, Lyon & Healy added unique features, including raised celluloid sound hole rings and decorative bridges.

the "Camp Uke" was based on a design licensed from W.I. Kirk who patented his design in 1930. The uke featured a round body, making it appear at first glance to be a banjo uke. A 1920s instrument catalog described the instrument as "The latest and daintiest of the ukulele family." Camp Ukes featured the same smile-style bridges used on many of L&H's regular ukes. The model came in several variations, ranged in price from $16.00 to $29.35. Some models came with body bindings and gold leaf decoration, some with f-holes, some with thick, lathe-turned "resonator" backs (top photo on pg. 65). Lyon & Healy also produced (or licensed production of) a more decorative Camp Uke model featuring a black-painted body bound front and back with white celluloid and adorned with golden Asianthemed decals.

One of the more oddball L&H models, designed in 1925 by Marquette Healy, the son of company founder Patrick J. Healy, was the "Venetian Ukulele." Marquette obtained a U.S. Design Patent for the design in 1928 (see pg. 197 in Section 5.1) The instrument's small teardrop-shaped body doesn't produce a lot of volume, but at least it could conceivably serve as a canoe paddle in a pinch.

LEFT: Besides being shapely, the bridge on L&H Superb model 5318 is unusual for a soprano uke, as it secures the strings with small celluloid pins.

BELOW: L&H's Solo model 5317 bears a lovely gold-green decal of oak leaves below its "Patent Applied for" bridge.

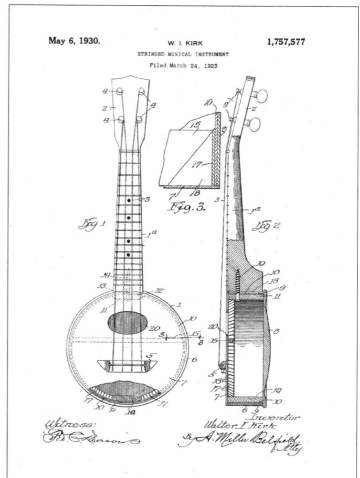

LEFT: The top-of-the-line L&H model 5320 Super Deluxe soprano koa uke features fancy inlays and ivorine and pearl bindings and purfling around its top, back and sound hole ring.

ABOVE: The design shown in W.I. Kirk's 1930 patent was licensed for Lyon & Healy's Camp Ukes.

But the most unique—and collectible—ukuleles Lyon & Healy created were undoubtedly their Bell and Shrine models. First produced in the mid 1920s, Lyon & Healy's model 5325 "Bell" ukulele, named for its bell-shaped body, was a concert-sized instrument with a mahogany body and neck, smile-style bridge, rosewood fingerboard with 17 German silver frets. It also featured ivorine (synthetic ivory) body bindings and a raised sound hole ring and kite-shaped headstock inlay. In advertisements, the bell was hailed as an instrument with "the unique shape (that) appeals immediately to the purchaser who is seeking the novel and the individual." The inspiration for the instrument came from the Washburn Bell guitars L&H produced in the mid 1920s. They also made a Bell tiple in the early 1930s.

Introduced in 1927 or 28, the style 5330 Shrine uku-

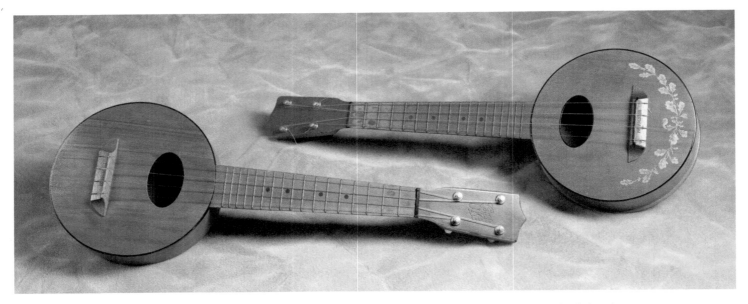

L&H Camp Ukes came in several styles, including a fancier version adorned with the same oak leaf decal used on their Solo model.

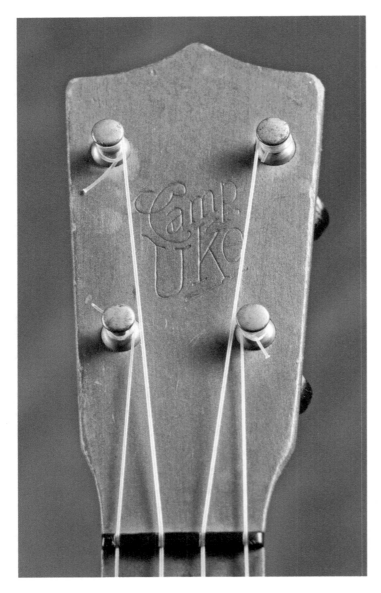

The "Camp Uke" moniker stamped into the front of the headstock.

A 1924 studio photo of two young women holding Lyon & Healy Camp ukes.

RIGHT: Some L&H Camp Ukes featured a tupelo wood "resonator back" which was turned on a lathe.

BELOW - LEFT & RIGHT: Lyon & Healy produced (or licensed production of) a Camp Uke model featuring a black-painted whitewood body bound front and back with white celluloid bindings.

Gold colored decals depict a pagoda, mountains and other Asian themes.

Shaped a bit like a canoe paddle, the L&H "Venetian Ukulele" was designed by Marquette Healy who obtained a US Patent for his design.

Lyon & Healy's model 5325 "Bell" ukulele stylish mahogany body features ivoroid bindings and a raised ivoroid sound hole ring.

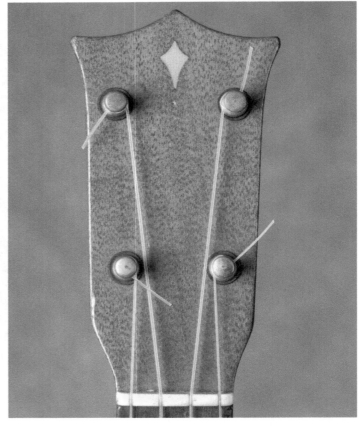

An ivoroid "kite" inlay decorated the top of the Bell uke's headstock.

Shrine Model

This is a professional instrument of the highest order, unique in shape, convenient to handle, and, above all, possessing a tone quality sweeter, more resonant and far-carrying than any ukulele you have ever heard. You will be amazed at the tone quality of this instrument. Scientifically built in every respect, and pronounced by discriminating players everywhere as in a class by itself.

Description

The body is made of extra fine genuine mahogany in beautiful satin finish; width of lower bout, 9 inches; length of entire instrument, 21½ inches. Top, back and sound hole edges bound with green celluloid, giving a very pleasing appearance; new model end extension bridge which allows freest possible vibration; genuine ebony fingerboard with 17 German silver frets and 4 round green celluloid position marks; genuine mahogany neck, beautifully modeled and finished; rosewood veneered headpiece with inlaid green celluloid design; equipped with special model patent pegs of our own exclusive design; strung with finest quality gut strings. This instrument absolutely possesses the last word in tone quality. Highly recommended for solo work.

No. 5330   Made of mahogany. Price, each........................$20.00

No. 5331   Same as No. 5330, except made of specially selected birch, mahogany finish. Each 15.00

Shrine Model Ukulele Cases

Made of 3-ply veneer covered with walrus grain waterproof black Keratol; steel valance; side opening; velvet lined; nickel plated brass lock, clasps and protectors; leather handle; durable workmanship throughout.

No. 6412   Price, each $10.50

No. 6410   Black walrus grain Keratol; fiberboard body; side opening; flannel lined. Each................................. 6.00

ABOVE: A page from the Tonk Brother's 1928 musical instrument wholesale catalog shows two different models of L&H's unique "Shrine" ukulele.

LEFT: The Shrine model 5330 ukulele has distinctive green celluloid bindings and fretboard dots and a uniquely shaped "gondola" pin-style bridge.

The Shrine ukulele's odd body required a specially shaped case made from a leather-like material called Keratol.

lele sold for the princely sum of $20—a lot of money in those days! It sported a three-sided balalaika-like body that the company claimed was "scientifically designed," perhaps referring to the fact that a triangle is a very strong shape. A 1930 advertisement described the shrine as "a professional instrument…possessing a tone quality sweeter, more resonant and far carrying than any ukulele you have ever heard." The mahogany-bodied concert- and less common tenor-sized shrine ukes featured distinctive green celluloid bindings, fretboard dots and headstock inlays, as well as uniquely shaped "gondola" bridges with four small celluloid pins securing the strings. L&H produced four variations of the shrine: the model 5330 mahogany concert (which sold for $20), the plainer birch-bodied model 5331 concert (which was $5 less) and two fancier tenor models; the 5350 Grand Symphony and the model 5355 DeLuxe. The later featured a figured koa body and neck, flashy pearl and ivorine inlays and gold leaf decal decorations.

Since the Shrine uke didn't fit into any standard uke case, L&H offered a special laminated wood hard case covered with "walrus grain waterproof black Keratol,"

an imitation leather-like material made from fabric treated with phenolic resin. No doubt due to its elaborate shape, the shrine case cost half as much as the uke it was designed to hold.

Unfortunately, Lyon & Healy's foray into the ukulele market was short lived; in 1928, all of their fretted instrument manufacturing equipment was sold to J. R. Stewart, a former L&H employee. Stewart then went bankrupt in the Wall Street crash of '29.

Schireson Brothers Jack and Nathan opened their first music retail store on South Broadway Street in Downtown Los Angeles in 1902.

2.5 Schireson's Hollywood Ukes

If you set a dozen standard soprano or concert ukes on a table face-side down, it's usually pretty hard to tell who made them; the basic body shape of Martins, Gibsons, Kamakas, etc. are all pretty similar. But there's one concert-sized vintage uke that's easy to differentiate from all the rest: the Hollywood ukulele. Although its body follows the classic Spanish form (a figure eight shape with the lower bout slightly larger than the upper), Hollywood ukes have a more voluptuous rounded shape with a noticeably larger lower bout (in contemporary terms, this uke has a big booty!). I'm not sure how this body shape affects the instrument's tone, but Hollywood ukes sound a bit warmer and mellower than other concert-size ukes I've played.

The Hollywood uke story starts in 1902, when brothers Jack and Nathan Schireson (pronounced "Shearson") opened a small music retail store in Los Angeles. In the early days, they didn't make ukuleles, but sold all sorts of musical good ranging from sheet music to guitars and band instruments to electric radios. In the decades to come, Schireson Bros. expanded their business to include ukuleles, guitars and mandolins they had manufactured under their Hollywood brand name (Hollywood isn't far from where their stores were in downtown L.A.) Building their own instruments was likely the idea of brother Nathan, who was an inven-

One thing that distinguishes Schireson Brother's Hollywood brand ukuleles is their voluptuous rounded bodies which display a noticeably larger lower bout than found on other ukes.

tor familiar with the mechanics of lutherie. He experimented with magnetic pickups for guitars and in 1932, was granted a U.S. patent for a steel cone guitar resonator device. Unfortunately, his design was similar enough to one patented by John Dopyera (founder of National String Instruments) that the case went to court; Nathan eventually lost.

Schireson's Hollywood ukuleles were built by Robert E. Pearson, an English luthier who was once a well-known banjo uke builder in England and also had worked for Martin Guitar prior to moving out to California to work for the Schireson Bros. The Hollywood uke line consisted of at least four models: #6, #8, #9 and #10. Their bottom-of-the-line #6 uke featured

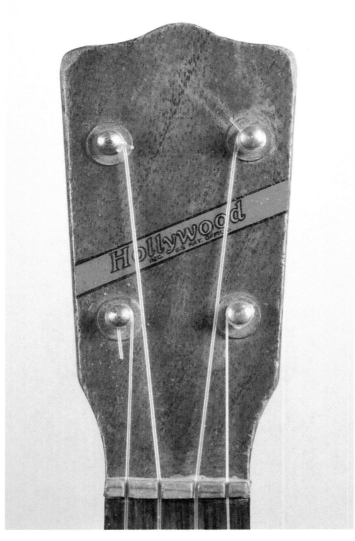

The bottom-of-the-line Hollywood #6 uke featured all-mahogany construction a rosewood fingerboard, no bindings; and a Hollywood brand decal on the headstock.

The Hollywood #10 features a curly koa body, abalone purling and an ivoroid-bound ebony fingerboard with fancy pearl inlays.

all-mahogany construction with a rosewood fingerboard and no bindings; just a simple black-white-black inlay around the sound hole and a Hollywood logo decal set diagonally in a red band across the headstock. Their premier #10 uke had features that rivaled Martin's coveted 5K model: A curly koa body with abalone purling and sound hole rosette and a mahogany neck with an ivoroid-bound ebony fingerboard with fancy pearl inlays. The headstock has two fancy pearl inlays as well as the "Hollywood" logo done in pearl. To top it off, this uke's bridge and nut were carved from real ivory, as well as the bridge pins (the fancy uke seen here lacks an ivory bridge and pins. It may be a model variation, or it had its original bridge replaced).

Other Hollywood concert ukuleles sport a variety of

RIGHT: Hollywood brand ukulele strings were made in Germany.

THE ART OF VINTAGE UKULELES • SANDOR NAGYSZALANCZY

Jack Schireson's grandson Gary holds a one-of-a-kind Hollywood uke with "Schireson" inlayed in pearl on the headstock.

different features, including models with spruce tops on mahogany bodies and those with rope bindings. Besides body shape, one thing all Hollywood concert ukes have in common is that their body sides were all bent from a single piece of wood—most ukes have a seam at the bottom of the lower bout where the upper and lower sides are joined. I contacted Jack Schireson's grandson Gary, who, unfortunately, didn't have any specific information about Hollywood's model numbers and how they were specified or may have changed over the years of production. You can see him holding a fancy one-of-a-kind Hollywood uke (with "Schireson" inlayed in pearl on the headstock) in the photo at left.

Schireson also produced Hollywood banjo ukes, mandolins and guitars although it's unclear whether or not Pearson supervised construction of these, or they had someone else manufacture these and simply gave them the Hollywood brand. They even had their own line of Hollywood-brand uke strings.

An interesting footnote to the Schireson Bros. story: Just after WWII, a man walked into one of their stores and asked to speak with Stanley Schireson, Jack's son. He showed him a line of transistor radios that his company produced in Japan. Stanley liked the radios and agreed to carry them in his stores. That man's name was Morita Akio and the radios he sold were built by the company that he co-founded: Sony. The deal they struck made Schireson Bros. the first Sony dealer in America! Over the years, Schireson expanded their home and musical electronics business and eventually changed their name to Volutone. They're still in business today, working as an electronics distribution company in Southern California and Nevada.

The Harmony Company of Chicago produced countless budget-priced ukuleles with good-to-decent playability, most made of stained-whitewood adorned with stenciled or decaled decorations.

2.6 Harmony:
Prolific Ukulele Manufacturer

Ever since I started collecting ukuleles many decades ago, musician friends have asked me what exactly constitutes a "great" uke? Does it have to be fancy, finely crafted or have some kind of historic value? The simple answer is no, it just has to be interesting in some way. A good example of this is the ukuleles produced by the Harmony Company of Chicago Il. Most were budget-priced instruments with good-to-decent playabili-ty that anyone could afford. When most folks think of a Harmony uke, I imagine they picture a cheap painted or stained-whitewood instrument with stenciled or decaled decorations. But did you know that in their heyday, Harmony was the largest musical instrument company in America, and that, in addition to their inexpensive models, Harmony made top-quality instruments endorsed by some of the finest musicians of their time?

The Harmony story begins with Wilhelm Schultz, a German immigrant who came to Chicago in 1882. Though he had been a builder of cabinets and staircas-

Mail order giant Sears & Roebuck sold many thousands of Harmony-built ukuleles under the Supertone brand name.

Among the many Harmony Supertone-brand ukes that featured charming decals, their "Drowsy Waters" model was one of the most popular.

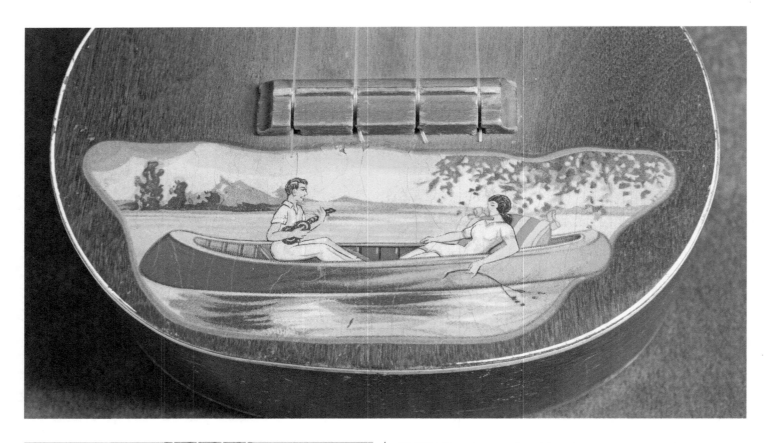

ABOVE: The theme of a girl and guy on a romantic canoe ride is displayed on another of Harmony's decal-decorated soprano ukuleles.

LEFT: Tropical themes were also commonly employed on Harmony's ukes, including this stenciled Supertone model which features flying Macaws as well as palm trees and a canoeing couple.

es, he decided to follow his passion for music and got a job building stringed instruments. After acquiring lutherie skills working at Lyon & Healy, Schultz struck out on his own, creating the Harmony Company in 1892. Starting with just 4 employees, Schultz initially built violins and guitars, and then mandolins and banjos. Always mindful of the musical trends of the time, Schultz soon added ukuleles and Hawaiian-style guitars to their production. By 1915, Harmony had 125 employees and became the first large-scale ukulele manufacturer in the country.

One of Harmony's largest customers was Sears & Roebuck, who sold many thousands of their ukuleles, guitars, etc. under the "Supertone" brand name through their mail-order catalogs. The Supertone line included both traditional Hawaiian-style ukes made from mahogany and koa, as well as inexpensive models featuring eye-catching decorations, such as the decaled "Drowsy Waters" uke, shown on previous page.

ABOVE: This Harmony uke is decorated with a decal depicting a pagoda in an Asian garden setting.

LEFT AND BELOW: This model, known as "The Vagabond," features a brown-burst finished body with decorative decals and a pearloid-covered fingerboard.

The Vagabond's body decals show a jolly band of gypsies playing and dancing in an idyllic forest glen.

The Harmony Blue Bird model soprano uke has a colorful geometric painted finish with a stenciled bird and floral decoration.

Harmony produced ukuleles sold under many different brand names, including the ones shown here.

THE ART OF VINTAGE UKULELES • SANDOR NAGYSZALANCZY

Evidently the "girl and guy on a romantic canoe ride" motif was popular, as Harmony produced a few other canoe-themed ukes.

In 1916, Sears decided to up their ante in the ever-growing ukulele market by buying the Harmony Company and thus securing their entire output of instruments. In addition to the Supertone ukes, Harmony built inexpensive ukes for the Sear's Silvertone brand, including various models with simple stencil-painted decorations—water skiers, canoes, palm trees and various tropical and fantasy motifs. One of the coolest Harmony models has to be their "Vagabond" uke that features colorful decal of gypsies playing and dancing in a lush forest. Bold colors and a geometric motif adorn Harmony's "Blue Bird" uke. Another fun model they made features graphic characters from Max Fleishman's Betty Boop cartoons, popular in the 1930's.

In the late 1920s, Harmony's ambitious president Jay Krause directed the company to build ukes and other instruments for outside vendors. Any customer requesting 100 instruments or more could contract Harmony to build them. This business was so successful that, in the coming decades, Harmony bought up many of their competitors and took over production of their lines of instruments. Thus, lots of Harmony-made ukuleles bear other brand names, including: Airline, Holiday, Kay, La Scala, Nonpareil, Stella, Sovereign, Valencia, Vogue and Rainbow. The Rainbow uke was one in a whole line of decorative "Art Moderne" models that Harmony produced (see Section 3.3) Harmony also continued building ukes bearing their own brand name, though their headstock labels changed in design several times over the decades.

Some of the very best ukuleles that Harmony manufactured were the special models created for Roy Smeck and Johnny Marvin—two very talented and popular vaudevillian ukulele players and performers. The Smeck signature model was the first of a new line of "Vita" brand instruments which included guitars and mandolins. The Smeck "Vita-Uke" had a distinctive lute-shaped body made from beautiful Cuban mahogany with a spruce top (see Section 4.9). Harmony's relationship with Smeck continued for many decades, resulting in several other Smeck signature models, including the "Professional Concert Uke," shown here

LEFT: Harmony's Betty Boop uke features characters from Max Fleishman's popular 1930's comics.

This Nonpareil uke, made by Harmony, features multi-colored wood bindings.

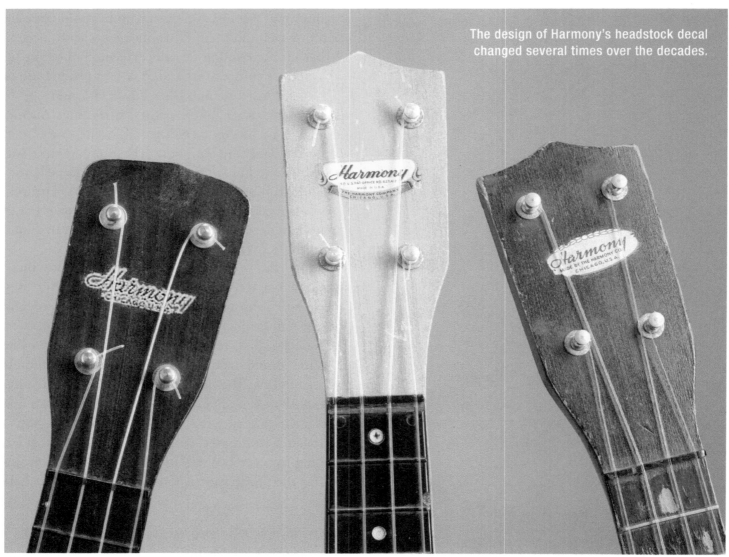

The design of Harmony's headstock decal changed several times over the decades.

ABOVE: Some of the better-quality ukuleles made by Harmony include (top to bottom): the Johnny Marvin Professional, the Roy Smeck Vita Uke and the Roy Smeck Concert Uke.

LEFT: This page from Harmony's 1958 catalog shows the full line of ukuleles they produced at the time.

The "Johnny Marvin Professional Tenor" uke (which actually had a concert-sized body) came in two models: the regular one (seen above) made from flame grained mahogany, and the "Prince of Wales" model, made from figured koa and featuring gold-plated tuning pegs. Both models were fitted with a patented airplane-shaped "aero bridge," designed to capitalize on the popularity of Charles Lindberg's historic flight across the Atlantic.

In December of 1940, Kraus staged a buyout of Harmony from Sears, moving the company to a larger plant to allow them to expand, although most of that growth was in guitar production: In 1941, they built a third of the total number of fretted instruments made in the U.S., but 75% of that total was guitars and only 10% ukuleles.

A simple stencil of "my dog has fleas" notes and painted-on "bindings" decorate the top of Harmony's "Classmate" ukulele.

The end of WWII saw a resurgence of interest in the ukulele—in 1949, Harmony sold nearly 150,000 ukes. The majority of there were inexpensive white wood instruments with molded plastic fingerboards and decorated with simple stenciled designs. But the American folk revival and the advent of rock n' roll drove Harmony to focus the majority of their production efforts on guitars— flat-tops, arch-tops, and electrics. Between 1945 and 1975, Harmony produced an astounding 10 million guitars—more than any other company in the world.

Ironically, it was foreign competition and Harmony's commitment to quality that led to their ultimate demise. While companies worldwide built instruments using automated equipment, Harmony's instruments—even the least expensive models—were built by skilled craftsmen using traditional hand labor methods. By the mid 1970s, the market was flooded with cheaper instruments, many manufactured in Japan. After 83 years of building quality instruments, the Harmony factory closed its doors in 1975. Fortunately, the legacy they leave behind includes an unimaginably large number of ukuleles; some frivolous, some fancy, but all crafted with pride by a company that remains an American legend.

The Regal Musical instrument Manufacturing Company of Chicago produced a staggering number of different model ukuleles between 1924 and 1954.

2.7 Regal's colorful Ukes

Another ukulele-manufacturing juggernaut possibly only second to Harmony in instrument output, The Regal company was started back in 1896 by an Indianapolis retailer named Emil Wulschner. Initially, his company "Emil Wulschner & Son" built only guitars and mandolins under the Regal, University and 20th Century brand names. After a couple of changes in ownership, Lyon & Healy bought Regal in 1904 and eventually re-launched it in 1924 as the "Regal Musical instrument Manufacturing Company of Chicago." As America's ukulele craze was exploding at the time, the newly independent Regal focused production on ukuleles, as well as tenor guitars. In the decades that followed, Regal made untold numbers of ukes with a staggering variety of different models, the reason being that the company was run mostly as an "original

RIGHT: The paper label found inside Regal ukuleles, bearing the motto "The Mark of Better Instruments."

Three of the different headstock labels Regal used over decades of ukulele production.

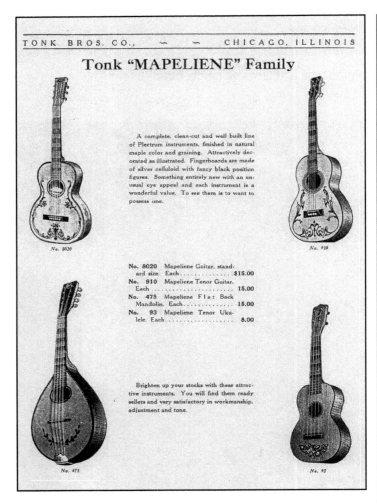

Most Regal ukes were commissioned by wholesale companies including the Tonk Brothers, who sold Regal's Mapeliene ukes.

equipment manufacturer." In other words, they built most of their instruments for wholesale companies, like N. Shure Company and Tonk Brothers, which commissioned and sold them. Unfortunately, because they often produced the same model ukes for the same wholesalers as other instrument companies such as Harmony, it can be hard to distinguish Regal-built ukes from those made by their competitors.

In the 30 years that the independent Regal company was in business (their operations ceased in 1954), they produced a staggering number of different ukuleles, many of them highly decorated. The great majority of their soprano-size and concert-size ukuleles were inexpensive instruments built from white woods, such as birch or basswood. They also had several models of banjo ukes, including a "Le Domino" model (see Section 3.5). Most Regal instruments were not expensive or of high-quality, but rather were made to be visually appealing and affordable. Regal's cost-effective production strategy was to build basic ukes, then send them out to be painted and stenciled and/or decaled by firms specializing in applying decorations.

Regal's inexpensive models include some of the coolest ukes made in the 1920s and 30s. Three great examples are the "Le Domino" the "Red Dragon" and the "Egyptian." All three models were decorated with decals applied atop the painted instrument. The Le Domino model came in both black-bodied and blonde

Three of Regal's most recognizable uke models are (left to right)
the Red Dragon, Le Domino, and Egyptian.

The Red Dragon's Asian motif decals on the uke's painted top.

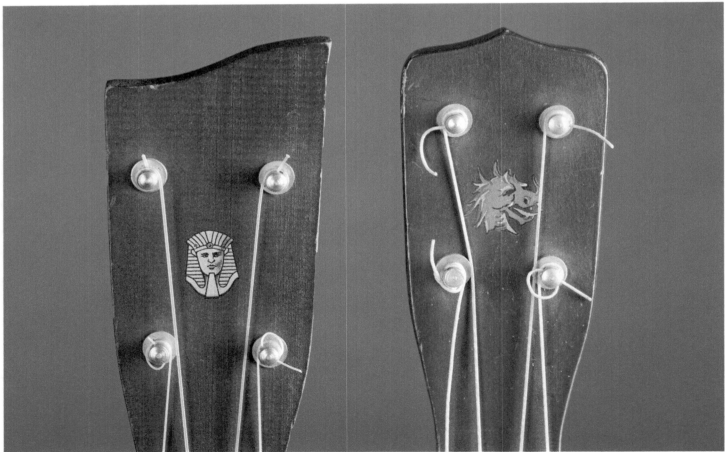

Headstock decals on Regal's Egyptian and Red Dragon ukes.

THE ART OF VINTAGE UKULELES • SANDOR NAGYSZALANCZY

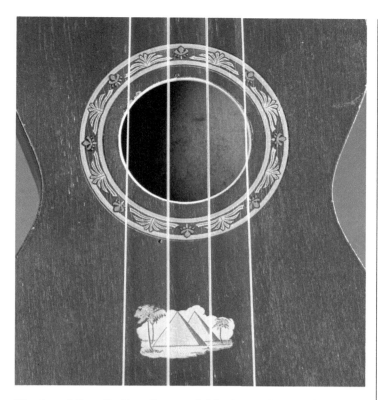

The top of Regal's Egyptian model features decals of pyramids and palm trees and a decorative floral sound hole ring.

bodied versions, featuring decals of dominos on both the body and fingerboard (see Section 3.5). The Red Dragon model has a large and extremely elegant dragon decal on the body, as well as a smaller decal of the Dragon's head on the headstock. This model came with either a maroon or an olive green and black burst painted finish. The Regal "Egyptian" model's decals that were applied onto a painted (either maroon or green) wood body included a small scene of pyramids and palm trees on the top above the bridge, decorative sound hole ring and the golden funerary mask of a pharaoh on the headstock. Originally designed by uke manufacturer J.R. Stewart (whose company was taken over by Regal in 1930), the Egyptian model was, no doubt, created to take advantage of America's fascination with British archaeologist Howard Carter's remarkable 1922 discovery of the tomb of King Tutankhamen.

A great many of Regal's ukuleles were decorated with painted-on designs applied via a stencil, which is basically a sort of mask with a cut-out design that's temporarily fixed in place over the instrument's sur-

A simple stencil was used to add a painted clown and monkey design to the top of Regal's model No. 86 uke.

The three-color design atop Regal's wartime Victory model were applied using the silk screen method.

Regal sometimes used the same stencils to apply designs using different paint color schemes.

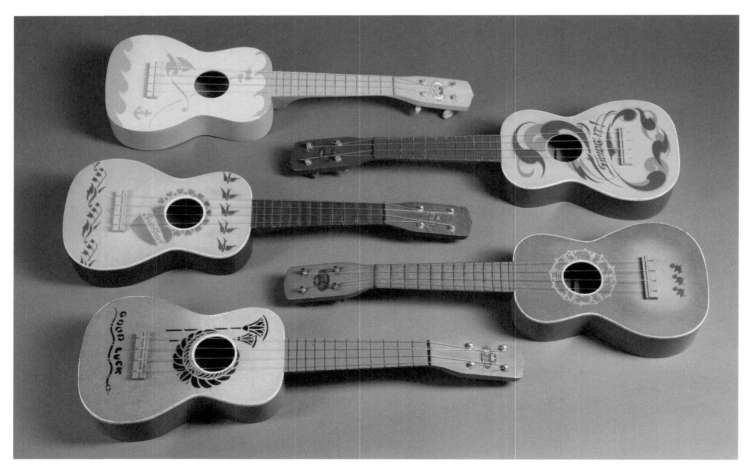

An assortment of Regal's stencil-painted ukes include (top to bottom): the Nautical, Swing it, Sweetheart, Animal Parade and Good Luck models.

THE ART OF VINTAGE UKULELES • SANDOR NAGYSZALANCZY

Regal's use of bright colors no doubt helped increase the visibility of their instruments quite literally.

Cute animal decorations no doubt increased the sales appeal of Regal's Doggone and Panda model ukuleles.

The visual appeal of many Regal ukuleles were enhanced by the addition of sparkly pearloid fingerboards, including the Dorothy Dean and Silhouette models shown here.

THE ART OF VINTAGE UKULELES • SANDOR NAGYSZALANCZY

The back of the Silhouette uke features a stenciled image of a Columbus-era sailing ship.

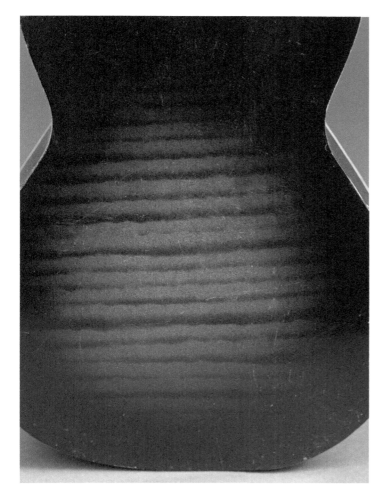

Regal sometimes used faux painting techniques to make their inexpensive white-wood ukes appear to be made of mahogany or koa, including the FOA model shown here.

Made sometime around 1928, Regal's "Ha Ha The Laffing Uke" features a hand-painted image of a minstrel, which was considered to be socially acceptable at the time.

face. When paint is sprayed over the mask, it's only applied to the cut-out areas, hence rendering the design. Designs featuring several colors were created by using two or more stencils in separate steps. Stenciling allowed decorations to be applied very quickly and repeatably; perfect for mass produced instruments. Silk screen printing methods were used for more complex multi-colored images, such as found on the body of Regal's war time "Victory" ukes (see Section 6.2). Variations in some models were done by using the same stencils and simply changing paint colors. In fact, Regal manufactured and sold untold numbers of stenciled ukuleles in a wide range of decorative styles. Some of the more popular stenciled models include the "Sweetheart," "Good Luck," "Swing It," "Nautical" and "Animal Parade." Two of the cutest models from this time period have to be the "Doggone" and "Panda" ukes. To add more flash to some models, Regal fitted them with Pyralin pearloid finger boards.

Besides using paint for decoration, Regal also employed faux painting techniques to make their white-wood (usually birch or basswood) constructed ukes appear to be made of mahogany or koa. One of these, they called the "FOA" model, I'm guessing that FOA stands for "Faux" in this case, as this uke's painted brown finish created the look of the wood grain present in flamed or fiddle-back mahogany. Their "Mapleiene" line of ukuleles (as well as guitars and mandolins)

The entire body of the Regal Jungle uke is covered in a thick layer of faux leopard fur.

Regal's spruce-topped F-hole model has a body that looks more like a mandolin than a ukulele.

featured bodies painted and faux-grained to resemble natural maple wood. They also used faux wood graining to create the look of koa wood on both the less expensive version of their Wendell Hall "Red Head" ukes and the "Ha Ha The Laffing Uke." The latter featured a hand-painted black minstrel figure that was appropriate at the time, but is now an image that's extremely distasteful and politically incorrect.

Regal used another kind of faux finish for their "Crystaline" model ukes, which were coated in a special paint that, when dry, made the instrument look like it was covered in mineral-like crystals. But for their ultimate faux finish, Regal did away with paint entirely: Their wonderfully wild "Jungle Uke" model, featured a wood body entirely covered with fake leopard fur (also see Section 5.6).

Despite Regal's reputation as the maker of cheap, decorative yet poorly constructed instruments, they also produced their share of better-quality ukuleles, including the Wendell Hall "Red Head" and "Master Crown" (see section 4.5), the Sterling-brand "Marquetry Uke," the Regal "Superior," the "Tonk American" and the mandolin-shape-bodied "F Hole" model. These were made of either mahogany or koa, with either celluloid or wood body bindings. Despite their best efforts, none of these models matched up to the quality of instruments produced by Martin, Gibson and Lyon & Healy.

In the 1930s, Regal licensed the use of Dobro's patented resonator mechanism and produced their own line of "amplifying" guitars, mandolins and ukuleles (see pg. 98 in the next section). WWII brought an end to the production of resonator guitars, and Regal ceased building all their fretted instruments in 1954. That same year, Regal sold their brand name and assets to the Harmony Company. Fender took over the brand in the late 1950s.

Chicago, 1920s.

2.8 National & Dobro Resophonic Instruments

Question: When is an acoustic ukulele, arguably the world's quietest stringed instrument, not so quiet? The answer is, when it's a resonator uke. Instead of relying on a thin wood top to naturally amplify the vibration of its strings, a resonator uke, (or guitar, mandolin, etc.) transfers string vibration to a speaker-like thin metal cone housed inside the body. In addition to being louder than a standard acoustic uke, a resonator ukulele has a distinctive, bright metallic sound that lends itself well to certain styles of music, including the blues and Hawaiian jazz.

Resonator instruments were invented at a time when acoustic instruments (primarily guitars) just weren't loud enough to be heard in bands that featured brass instruments. Credit for their invention goes to a Czech immigrant and luthier named John Dopyera who, along with his brothers and musician/inventor George Beauchamp founded the National Stringed Instrument Corp. in 1927. Based in Los Angeles, California, National's earliest products were round-neck Spanish guitars for regular playing and square-neck Hawaiian guitars for playing with a slide bar, like a lap steel. Both types sported heavy metal bodied and came in both single-cone and tricone models, the latter featuring three smaller cones instead of a single, larger cone. In

The cover of National's 1929 catalog of resophonic instruments.

Triolian Mandolins and Ukuleles

In an amazingly short time NATIONAL instruments have become famous in all parts of the world. This has been accomplished not only through personal audiences but through the medium of radio, which demands for perfect reception the ultimate in quality and tone clarity.

Triolian Mandolins and Ukuleles, like the Triolian Guitars, surpass all other instruments of similar price in volume and tone quality. They are made from an alloy metal which will not deteriorate in any way, is not affected by moisture or temperature, and with reasonable care will last a lifetime. Finished in modern two-tone brown walnut.

Triolian Mandolin (as illustrated)..........$40.00
Triolian Ukulele (not illustrated).......... 25.00

National's first catalog listed just two ukulele models: the "Silver" and the pear-shape-bodied "Triolian" which was offered as both a four-string uke and an eight-string mandolin.

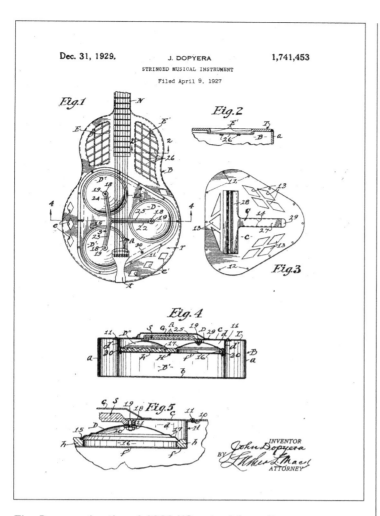

Dec. 31, 1929. J. DOPYERA 1,741,453
STRINGED MUSICAL INSTRUMENT
Filed April 9, 1927

The Dopyera brothers' 1929 US patent for a three-cone resonator guitar design, which they employed for guitars and mandolins, as well as some of their earliest ukuleles.

Duco" finish. Duco paint was a durable nitrocellulose lacquer that was then a popular paint for automobiles and other metal products. Polychrome finished ukes were painted with three different colors, dark yellow, orangish red and light green, sprayed over the entire instrument, including the fingerboard in a seemingly random fashion, creating a rather splotchy look. The back of these instruments featured a lovely image of palm trees on a tropical beach, stencil painted in black and reddish orange.

National's line of Silver model ukuleles also had but a single cone centrally located inside the instrument's

National's Triolian ukes originally came with a two-tone brown walnut painted finish, but were later offered in brightly plated "German silver."

1928, at the peak of America's first uke craze, National introduced their first resonator ukuleles as well as a line of plectrum guitars, tenor guitars, and mandolins.

National's first catalog listed just two ukulele models: the "Triolian" and the "Silver." The Triolian model, which was offered as both a four-string ukulele and an eight-string mandolin, had an odd pear-shaped body that housed three metal cones, an arrangement based on the Dopyera brother's three-cone resonator guitar design for which they were granted a US patent in 1929. The Triolian's body, which was made of "alloyed metal," was painted with a two-tone walnut finish. In subsequent years, National offered the pear-shape Triolian ukes with a "German silver" brightly plated finish.

At some point, possibly as early as 1930, National made Triolian ukuleles with standard Spanish style figure-eight shaped metal bodies that housed a single resonator cone. These were available with either the standard two-tone walnut finish, or a "polychrome

As early as 1930, Triolian ukes were fitted with Spanish-style bodies. They came in two finishes, the fancier being a polychrome Duco lacquer with stenciled palm trees on the back of the body.

The NATIONAL Silver Ukulele

Those haunting Hawaiian strains played on the Ukulele . . . how they exalt the emotions!

Thousands of Ukulele players have pronounced the NATIONAL Silver Ukulele an instrument that will delight you. It has the same beautiful German silver finish as our Guitars and Mandolins, and the unique NATIONAL feature of amplifying the volume while retaining all the softness and beauty of tone.

Made in three styles, priced as follows:

Style 1—(plain) each $55.00
Style 2—(beautifully hand engraved) 70.00
Style 3—(Artistic floral design) 85.00

Spanish figure-eight-shaped body. All Silver ukes had shiny nickel-plated metal bodies and came in three styles: Style 1 instruments had plain, un-engraved bodies while Style 2 instruments were fancier, with a hand-engraved floral design commonly known as the "wild rose" pattern on both the front and the back of the body. Style 3 National ukes sported an even more elaborate "lily of the valley" floral engravings. Early models came with five diamond-shaped, screened holes in the cover plate, as seen on the body of the Style 3 uke shown p. 96 . National later changed the cover plates, so that the five diamond openings are formed by a series of small holes (see the lower left photo on pg. 96). All three models had stylishly shaped headstocks overlayed with rosewood veneer and bearing "National Trade Mark" decals (sometime in the early 30s, they topped the headstocks with pearly ivoroid plastic). In National's 1929-30 catalog, plain Style 1 ukes are listed as selling for $55, Style 2 ukes were $70 and top-of-the-line Style 3 instruments were $85., which made them quite expensive in the depression era; for comparison, an exquisitely fancy Martin 5K then sold for $55.

Early National ukuleles were what we now consider "concert sized," with 11 1/8" long metal bodies and wood necks with 14 7/8" scales. In 1931, they revised these ukes, changing to a smaller soprano-sized (9 3/4" long) body with a 13 3/4" scale. Both size ukeleles feature the same resonator cone and cover plate. The engraved designs on the Style 2 and 3 ukes were basically a smaller version of the same designs found on the back of their same-style guitars, although the proportions of the floral elements are different. Large- and small-bodied Style 2 ukes have a slightly different engraving pattern on the front of the body, between the cover plate and the end of the fretboard.

Construction wise, all early National ukes featured German silver bodies. Also known as nickel silver or white brass, German silver is an alloy that's typically 65% copper, 10-23% zinc and 10-20% nickel (National switched to using yellow brass in the early 1930s). Constructed from several separate sheet metal pieces silver soldered together, the bodies of all Style 2 and Style 3 ukes were first engraved, then received a thick layer of nickel plating that was polished to a bright, mirror-like finish.

The resonator cone used in National ukuleles was a

National's Silver Style 2 ukuleles are adorned with a hand-engraved floral "wild rose" pattern on both the front and the back of the body.

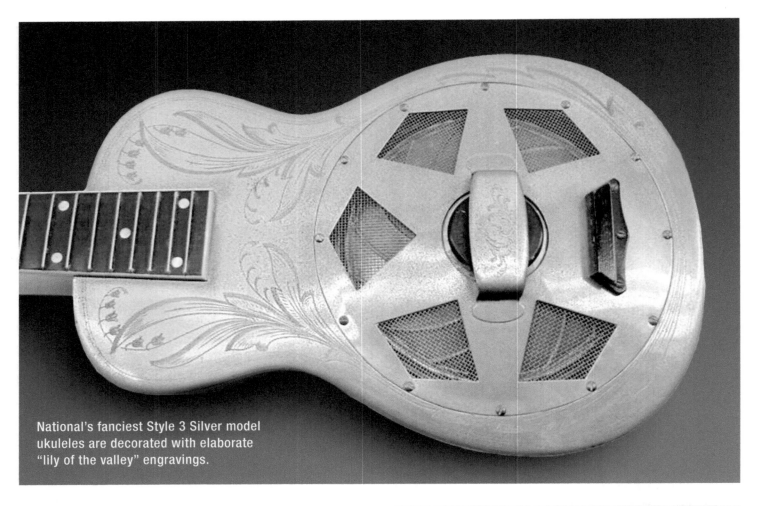

National's fanciest Style 3 Silver model ukuleles are decorated with elaborate "lily of the valley" engravings.

Later Silver model ukuleles, including this Style 2 model, sport cover plates where the diamond openings are formed by a series of small holes.

The headstocks of early National ukuleles all feature a decal of their company logo.

slightly trimmed down version of the same cone used in their tricone guitars. Each cone was made from a disc of thin (.005-.007" thick) pure aluminum that was first spun to shape on a lathe, then stamped with a series of spiraling ridges to lend greater strength. Each cone was also crimped around its outer edge, to give it greater flexibility.

The Dobro logo of the Dopyera Brothers resonator instrument company they formed after brothers Rudy, Emile, Robert and Louis left National.

Dobro

Unfortunately, at the same time that National was building their beautiful "amplifying" ukuleles (as they were referred to in their catalogs), the business foundations of the company crumbled due to conflicts involving intellectual property of the single-cone resonator instrument design. John Dopyera and his brothers Rudy, Emile, Robert and Louis left National and formed their own company which they named "Dobro," a contraction of "Dopyera Brothers" (coincidentally, the word "dobro" means "good" in Slovak, the Dopyera's native language). The Dobro Company thus became independent and a competitor of its original parent company, National.

To avoid infringing on the resonator instrument patents still owned by National, Rudy Dopyera developed his own, new design for a single-cone resonator, where the cone was inverted (hollow side up) surmounted by a multi-legged "spider" bridge which transmitted the energy of the instrument's vibrating strings to the cone which amplified the sound (he was awarded US patent #2,045,265 for his design in 1936).

In the early 1930s, Dobro built a wide variety of metal- and wood-bodied single-cone guitars, mandolins and ukuleles. The bodies for their wood instruments were actually produced by Regal, who also licensed Dopyera's inverted-cone-and-spider design for their own line of resonator instruments. The two most popular ukulele models Dobro produced were the Models

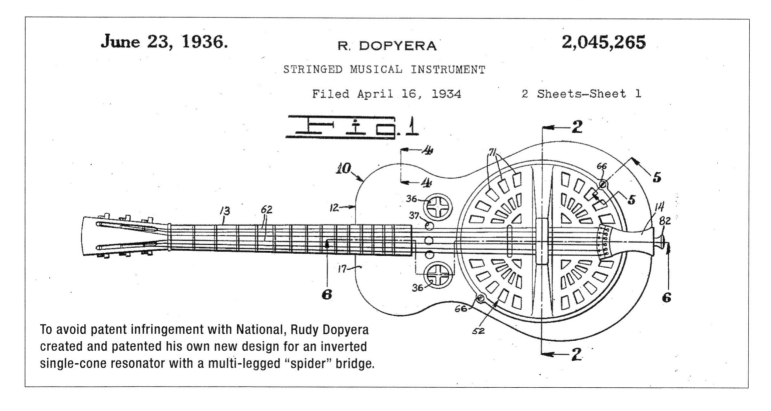

To avoid patent infringement with National, Rudy Dopyera created and patented his own new design for an inverted single-cone resonator with a multi-legged "spider" bridge.

$15.00

Greatest
Amplifying
Ukulele
Value

No. 15. Ukulele; mahogany body and neck; rosewood fingerboard; dark mahogany finish in satin rubbed effect. Each.................$15.00

Regal licensed Dopyera's inverted-cone-and-spider design for their own line of resonator instruments.

A-15 and A-30. Both of these were tenor-sized instruments with mahogany plywood bodies and solid mahogany necks with rosewood fingerboards. They also both sported 6-inch diameter single cones and eight-legged spider bridges contained beneath a chrome plated cover plate perforated by four sets of holes, each arranged in a fan shape. The difference between the two models was the number of additional screen-covered holes at the top of the body above the cover plate: The A-15 had two holes astride the end of the fingerboard while the A-30 had only one centered hole, thus facilitating its nickname: "The Cyclops" (they also produced resonator ukes with a pair of F-holes in the upper bout, but I'm not certain of their model number) Not only were Dobro's single-cone ukes louder than the tricones made by National, but they were cheaper to produce. In addition to producing instruments under their own brand name, Dobro licensed their designs and supplied parts to other manufacturers and vendors including Kay-Kraft, Regal, Harmony (for Sears) and Montgomery Ward.

After numerous clashes in court between National and Dobro in which Dobro prevailed, the Dopyera Brothers regained control of National in 1934, at which point it became the National-Dobro Corp. Not only did their new company produce a full line of acoustic

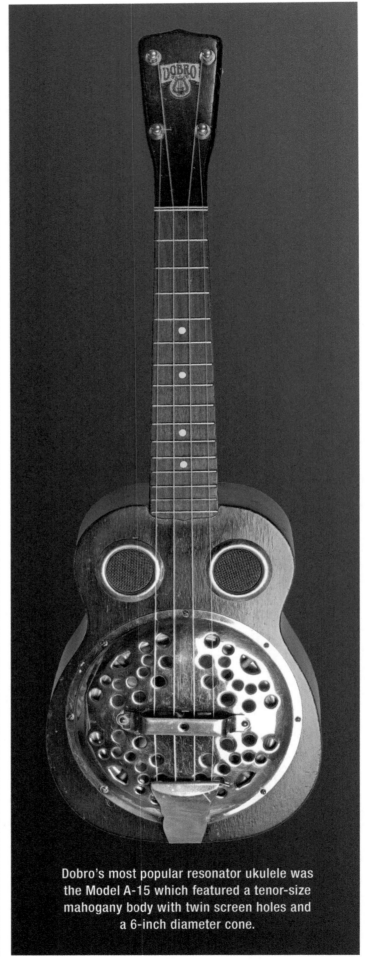

Dobro's most popular resonator ukulele was the Model A-15 which featured a tenor-size mahogany body with twin screen holes and a 6-inch diameter cone.

After the Dopyera Brothers regained control of National in 1934, their National-Dobro Corp. sold a full line of acoustic resonator instruments, as well as amplifiers made for them by the Webster Electric Company.

resonator instruments, but they also produced electric lap steels and amplifiers (made for them by Webster Electric). As a result, National founding partner George Beauchamp left the company and paired up with Adolph Rickenbacker, whose company had previously supplied cones and steel bodies for National and the cones and spider bridges for Dobro. Together, they founded a guitar company that eventually became Rickenbacker Guitars.

The National-Dobro Company moved to Chicago in 1936-37, and in 1940 was purchased by Valco, a new company formed by three former owners of National-Dobro, including Louis Dopyera. The Valco name is a combination of the three partner's initials. Their success was short lived, as production of all metal-bodied resonator instruments ceased following

the US entry into the Second World War in 1941. After a number of revivals and changes in ownership, the Dopyera bothers sold their company and the Dobro name to the Gibson Guitar Corporation In 1993.

Chapter Three
Ukulele Decorations and Details

Whether they're stenciled, decaled or hand painted, decorated ukes are simply charming.

Wⁱhat separates cheap instruments from more expensive models? Or cool and visually exciting instruments from boring plain vanilla ones? It's all in the details. Sometimes details are functional features that affect the way a uke plays or sounds, such as a novel bridge or patent tuners. But more often, details are purely visual elements; eye candy that delights, like a whimsical decal or a sparkly celluloid fingerboard.

Fancier vintage ukuleles made from nice figured hardwoods, like koa or mahogany, typically featured classic details, such as elaborate pearl fingerboard and headstock inlays or showy rope or colorful wood marquetry body bindings. Such details gave these ukes a lot more visual interest and an air of class. Simply owning and playing one implied that you appreciated—and could afford—a fancier, high-quality instrument.

In contrast, most inexpensive ukes were made of white woods typically painted overall and adorned with decals or stenciled images, both of which were quick and economical to apply. Such decorations often had a theme that gave the uke its brand name. For example, the Le Domino uke featured numerous domino decals on both body and fingerboard (see Section 3.5). Other popular decorative themes included paradisical islands (palm trees, hula dancers, etc.) College sports and cartoon strip characters. The decorations on these cheaper ukes made them more desirable and fun

The Art of Vintage Ukuleles • Sandor Nagyszalanczy

than plain wood or painted ukes. If the sheer number of different vintage models of both fancy higher-quality ukes and decorated, inexpensive ukes that were produced in the 1920s is any indication, these ukes were very popular indeed.

3.1 Ukes from Paradise

I've always wondered if the ukulele would have become so popular if its country of origin had been, say, Sudan, Finland or Bosnia? Certainly, the fact that ukuleles came from a tropical island paradise had a significant influence on how quickly interest in these instruments grew in the early part of the 20th century. Just try to think about Hawaii without conjuring a vision of swaying palm trees, sparkling waters at sunset and sandy beaches replete with dancing Wahines and uke-strumming Kanes.

But where did all these images of paradise come from? Before Hawaii became an official U.S. territory in 1898, few Americans had actually visited the islands, as early sailing ship journeys were long and treacherous. American author Mark Twain did brave the passage to Hawaii in 1866 and later offered his praises in an 1899 speech: "No alien land in all the world has any deep strong charm for me but one, no other land could so longingly and so beseechingly haunt me, sleeping and waking, through half a lifetime, as that one has done. For me its balmy airs are always blowing, its summer seas flashing in the sun; the pulsing of its surfbeat is in my ear." Little wonder that Hawaii came to be known as the "Paradise of the Pacific."

It wasn't until regular steamship routes were established between California port cities and Honolulu that tourism become practical, safe and affordable. By the 1920s and 30s, the Matson company had droves of tourists buying tickets for the 5-day voyage to Hawaii aboard one of their growing fleet of gleaming white

The fact that the ukulele is directly associated with Hawaii, a true tropical paradise, no doubt had an impact on its growing popularity in mainland America during the early part of the 20th century.

In the 1920s and 30s, it took 5 days to get from the mainland to Hawaii aboard one of Matsons luxurious steamships, plenty of time to learn a few chords on the ukulele.

The cover of one of the menus on a Matson steamship bound for Hawaii features the ukulele.

luxury passenger vessels, including the S.S. Lurline, S.S. Mariposa and S.S. Monterey. Matson's travel brochures and advertisements enticed potential customers with colorful, tantalizing images that portrayed Hawaii as the ultimate tropical destination. Once aboard, passengers were exposed to more paradisical imagery: everything from shipboard murals to the playing cards in the game room featured artwork depicting familiar island motifs such as native dancers, exotic flowers and outrigger canoes. In the dining room, a print of a colorful lei-draped ukulele graced the menu covers. This was most appropriate, as Matson passengers could take shipboard classes that taught them how to play the "jumping flea."

America's exposure to Hawaiian culture was significantly broadened thanks to two things: the 1915 Pan-Pacific International Exposition, which featured Hawaiian music and dancing, and Richard Walton Tully's musical play the "The Bird of Paradise." Set in Hawaii, Tully's play was so popular, it toured American cities for more than 10 years. Merchants, both on

the mainland and in the islands, were quick to capitalize on the public's fascination with all things Hawaiian, and they weren't shy about using paradisical imagery to boost sales. By the time the first big ukulele craze was in full swing in the 1920s, one could find all manner of products displaying island-themed graphics: aloha shirts, dresses and scarves, serving trays, dishes and glassware, and even cans of "Summer Isles" brand pineapple slices and boxes of "Hula" brand apples. The artwork ranged from quaintly picturesque to downright seductive. Some of the most colorful artwork was created for record jackets and the sheet music covers of Hapa Haole songs penned by Tin Pan Alley composers (see Section 8.2).

It didn't take long for mainland instrument manufacturers to get in on the action, producing untold numbers of ukuleles decorated with tropical theme graphics. Given the growing market for attractive yet inexpensive ukuleles in the 1920s and 30s (and again in the 1950s), it's certain that all the major mainland ukulele manufacturers produced them, including Har-

Several musical instrument companies, including Harmony and Regal, produced untold numbers of ukuleles adorned with tropical theme graphics.

The stenciled top of the "Playtime" ukulele features a typical tropical beach scene, complete with palm trees and a grass-skirt-wearing maiden.

Detailed tropical designs were applied to the tops of painted ukes using the silk screen method.

mony, Regal and Lyon & Healy. However, very few have labels or decals that identify who made them. Some instruments show only brand names, such as Collegiate, Supertone, La Pacific and Playtune. Still others lack any kind of labeling at all.

As a whole, the musical instrument industry cranked out thousands of inexpensive ukes that, frankly, looked way better than they played or sounded. Since these ukes were typically sold in Music Shops directly opposite well built, but more expensive Hawaiian-made koa ukes, their affordable prices and enchanting appearances kept them competitive. Thousands were sold, as first-time buyers were typically unwilling to pay big bucks for an instrument they likely didn't already know how to play. They were also sold in island shops as souvenirs and made decent beginners' instruments at best.

RIGHT: This beach scene decoration features kids playing in the sand, with mom and dad resting under canvas umbrellas.

THE ART OF VINTAGE UKULELES • SANDOR NAGYSZALANCZY

Not every topically-themed uke scene makes sense: Palm trees at an icy mountain lake? Fireflies on a spiderweb? Macaws in Hawaii?

To keep costs down, the majority of decorative ukes—both tropically themed and otherwise—were made entirely from whitewoods, such as birch and poplar. To hide the plain wood, they were first entirely painted in a solid color or stained with a dark wood-toned stain. Decorative scenes were then rendered on their tops using either a stencil or silk screen. Both techniques allowed fairly complex designs to be applied quickly and consistently. Simpler single-color graphics were usually spray painted on using a cardboard stencil temporarily affixed to the top of the instrument. When poorly applied, stenciled graphics often display blurry lines along the edges of their designs, as well as areas of overspray. More elaborate designs featuring one, two or more contrasting colors, were usually applied with the silk screen process using a finely detailed stencil attached to a mesh-covered frame.

The graphic designs found on island-themed ukes typically featured tropical beach scenes, often with palm trees, flowers and/or hula maidens set against a backdrop of volcanic mountains and/or ocean sunsets. One of my favorites is the red uke shown p. 104 which depicts a family having a fun day at the beach, complete with kids playing in the sand and dad and mom resting under canvas umbrellas.

Sometimes, the artists who created these ukulele graphics went a bit astray. Take, for example, the three ukes in the photo above. The one at left shows a lake scene one might see in upstate New York or Vermont, complete with a sailboat, light house and snow-capped peaks in the background… as well as a totally-out-of-

Two paradisical decorated plastic ukuleles: A Mastro T.V. Pal baritone (left) and Carnival "Aloha" Ukette (right).

place palm tree. In the center of that photo, there's the blue Harmony uke with the hula maid catching fireflies—insects which aren't found in Hawaii. Finally, at right is a Supertone ukulele featuring a couple taking a romantic canoe trip down a lazy river lined with palm trees while a flock of South American macaws flies overhead (perhaps the river is in Brazil?).

The next wave in America's love affair with the ukulele came in the late 1950s and early 60s, partially bolstered by the development of injection-molded plastic instruments. The new synthetic materials enabled manufacturers to churn out more low-priced ukes than ever— Mario Maccaferri's Mastro company alone made more than nine million plastic ukuleles! Jovial island graphics

A pair of Silvertone ukuleles sold by Sears & Roebuck: The Water Skiers (left) and Ukulele Hula Girl (right).

Musical instrument wholesaler P'mico sold an entire line of Peter Pan brand ukuleles, all featuring charming hand-painted figures and decorations.

adorned Mastro's cutaway baritone and Carnival's toy-sized ukette. Plastics also helped speed up production and reduce the cost of wood-bodied ukes via the use of injection molded fingerboards. A one-piece plastic fingerboard, complete with the nut and all the frets, could be simply screwed atop the uke's neck, thus reducing the number of steps needed to build a uke such as the Silvertone "water skiers" model sold by Sears & Roebuck (the uke at left in the photo on pg. 107).

3.2 Peter Pan Hand-Painted Ukes

Have you ever heard the saying "you can put lipstick on a pig, but it's still a pig"? That phrase comes to my mind when I play one of the decorative, yet inexpensive ukuleles that were sold by the millions from the 1920s to the 1950s. Most of these were built rather crudely from inexpensive "white woods," such as birch or poplar and lacked any of the fancy appointments—bindings, inlays, etc.—that more expensive models had. Typically, they were either painted or stained dark

A Dutch couple in traditional garb grace the top of this Peter Pan soprano uke.

to resemble more expensive woods. To add visual appeal, many such ukes were adorned with either colorful decals or painted stencils—both techniques that were quick and inexpensive to implement. Themes of decoration included sports (often football), exotic imagery (Japanese pagodas, Egyptian pyramids, etc.), romantic vignettes (such as lovers in a canoe), humorous or cartoon figures (Harold Teen, Betty Boop, etc.) and stylish Art Nouveau or Art Deco patterns.

At first glance, ukuleles branded as "Peter Pan Ukes" are pigs with lipstick. They're constructed simply, with plain mahogany or stained whitewood bodies bound front and back with a single celluloid binding, frets set directly into the neck and friction pegs. But upon closer inspection, what sets them apart from other "lipstick" ukes are the hand-painted figures on their bodies. The figures are based on popular themes of the era, including a Dutch boy and girl dressed in traditional garb, an animated harlequin couple, circus clowns, hula girls and palm trees, whimsical dancers and more. Even though these decorative themes were repeated on numerous instruments, each uke was individually

LEFT: The Peter Pan uke features a pair of Harlequin figures and lantern decorations, each painted by hand.

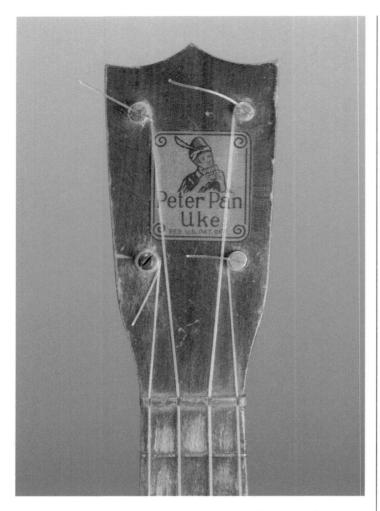

A Peter Pan Uke headstock decal depicts Peter wearing a feathered cap and playing a South American pan flute.

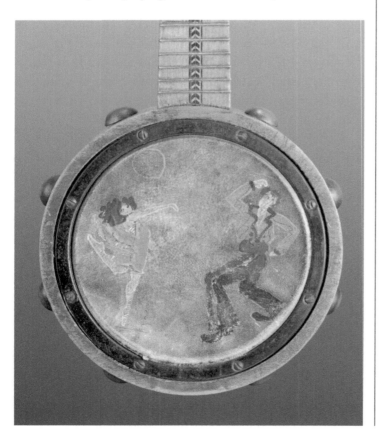

The head of this banjo uke from P'mico's Peter Pan line shows a flashy-dressed couple dancing the night away. A trio of painted dots mark the uke's 11th, 12th and 13th frets.

hand painted—a process much more laborious than simply slapping on a decal or spraying paint with a stencil—and no two are exactly alike. In addition to the character figures, most Peter Pan ukes have hand painted fretboard position markers, which are clearly more decorative than functional.

Peter Pan brand ukuleles were a product of the Progressive Musical Instrument Corporation also known as "P'mico." Based in New York City, P'mico was not a manufacturer, but a wholesaler of all manner of musical instruments and merchandise. The products they sold to music stores and instrument dealers were manufactured by a great variety of companies. P'mico's list of uke brand names included: Armstrong, My Buddy, Buckaroo, Nobility and Collegiate.

P'mico first registered the "Peter Pan" brand name

LEFT: A dancing couple painted on the skin head of another Peter Pan banjo uke. Note the domed brass buttons that decorate the outside of the banjo's body shell.

THE ART OF VINTAGE UKULELES • SANDOR NAGYSZALANCZY

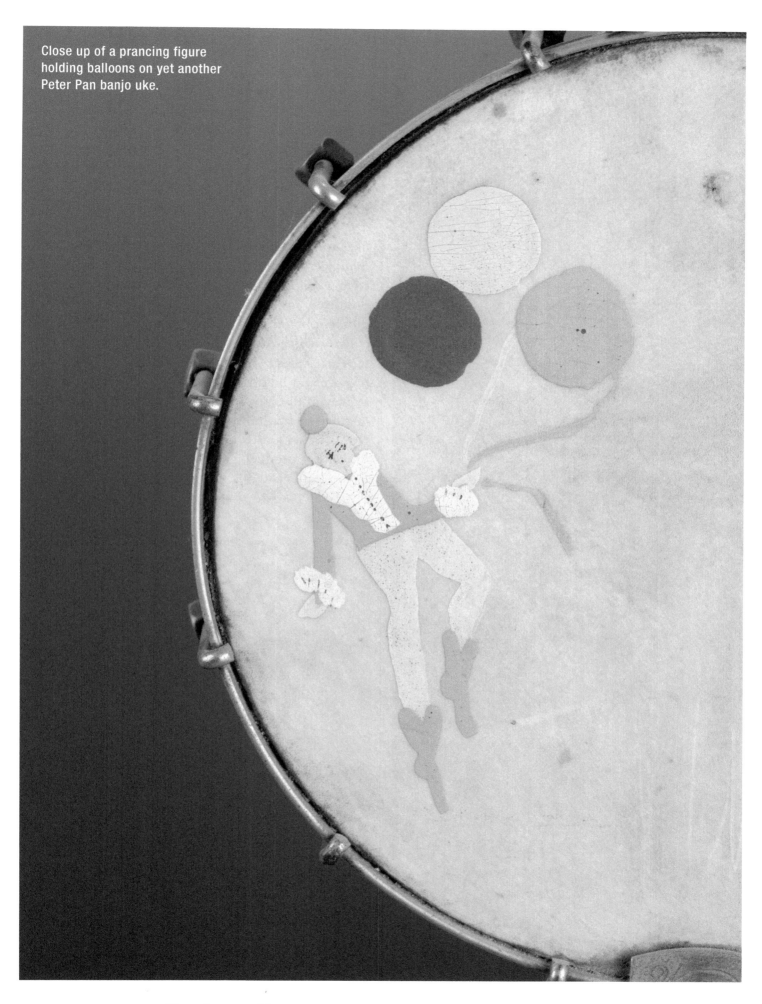

Close up of a prancing figure holding balloons on yet another Peter Pan banjo uke.

in 1926, but evidently sold these ukes as early as 1924. All these ukes bear a "Peter Pan Uke" decal on the headstock, which includes an illustration of Peter with a feather in his cap, playing a pan flute. The brand included both wooden soprano ukuleles as well as banjo ukuleles. Besides the hand-painted figures on their skin heads, many of these banjo ukes featured a herringbone stripe around the body and down the center of the fretboard, as well as domed brass studs surrounding a laminated-maple body.

It's likely that both Peter Pan soprano and banjo ukes were manufactured by one of the big instrument manufacturers such as Harmony or Regal, both located in Chicago. Between them, Harmony and Regal produced countless ukuleles sold under hundreds of different brand names.

P'mico also distributed a line of better quality "Peter Pan DeLuxe" ukuleles which were made from mahogany and had flashy pearloid fretboards, headstock overlays and body purflings. These were either manufactured by Harmony or Regal or possibly by John Rutan, a luthier located in St. Louis, Missouri. Rutan was known for producing some very high quality ukuleles in the 1920s and 30s.

LEFT: P'mico's best quality ukulele was the "Peter Pan DeLuxe" model which was made from solid mahogany and had a flashy pearloid fretboard, headstock overlay and body purfling.

3.3 The Art Moderne

Even if you have little interest in art or design, you've likely heard of Art Deco, a style popular in the early 20th century. But you might not be familiar with Art Moderne, a style that succeeded Art Deco in the 1930s during the Great Depression. While Art Deco made liberal use of decorative embellishments, Art Moderne embraced a much sparer design language that reflected the machine age, employing straight lines and streamlined and/or repetitive geometric forms that gave the architecture, furniture and indus-trially designed objects of the period the look of both efficiency and functionality.

While the great majority of Americans faced severe economic challenges during the Great Depression, it didn't stop them from purchasing inexpensive musical instruments, including ukuleles, which reached the peak of their popularity at the time. By the mid 1930s, the Harmony Company of Chicago, the largest producer of stringed instruments in the U.S., was producing dozens of different lines of ukuleles, as well as guitars, banjos and mandolins. Ever eager to capitalize on popular trends, Harmony created a new instrument model named for the Art Moderne design style it em-

Art Moderne model ukuleles first produced by Harmony in the mid 1930s were decorated with an array of geometrical forms which were derived from the Art Moderne design style.

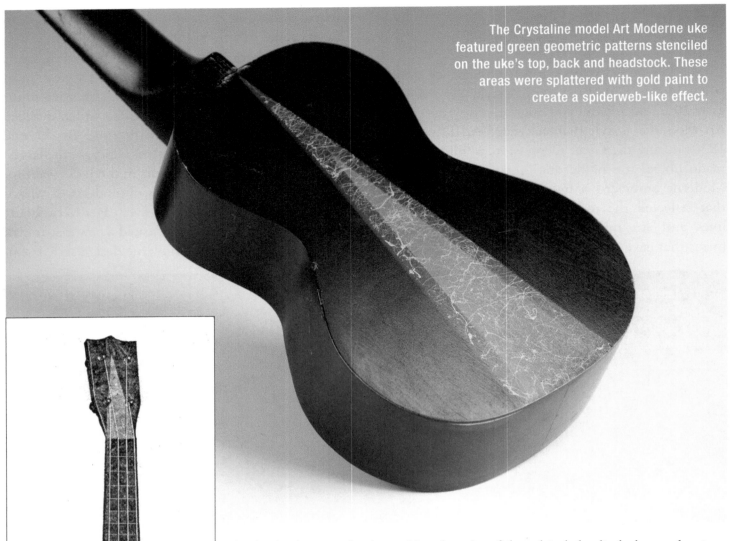

The Crystaline model Art Moderne uke featured green geometric patterns stenciled on the uke's top, back and headstock. These areas were splattered with gold paint to create a spiderweb-like effect.

Art Moderne Crystaline Ukulele. A new crystaline art moderne ukulele, in pleasing black and silver crystaline finish. Substantially constructed of birch with hardwook neck, accurately fretted and fitted with patent friction pegs. Packed each in box.
No. 3A7. Each..... 1.35

bodied. The tops, backs and headstocks of these birch-bodied ukes and guitars were decorated with an array of geometrical forms which were usually painted on using stencils to keep the patterns uniform. In 1932, these ukes sold for $1.35—the equivalent of $26.77 in today's dollars. Music stores purchased them through wholesale mail order houses like N. Shure of Chicago (which later became the Shure Brothers microphone company).

Art Moderne models were produced in both soprano and concert sizes and came in various color schemes and with a variety of features. The concert-sized uke seen at the center of the photo p. 113 has a painted black body and neck with gold stenciled decorations, white celluloid top and sound hole bindings and an ivory-color pearloid fingerboard. The decorations on the uke shown above are done in a "crystalline" finish: The green geometric patterns stenciled on the uke's top, back and headstock were splattered with gold paint, thus creating a spiderweb-like effect. Another variation in color schemes is displayed by the brown soprano uke on the next page. Its patterns were created by partially masking off shapes on the natural-color birch body and headstock, then staining them a darker color.

Probably the showiest of the Art Moderne ukes was branded as the "Rainbow" model (none of the other models in the line carried any labeling whatsoever). Sporting a bright green painted finish and distinctive green pearloid fingerboard, the Rainbow's geometric patterns were created by masking off

The geometric patterns on the top of this Art Moderne uke were created by partially masking off areas of the body and headstock, then staining them a darker color.

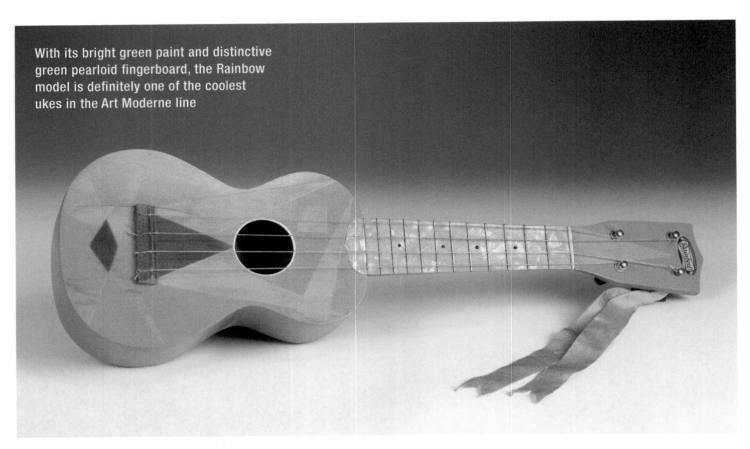

With its bright green paint and distinctive green pearloid fingerboard, the Rainbow model is definitely one of the coolest ukes in the Art Moderne line

sections on the top, back and headstock, thus allowing the natural color of the wood to show through. The dark shapes above and below the bridge were done by staining the wood in those areas. For added flair, this soprano-sized uke came with a pair of jaunty yellow and green ribbons tied to one of its friction tuners.

For some odd reason, the headstocks of Art Moderne ukuleles came in three different shapes, each commonly used on other Harmony models, including the Harold Teen and Cheer Leader ukes. Why the company changed headstock shapes over the course of manufacturing these instruments is likely to remain a mystery.

3.4 Harold Teen's Comical Uke

Only a handful of vintage American comic strips and their featured characters have managed to gain long-term popularity: Gasoline Alley, Popeye and Barney Google are each nearly 100 years old, and the Blondie comic turned 90 in 2020. The vast majorities of strips have their heyday, and then pass into inky obscurity.

One comic strip character that few remember today is Harold Teen. Created by cartoonist Carl Ed (pronounced "eed"), the strip ran from 1919 to 1959, debuting as "The Love Life of Harold Teen" in the Chicago Tribune. It starred high school student Harold "Teenzy" Teen, his sidekick Shadow Smart, bob-haired girlfriend Lillums Lovewell, her sometime rival Mimi Snatcher and Pop Jenks, proprietor of The Sugar Bowl soda shop, where the gang often gathered. Ed said he started the strip because, at the time, "…there was no comic strip on adolescence. I thought every well-balanced comic sheet should have one." Despite its obscurity today, Harold Teen was so successful at depicting teenage life in the day, that comic aficionados consider it a cultural icon of the Jazz Age.

The Harold Teen uke, first manufactured in the late 1920s/early 1930s by the Harmony Company, was a painted whitewood instrument that came in red, green or yellow. A sticker inside the body read "Genuine Harold Teen Ukulele made by The Harmony Co. Licensed by Famous Artists Syndicate." Despite the simple paint and basic construction, the ukes were bedazzled with colorful decals of the entire Harold Teen gang. Below the bridge, Harold is shown strumming and singing to Lillums, their thought bubbles declaring that "music self played…is happiness self made." Just above the bridge is Harold's jalopy "Leapin' Lena" which expels a musical note from its exhaust. On the uke's top bout, Pop Jenks and Mimi Snatcher are dancing and shouting "boop boop a doop." Harold, dressed in a cardigan sweater and baggy slacks, appears on the uke's headstock, while other minor characters are pictured the sides of the body.

Harmony-made Harold Teen Ukes sported a pearloid (aka "mother of toilet seat") fretboard with bullseye fret markers. Later models (likely built by

First produced by Harmony in the 1920s, the Harold Teen model ukulele was based on a popular comic strip of the same name.

Created by cartoonist Carl Ed in 1919, the Harold Teen comic starred high school student Harold "Teenzy" Teen, his girlfriend Lillums Lovewell and a host of other characters.

Decals on the uke's lower bout show Harold strumming and singing to his girlfriend Lillums, while imagining that "music self played…is happiness self made."

The decals on the uke's upper bout feature Harold Teen characters Pop Jenks and Mimi Snatcher dancing and shouting.

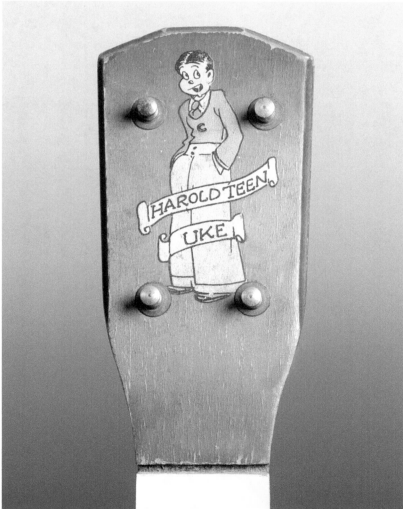

LEFT: The uke's headstock decal shows Harold in his signature cardigan sweater and baggy pants.

BELOW: This newspaper clip advertises the first film based on Harold Teen comics: a 1928 silent film that starred Arthur Lake as Harold.

Regal) had fretboards painted ivory white and bodies bound with dark celluloid purfling. Tuners were the typical "chess piece" style bakelite type found on many other ukes from this period.

Sonically, the Harold Teen uke isn't anything to write home about. Even when strung with modern nylon strings (it's original strings were gut), it lacks volume and harmonic richness. But nevertheless, it's snazziness makes you want to slip on a raccoon coat, strum a jazzy tune and yell "Yowsah," a slang term Harold often uttered in the frames of his comic strip.

Besides longevity, a strong measure of the popularity of any comic strip is how far their characters leap beyond the newsprint and into other media. Two films were made featuring Harold Teen: A 1928 silent film starring Arthur Lake as Harold and a 1934 musical starring tap dancer Hal Le Roy. A 1941 Harold Teen radio show on station WGN in Chicago aired hit records of the day. Numerous songs were written about Harold and his pals, including "Swinging at the Sugar Bowl" recorded by Bob Crosby (Bing's brother) and a tune by Kansas City pianist Joe Sanders' that proclaimed Harold as the "Don Juan of comic strip fame." There was certainly no shortage of Harold Teen merchandise, including toys, a board game, celluloid wind-up figures, pin-back buttons that came in boxes of Pep Cereal and Cracker Jack, and…one of the coolest ukuleles ever.

Vaudeville ukulele girls from the 1920s.

3.5 The Le Domino Line

Of all the hundreds of painted, stenciled or otherwise decorated ukuleles made in America during the "uke craze" of the 1920s, few are as attractive and instantly recognizable the Le Domino. Adorned with stylish decals of small dominos, this uke simply emanates charm and delight. In addition to a domino rosette bordered in gold surrounding the sound hole and a trio of larger dominos just below the bridge, miniature dominos also mark this uke's fretboard at the 3rd, 5th, 7th, 10th and 12th positions. Better still, each bears the same number of dots as the fret it marks--a three-dot domino at the 3rd fret, a five dot at the 5th, etc. The 12th fret domino (which is actually where the 13th fret would be, if the uke had one) is on a decal

LEFT: The iconic Le Domino uke was designed by James R. Stewart, a Chicago luthier who worked for the Harmony Company in the early 1920s.

BELOW: This Le Domino uke bears a gold and red "J.R.S Co." decal atop the its headstock, an abbreviation for the J.R. Stewart Company.

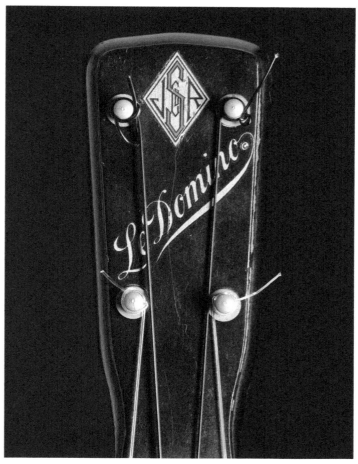

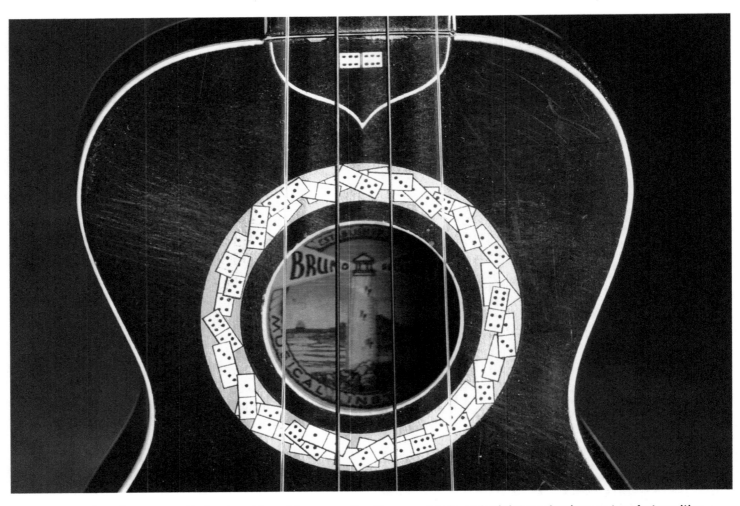

Decals of dominos form a rosette bordered in gold surrounding the sound hole and miniature dominos act as fret position markers, each bearing the same number of dots as the fret it marks.

A blond version of the black Le Domino uke and a Le Domino banjo uke.

Small domino decals surround the body shell of the Le Domino banjo uke.

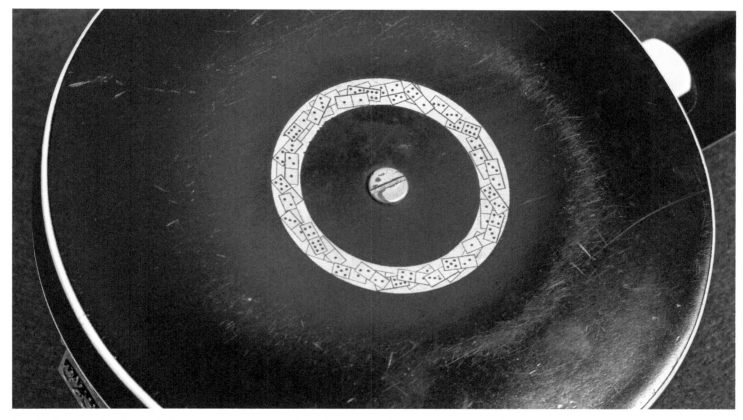

The Le Domino banjo uke's large wood resonator has the same gold rosette with dominos are found on the original black soprano model.

The well known Le Domino Guitars are made with either white or dark tops. Concert size. Neatly trimmed with white celluloid and decorated with domino decalcomania. Ebonized bridge with white pins.

No. 18   Dark top Le Domino Guitar. Each................$15.00
No. 19   White top Le Domino Guitar. Each................15.00
No. 911   Le Domino Tenor Guitar. Regulation size with full 23-inch scale. Ebonized bridge with white pins. Contrasting white celluloid binding around sound hole, both edges and fingerboard. Le Domino decorations as pictured. Each 15.00
No. 4500 Le Domino Flat Mandolin. An outstanding mandolin, well made and accurately adjusted. White celluloid guard plate and white celluloid bindings to correspond with other Le Domino numbers. Nickel-plated patent heads and tailpiece. Each.................................... 16.00

Le Domino Ukuleles in concert and tenor sizes. Made of well seasoned birch finished in jet black with contrasting white celluloid bindings as illustrated. Good quality strings. Patent pegs.
No. 125   Concert Size Le Domino Ukulele...$ 7.50
No. 127   Tenor Size Le Domino Ukulele.....12.00
No. 801   Le Domino Tiple. A beautiful instrument in jet black finish with contrasting white celluloid trimmings. Ebonized bridge. Hardwood neck. Nickel-plated patent heads. Each.......................$15.00

The Tonk Brothers wholesale catalog shows the whole line of Le Domino instruments, including regular and tenor guitars, a tiple, a mandolin and soprano uke and banjo uke.

that creates the illusion of a fingerboard extension.

Although the ukulele's painted body and neck were built from inexpensive birch wood, the Le Domino was a relatively well constructed instrument which featured some classy touches, including white celluloid binding around the top, back and soundhole, white bakelite tuners and a white/black/white celluloid nut. Even the original strings echoed the dark/light theme, with white strings top and bottom and two black strings in the middle. The Le Domino's solid-birch top employed an unusual fan bracing pattern that lent it a decent sound for ukulele not built from traditional tone woods like mahogany and koa. Curiously, it has an unusually long scale for a soprano-sized instrument: 14 1/8" long, as compared to the 13 3/4" long scale most commonly used on Martin, Gibson, Lyon & Healy and other soprano ukes of the period.

The Le Domino model was the brain child of James R. Stewart, a Chicago luthier who, in the early 1920s, had worked for the Harmony Company; the world's largest manufacturer of stringed instruments at the time. In 1925, he started his own J.R. Stewart fretted instrument company (you can see the "J.R.S Co." decal headstock decal on page 121). Within a couple of years, he had patented the Le Domino's unique headstock design and began producing his long-scale soprano ukuleles, which some music catalogs listed as a "concert size" instruments. With early success and sales, he expanded the line to include Le Domino tenor ukes and banjo ukes, as well as guitars, tenor guitars, tiples and mandolins. These featured all (or most) of the same decorations, appointments and constructions as the original soprano. For example, the Le Domino banjo uke sported domino fret markers, mini dominos surrounding its black body and a golden domino ring centered on the back of its resonator.

Despite his early success with the Le Domino line, J.R. Stewart's luck was soon to run out. In 1928, musical instrument manufacturing giant Lyon & Healy got out of the stringed-instrument-making business and Stewart bought their equipment and factory on the South Side of Chicago. Less than a year and half later, the U.S. stock market crashed and left J.R. Stewart--and well as most other manufacturers--scrambling. By the spring of 1930, Stewart declared bankruptcy and sold their entire business to musical distributors, the Tonk Brothers. Eventually, Regal, another Chicago-area instrument manufacturer, obtained the Le Domino instrument line, which they continued to manufacture for some years thereafter. In addition to the classic black-painted Le Domino ukuleles, Regal also made a cheaper, much plainer "blond" model (the top uke in the bottom photo on p. 122) that featured only a single triple-domino decal on the top below the bridge. The Regal-era instruments are distinguished by their headstocks, which are simpler and less elegant that Stewart's original patented design.

In the 1920s, college football was prominently played across the country and ukulele makers took notice, creating the Pep Leader, Cheer Leader and Touchdown models shown here.

3.6 Celebrating College Football

Watching contemporary football on a giant flat-screen TV, it's easy to overlook how far this game has come since its humble origins more than 150 years ago. From the late 1860s through the early 1900s, athletic clubs and colleges across the country formed teams that competed in a pigskin ball pitching and punting game that evolved from a modified form of English rugby. Players wearing un-padded clothing and soft leather skull caps battled each other in stadiums filled with excited fans. Male cheerleaders' shouting chants such as "rah, rah, sis boom bah" through their cardboard megaphones often whipped the crowds into a frenzy (women didn't participate in cheerleading until the 1920s). Well-heeled fans sported trendy raccoon coats and strummed their favorite team's songs on a uke, such as Duke's "Fight! Blue Devils Fight!" Clemson's "Tiger Rag" and Ohio State's "Buckeye Battle Cry." Popular tunes of the era included "After the Game is Over," "You Gotta Be a Football Hero (To Get Along with the Beautiful Girls)" and "Doin' the Raccoon" (which reportedly started the whole rac-

A leather helmet, football, and megaphone mark the Touchdown uke's 5th, 7th and 10th frets.

THE ART OF VINTAGE UKULELES • SANDOR NAGYSZALANCZY

The 1928 novelty song "Doin' the Raccoon" supposedly sparked the fad of wearing raccoon fur coats to college football games.

ABOVE: A decal just above the bridge on the "Touchdown" ukulele shows a pair of rival college players wearing leather helmets and padded uniforms which were common in the 1920s.

coon-coat-wearing craze).

The three vintage ukes shown here celebrate what's been called "The Golden Age of American Spectator Sports." In the 1920s up until the time of the Great Depression, the US economy was strong and many workers had more leisure time. Newspapers had increased coverage of sports and radio broadcasts of games made it easier for fans to follow their favorite teams. While college football was prominently played across the country, professional football's popularity was boosted by the founding of the American Professional Football conference, which became the National Football League in 1922

The football-themed "Touchdown" ukulele features a decal just above the bridge depicting a pair of rival college players wearing hardened leather helmets and padded uniforms which became more common in the 1920s. The uke's pearloid fretboard decals include a helmet, a football, and a megaphone marking the 5th, 7th and 10th frets respectively. There's white celluloid binding around the front of the body and ringing the sound hole.

Cheer Leader Ukulele. A high grade instrument handsomely decorated in colors with cheer leader decoration. A series of 12 miniature transfer pennants in authentic colors (size 2x1") of the leading schools (separate series for Eastern, Central and Western selling) free with each instrument. These transfer pennants are easily put on ukulele by the purchaser. Can be had with or without a 9x12 inch Collegiate Song Book consisting of 114 favorite songs from 106 colleges. This book has ukulele and guitar chords, piano accompaniment, harmonica symbols and words.

No. 3A1.
Ukulele, without book. Each..... **2.25**

No. 3A3.
Ukulele, complete with book. Ea.. **2.75**

ABOVE: A sheet of small stick-on pennants of various college teams came with the Cheer Leader uke, allowing the buyer to adorn their uke with the pennants of their favorite teams.

LEFT AND BELOW: The "Cheer Leader" uke's body decal depicts a megaphone-toting cheer leader leading a cheering crowd in a college football stadium.

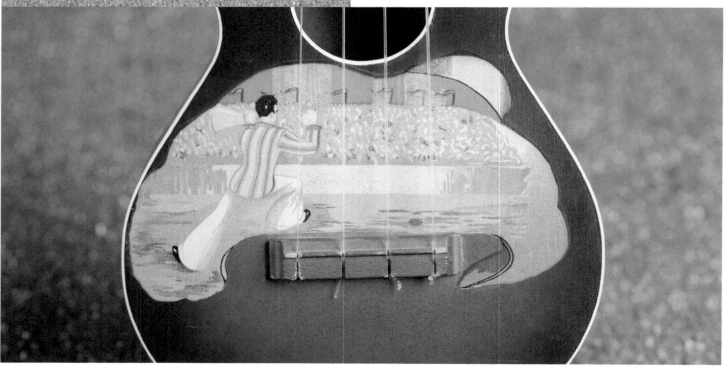

THE ART OF VINTAGE UKULELES • SANDOR NAGYSZALANCZY

The angular lines of the male cheer leader decal featured on the "Pep Leader" uke's lower body bout reflect the Art Deco design style that was popular in the 1920s.

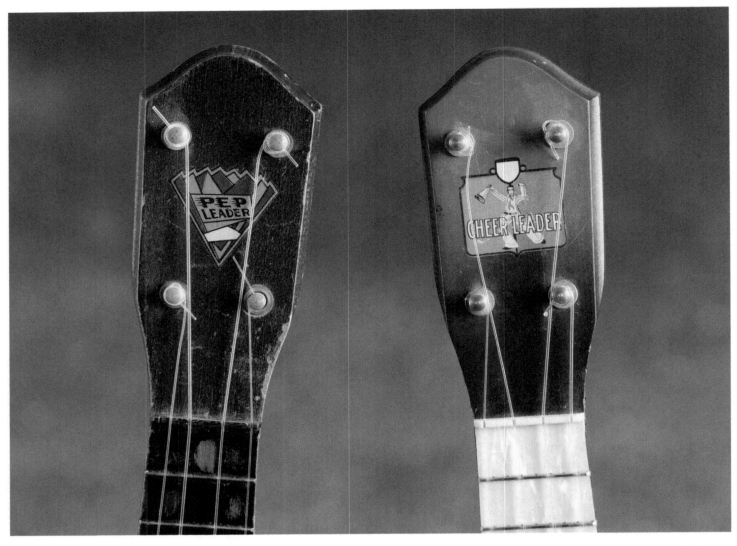

The characteristically shaped headstocks of the Pep Leader and Cheer Leader model ukes indicate that they were made by the Regal Musical Instrument Company.

The "Cheer Leader" uke's body decal depicts a megaphone-toting cheer leader wearing a brightly stripped jacket and white bell-bottomed pants in a college football stadium with a cheering crowd in the background. The instrument's pearloid-capped fretboard sports decals of crossed pennants marking frets 3, 5, 7, and 10. Like the Touchdown, it has white celluloid top binding and a sound hole ring. A tasseled cord tied to one of the uke's Bakelite tuning knobs adds a bit of flair. The instrument originally came in a box along with a "how to play" instruction booklet and a sheet of small stick-on pennants featuring the names of many college football teams of the era: Stanford, Washington, Northwestern, Michigan, Wisconsin, etc. The idea was that purchasers could adorn their ukes with whatever pennants they chose.

The colorful graphics on the "Pep Leader" uke's lower body bout also feature a male cheer leader, this one shouting through his megaphone. The angular lines of the figure are rendered in the Art Deco style that was popular in the 1920s. The uke's headstock Pep Leader decal is also done in this style. The snazzy purfling around the top and sound hole are made of alternating blocks of black and cream-colored ivoroid (an early plastic that imitated the look of ivory).

The tops, backs and necks of the Touchdown and Pep Leader ukes are made from inexpensive birch, with sides bent from mahogany plywood. Both ukes have a wood-tone sunburst finish on the top and back which is lighter in the middle and darker at the edges. The Cheer Leader is entirely made of birch that's been painted black and green. Judging from the rounded shape of their headstocks, the Cheerleader and Pep Leader ukes were made by the Regal Musical Instrument Company, while the Touchdown uke was likely made by Harmony.

3.7 It's all in the Details

Renowned modernist architect Ludwig Mies van der Rohe once said that "God is in the details." Best known for the stark yet sleek metal-and-glass skyscrapers he designed in the 1950s and 60s, one can only imagine what he would've thought had his phrase been applied to ukuleles. But like all other things made by man and nature, details are a critical part of the overall effect that an object—animal, mineral or made of mahogany—has upon those who behold it (or in this case, strum it).

This article is an exploration of all the little things that make vintage ukes both attractive and functional: Oddly-shaped bridges, inlayed headstocks, beautiful fingerboards, unusual tuners, complex bindings and decorative sound holes. In addition to intimate photos showcasing these details, I offer some history and bits of trivia about the ukuleles they enhance.

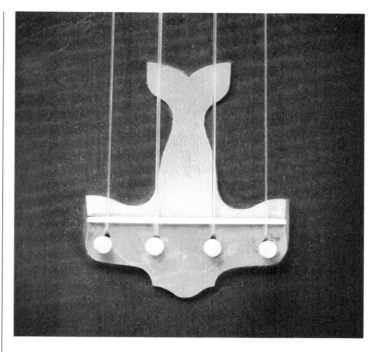

The airplane bridge on the Johnny Marvin Professional ukulele was fashioned as a tribute to Charles Lindberg's solo flight across the Atlantic.

This collection displays some of the more unique and interesting bridges found on ukuleles. From lower left clockwise: Aero, Bell, Shrine and Johnny Marvin Professional models.

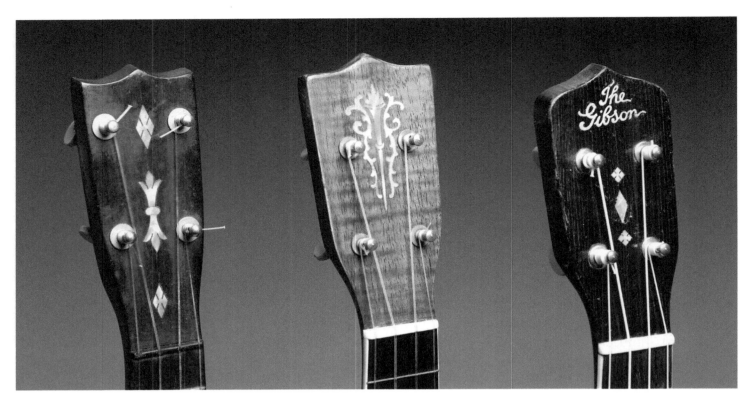

Three fancy soprano headstocks, from left to right: Gretsch, Martin 5K, and Gibson Style Uke-3.

Bridges

Whether they were originally inexpensive or pricey, around 98% of all vintage ukes have basic bridges that are typically a short rectangular strip of wood with a small raised saddle and slots at the strip's rear edge used to secure the knotted ends of the strings.

But Lyon & Healy had a more aesthetic goal in mind when they created the shapely and unique bridges for their entire line of ukes. The photo on previous page, shows Lyon & Healy's Bell Uke (top left) and Shrine Uke (top right). The strings on both of these soprano-size ukes are secured via small ivoroid bridge pins, a unique approach employed on their soprano- and concert-sized ukes.

Four Hawaiian koa ukuleles with distinctive headstocks, from left to right: Akai, Malolo, Cox and Niu Kani.

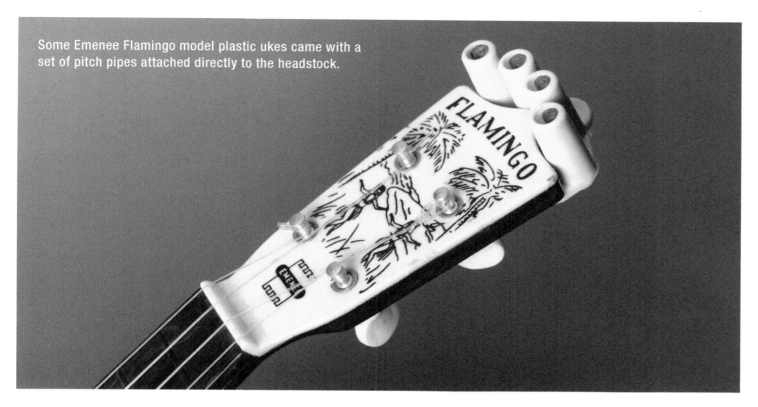

Some Emenee Flamingo model plastic ukes came with a set of pitch pipes attached directly to the headstock.

An entirely different kind of ukulele bridge design found its inspiration from a surprising source: Charles Lindberg's solo, non-stop flight across the Atlantic in 1927. His unprecedented accomplishment was so significant that merchandisers seeking to capitalize on its popularity created all manner of products featuring Lindberg and his Spirit of Saint Louis airplane: commemorative coins, buttons, picture puzzles, souvenir beanies, and the concert-sized "Aero Uke," made by the Stromberg-Voisinet Company of Chicago Illinois (See Section 5.5). The Aero's wing-like bridge has a unique screwed-on metal bar that serves to hold the strings in place. The sizeable maple bridge on Harmony's Johnny Marvin signature model ukulele is shaped to resemble a top view of Lindberg's plane (page 131).

Headstocks

I've seen plenty of vintage guitars and banjos with fancy-shape headstocks (aka pegheads) inlayed with intricate designs rendered in pearl or abalone. While such headstocks are relatively rare in the ukulele world, there are some examples worthy of mention. The three shown in the photo on page 132 are all high-end models made (left to right) by Gretsch, Martin and Gibson.

Over its long history, New York musical manufacturer Gretsch produced a wide range of instruments, including drums, guitars, basses, banjos and ukule-les. Their line of ukes produced in the 1920s and 30s ranged from a very plain Style 1, to the exceedingly rare koa-bodied Style 3 modeled after Martin's Style 5K. Their penultimate model, shown on the previous page, featured a pair of diamond-shape pearl inlays flanking a double ended floral decoration. The top of this model's mahogany head is covered in rosewood veneer which matches its rosewood fretboard.

Introduced late in 1921, Martin's top-of-the-line Style 5K featured a headstock topped with figured koa veneer inlaid with an attractive pearl "scroll" inlay. This curly-koa-bodied, pearl-encrusted model retailed for the princely sum of $50, equivalent to about $860 today. Martin dropped the 5K in 1940, evidently due to shortage of koa wood during WWII. They made a mahogany version of the Style 5 in 1941, but it was only in production for two years.

Although Gibson's model "Uke-3" was the company's fanciest stock model produced in the late 1920s (Gibson did occasionally build custom ukes on special order), it's appointments—bindings, inlays, etc.—didn't measure up to other top-shelf ukes made by Martin, Lyon & Healy and others. The Uke-3, which sold originally for $20, featured a headstock with "The Gibson" script logo done in silver paint above a pair of pearl diamonds with a pearl square in the middle.

The headstock shape of the great majority of ukuleles is generally known as the three-peaked "crown." However, early Hawaiian luthiers often created their

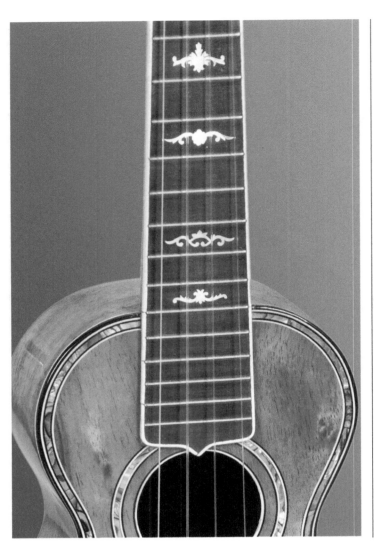

own unique headstock shapes. Take, for example, the four ukuleles shown on page 132. The first one on the left is an Akai made at the Aloha Ukulele Manufacturing Company in Honolulu. The next one over is a 1920s vintage Malolo, which is said to have been given away to steam liner passengers of the Matson Line Steamship S.S. Malolo. The two ukes at right are both "cocoleles" with bodies made of coconuts. The far right uke with the swallow-tail headstock is a Niu Kani, while the one with the pointy head next to it is a Cox Cocolele, made in Honolulu by inventor and part-time auto mechanic Anthony G. Cox.

Most uke players have heard the tongue-in-cheek phrase "You should tune your ukulele once a year, whether it needs it or not." But back in the early 1960s, toy and instrument maker Emenee Industries came up with a clever way of making it easier to keep their ukes in tune: Some of Emenee's "Flamingo" model plastic ukes came equipped with a set of pitch pipes attached

LEFT: The fingerboard of Schireson Brother's Hollywood's #10 uke features some of the most elaborate pearl inlays ever done on a ukulele.

BELOW: Vintage Hawaiian-made ukuleles often sport rope bindings on the body, while the fancier ones also have a rope-bound necks and rope center stripes on their fingerboards.

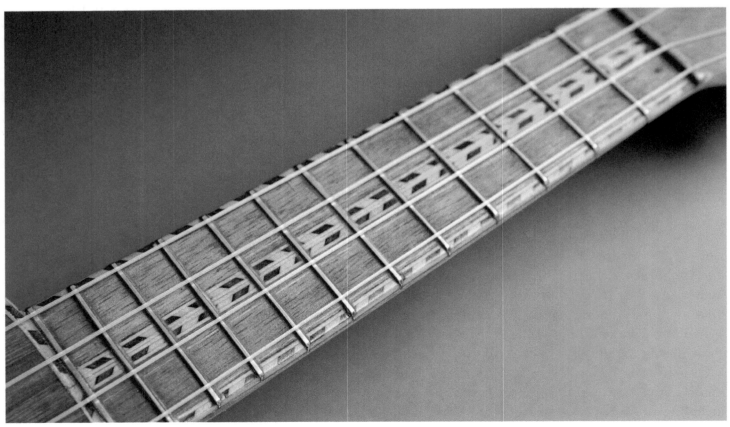

THE ART OF VINTAGE UKULELES • SANDOR NAGYSZALANCZY

ABOVE: Fancier, better-quality ukes often have fingerboards that extend over the top of the instrument. Here, from left to right are: a Martin 5K, a Gibson UKE-3 and a Martin 3K.

BELOW: Also known as "mother of toilet seat," pearloid is a celluloid plastic laminate that was commonly overlayed on ukulele necks, to give them more sparkle and appeal.

In addition to its cool extended fingerboard, this no-name ukulele has unique celluloid fingerboard overlays that act as fret position markers.

THE ART OF VINTAGE UKULELES • SANDOR NAGYSZALANCZY

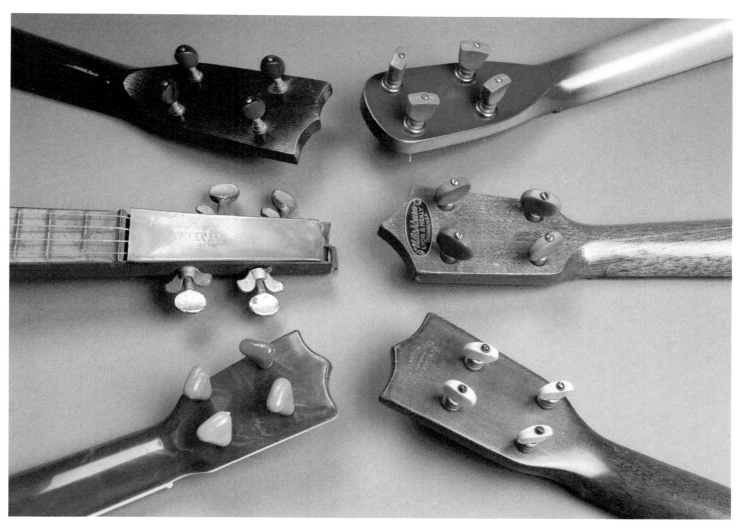

These six ukuleles all have tuners that are noteworthy. The brands are, clockwise from lower left: Fin-der, Rexcraft, P'mico, Gretsch, Washburn and Martin.

directly to the top of their headstocks. The four pipes are pitched G – C – E – A, which was—and still is—the standard tuning for soprano ukes.

Fingerboards

Fancier ukuleles not only have fancy headstocks but often more elaborate fingerboard inlays as well. The best examples, such as found on the Hollywood's #10 uke (page 134) feature arabesque pearl inlays similar to those found on the fanciest banjos of the era. Fancier models of early Hawaiian ukuleles often featured a multi-wood rope or herringbone center stripe and bindings on the edges of their fingerboards.

The extended fingerboards of the three soprano ukes in the photo on page 135 showcase more common styles of decorative inlay patterns. The ebony fingerboard, at left, belongs to the celebrated Martin 5K which sports a pearl snowflake at the 3rd fret and

various combinations of pearl diamonds, squares and eyelid-shape inlays at the 5th, 7th, 10th, 12th and 15th frets. The rosewood fingerboard of the Gibson Uke-3 (center) features four groups of shiny pearl diamond-shape inlays at the 5th, 7th, 10th, 12th frets. At right, Martin's style 3K uke has a simpler pattern of squares and diamonds at the 5th, 7th, 10th frets. The ebony fingerboards of 3K ukes produced before 1950 also features a center stripe which matches the instrument's black and white binding and sound hole ring.

To bring a bit of bling to less expensive models, many ukulele manufacturers produced instruments with fingerboards entirely covered in pearloid. Also known to luthiers as "mother of toilet seat," pearloid is the generic name for celluloid plastic laminates that give the overall look of real mother-of-pearl or abalone. To make pearloid, celluloid plastic chunks are swirled together in a solvent, then cured, sliced into sheets and bonded to backing laminates. Dyes may be added to create different colors (see the photo on page 135) or

Fancy bindings and purflings add lots of visual appeal to a ukulele. The uke's here are, clockwise from lower left, made by: Tru Fret, S. S. Stewart, Akai, Martin (Style 3) and Martin (Style 5K).

THE ART OF VINTAGE UKULELES • SANDOR NAGYSZALANCZY

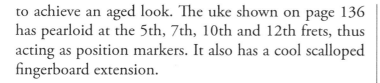

In lieu of a standard round sound hole, the Regal model at left has F holes, while the Roy Smeck Vita Uke next to it has a pair of holes shaped like circus seals.

A three-peaked crown-shaped sound hole is the hallmark of the Wendell Hall "Professional" model concert ukulele.

to achieve an aged look. The uke shown on page 136 has pearloid at the 5th, 7th, 10th and 12th frets, thus acting as position markers. It also has a cool scalloped fingerboard extension.

Tuners

Decades before ukulele makers dared to fit their instruments with geared tuning machines, ukuleles came with one of two types of tuners: Early Hawaiian instruments typically had wooden tuning pegs similar to those used for violins, while mainland ukes employed metal friction tuners with Bakelite knobs usually shaped like chess pieces. As you might guess, pricier models featured better, sometimes fancier tuners. Of the ukuleles shown in the photo on page 137, the Martin Style 2M and the Lyon & Healy Style 703 (bottom and center right) both have better quality

Grover brand friction tuners fitted with stylish knobs: ivoroid on the Martin and tan Bakelite on the 703. The Finder plastic uke at bottom left is distinguished by its unique multi-colored plastic tuning knobs. These are sometimes called "Chicklet" tuners, as their shape is reminiscent of the puffy shape of that once-popular brand of chewing gum. The Kluson brand tuners on the Gretsch WWII era "Army Uke" (top right) are noteworthy for their quality and vivid red color. The Cliff Edwards signature model uke (top left) has tuners with internal springs to keep them from slipping, yet allow easy tuning. Finally, the Rexcraft all-metal ukulele at center left features tuners that are crude in appearance, yet are unique and effective in their function. Each string wraps around the end of a standard thumb screw which facilitates tuning. Once set, a wing nut threaded onto the thumb screw locks its position in place.

With a triangular body that resembles a Russian balalaika, the Uka Lyka's odd sound hole is shaped like a club playing card symbol.

Body Bindings

Better quality ukes have always featured binding around the top of the body, and sometimes around the back as well. While it's functional purpose is to protect the edges of the wood body from impact and possible moisture damage, it also lends an instrument more visual impact; the more elaborate the bindings are, the greater the effect. Early Hawaiian ukuleles typically featured so-called "rope" bindings made up of alternating pieces of light and dark woods (the top left uke in the photo on page 138). Herringbone-style binding graces the edge of the S.S. Stewart uke (center left). These are made up of alternating pieces of wood dyed in four different colors with a single black binding strip surrounding the pattern. The Tru-Fret ukulele (bottom left) has an even more elaborate parquetry binding done in a neoclassical style. It's protected by a white celluloid binding that encircles the top of the uke. (Also

THE ART OF VINTAGE UKULELES • SANDOR NAGYSZALANCZY

Three cool sound holes on, from left to right, a Mastro Islander Deluxe, a Lyon & Healy/Washburn Superb and an S.S. Stewart Marquetry uke.

check out the cool checkerboard binding on the Pep Leader uke in Section 3.6, page 129).

One of the most distinctive edge bindings is found on Martin's Style 3 uke (top right). Seven layers of alternating ivory and black strips form the wide binding and also surrounds the sound hole. Both koa Style 3K and mahogany Style 3M models feature a distinctive ivory-color celluloid inlay on the top edge below the bridge known as a "parend," "shield," or "mustache." Both the top and back of Martin's style 5K uke (bottom right) are rimmed with a band of abalone bordered by white and black celluloid bindings. When the light catches it just right, a 5K simply sparkles.

Sound Holes

If there's one thing that every single uke has, it's a sound hole. The vast majority of holes are round and either totally plain or rimmed with a single ring of paint or celluloid. There are, of course, exceptions: Harmony's Roy Smeck signature uke (at right, page 139) showcases a pair of holes shaped like circus seals, while the Regal uke at left sports the kind of F-holes you'd find on a jazz guitar or violin. Wendell Hall's "Profes-

sional" model concert uke (page 139) had a sound hole the shape of a three-peaked crown and the Shrine uke , (pg. 131, upper right) has a triangular sound hole with convex sides. Vintage models adorned with stenciled or painted decorations often feature a rosette-like decal surrounding the sound hole. A great example of this is found on the English-made triangular-bodied "Uka Lyka" (previous page) whose sound hole is basically the shape of a club suit playing card symbol.

Beyond mere paint and decals, some of the coolest looking ukes feature other forms of sound hole decoration. Take, for instance, the uke at far left in the photo above. This plastic Mastro Islander "De LUXE" soprano boasts a toothed ring of dark brown plastic, as well as a really cool bridge and extended fingerboard. The Lyon & Healy soprano uke at center of the photo is part of a line that featured raised celluloid rings around their sound holes. The one shown here is made of ivoroid, colored and grained to imitate real ivory. Other models sported raised rings of black celluloid to match their black saddles and nuts. At right in the photo, the S.S. Stewart's herringbone sound hole rosette matches its binding and fingerboard center stripe. I also love the unique shape of its shapely finger board extension.

The skin heads of banjo ukuleles provided a perfect canvas for ukers to personalize their instruments.

THE ART OF VINTAGE UKULELES • SANDOR NAGYSZALANCZY

3.8 Banjo Uke Head Art

Venerated American naturalist, poet, philosopher and author of the classic treatise "On Walden Pond" Henry David Thoreau once said: "This world is but a canvas to our imagination." Evidently, quite a few early banjo ukulele enthusiasts took Thoreau at his word, using the tightly-stretched skin heads of their instruments as canvases for their own artistic expressions. The wide range of visual creations found on the heads of vintage banjo ukes is abundant enough to make banjo head decoration its own musical instrument art form. While ukers in the 1920s and 30s occasionally painted, drew or carved on regular, wood-bodied instruments, relatively few vintage examples exist, especially when compared to the plentiful examples of user-decorated banjo uke heads.

While I've seen all types and styles of banjo ukes with decorated heads, including a high-end Gibson UB-4, the great majority of these instruments are less expensive models with wooden shells (bodies) and smaller 6-inch to 8-in. diameter heads. The majority of these had a wooden shell (the name for a banjo's round body), although banjo ukes with metal shells were also common. During the ukulele's heydays, such banjo ukes sold for as little as a few dollars. Some common brand names of the era include La Pacifica, Luxor, Bruno, Maxitone, Perfactone, U-King and Sammo. A great many other banjo ukes are so-called "no name" instruments, as they bear no label or brand name.

Having seen many dozens of artfully adorned banjo heads over the years, I've observed that the majority fall into one of several categories based on their type of imagery:

• A particular individual, almost always female, either a spouse, girlfriend or a "fantasy woman" (mermaid, goddess, forest spirit, etc.). These are usually done as portraits showing only the head or the head and shoulders of the subject, although full forms are also seen, often wearing a bathing suit (some of these were pretty racy). Of course, the women are depicted with hairdos that were popular in the era, like the "Windswept Bob" and "Pringle Shingle." Some are decked out in period attire: Cloche hats, feathered headbands, flapper dresses and such.

• A couple, clothed in fancy dress or party attire, often kissing. Such artwork often celebrates a particularly significant event, such as an engagement, marriage or anniversary. The date of the event is usually present as are the names or signatures of friends, family and/or party guests. Sometimes, on open-backed banjo ukes, these names/signatures are found written on the back side of the skin head.

• Children, either at play or singing or dancing. The

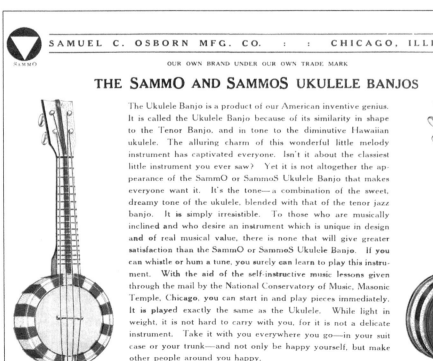

SammO was only one of dozens of different brands of banjo ukuleles available during the uke's heyday in the early 20th century.

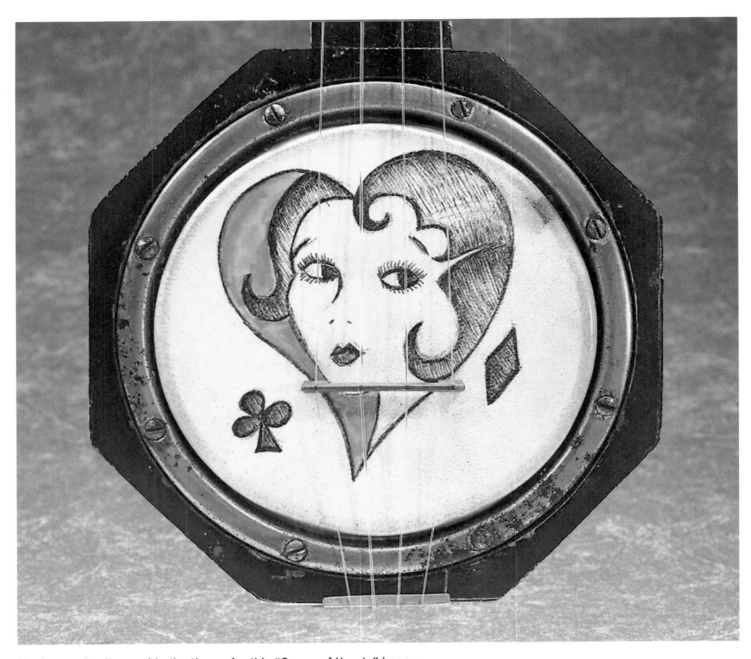

Playing card suits provide the theme for this "Queen of Hearts" image.

kids may be in plain dress or wearing uniforms of a youth organization, such as the Boy Scouts or Girl Scouts.

• A character from a popular cartoon of the era. Drawn from either comic strips or animated short films, some of the more popular candidates for banjo head art included: Felix the Cat, created in 1919 by Pat Sullivan and Otto Messmer during the silent film era, and Jiggs and Maggie, from a comic strip called "Bringing Up Father" created by cartoonist George McManus around 1913.

• Initials or insignias, such as pennants, of a par-

ticular college, university, academy, or fraternity organization, most likely the uke player's alma mater. These often include the school's sports team's colors, mascots, players or other sport-related imagery, mostly football, as most football games of the era were played at colleges and universities.

• Military imagery (soldiers in uniform, guns, knives, etc.) along with the soldier's name and members of their military unit. I saw one such banjo uke with artwork done in commemoration of a soldier who was killed in the first World War.

• Pastoral or fantasy images; a cabin in a lush for-

The dress, hairdo, pearls and cigarette holder identify this figure as a 20s era lady.

est, a tropical paradise, a romantic canoe ride, etc. These are sometimes signed and dated by the artist.

Of course, there are plenty of examples of banjo head artwork that doesn't fall precisely into any of these categories. For example, the banjo uke shown on page 153 depicts a fellow leaning against a lamp post. There's a bottle in his back pocket and he's clearly intoxicated. Perhaps this image was created as a joke or as a less-than-flattering self-portrait. Another example is seen in the photo on page 153 of a pair of young women, one holding a banjo uke with a head decorated with an image of a spider web that's ensnared a woman. Note also, that the banjo girl's swim suit

features spiders and webs. Clearly, there are no limits to personal expression.

Banjo head artists rendered their images using a great variety of art media, including pencils (both regular "lead" and colored) ink pens, and brushed-on watercolor and oil paints. Commonly, images are created using a mix of media. For example, the stylish female figure shown in the photo above was outlined in ink, then filled-in with colored pencils or paints. The quality of artwork ranges from rank amateur to seasoned professional. Unfortunately, the artwork on well-played instruments is often heavily worn or damaged or has accumulated dirt and grunge, making images hard to see, as is the case with the Valencia banjo uke

This handsome drawing of a couple on the head of a no-name banjo uke likely was done to celebrate a special occasion.

shown on page 156. Although it's hard to make out, if you look closely, you can see the pencil drawing of a wedding couple standing before cupid, who is holding an arrow. Some players simply skipped the hassle of drawing or painting by adorning their banjo uke heads with stick-on decals: Animals, college pennants, pin-up girls, etc.

Decorated banjo heads are often signed and dated by the artist, sometimes with a dedication. Many of these ukes include the names and/or initials of the player's friends, or perhaps, members of their club or sports team. Some include personal information about the artist or player, like their nick name (or those of their friends) and/or street address. There are also plenty of ukes with written comments or phrases that only the artist or player/owner would have understood. Like ancient cryptic scriptures, their meanings are lost to the sands of time.

One interesting aspect of banjo head art is how artists chose to orient the images on the instrument. Some

THE ART OF VINTAGE UKULELES • SANDOR NAGYSZALANCZY

Dressed in what looks like a scout uniform, this young lad sings along with a gal playing a banjo uke.

THE ART OF VINTAGE UKULELES • SANDOR NAGYSZALANCZY

A nice multi-colored drawing of Felix the Cat, a very popular cartoon character created during the silent film era.

THE ART OF VINTAGE UKULELES • SANDOR NAGYSZALANCZY

Vintage comic strip characters Jiggs and Maggie were featured in a comic strip called "Bringing Up Father" which ran in newspapers from 1913 to 2000.

This painted banjo uke head features "Willie the Wildcat" which was first adopted as the sports mascot of California's Chico State Teachers College in 1924.

The artwork on this banjo uke commemorates the 32nd Army Infantry Division formed from Wisconsin and Michigan Army National Guard units who fought in WWI and WWII.

show the picture level when the uke is held in playing position, while others show the image level when the uke is hung on the wall or set on an instrument stand. Still others have images oriented so that they're right-side-up to the player, but upside down to the audience. I've even seen one example where the image is upside down when the uke is held up vertically. It's possible (although unlikely) that with some of these vintage instruments, the head and tension ring assembly may have been rotated, perhaps when the instrument was repaired?

Artistic players weren't the only ones to decorate

Pastoral images, like a romantic canoe ride down a scenic river, were popular themes for banjo uke head art.

The Art of Vintage Ukuleles • Sandor Nagyszalanczy

ABOVE: Perhaps done as a joke, this colored pencil drawing depicts a drunk red-haired man leaning on a lamppost, apparently counting on the post to keep him upright.

LEFT: The head of the banjo uke this young woman holds is decorated with a spider web that's ensnared a woman.

Banjo head artists rendered their images using a variety of art media, including oil paints which were used to create this tropical scene.

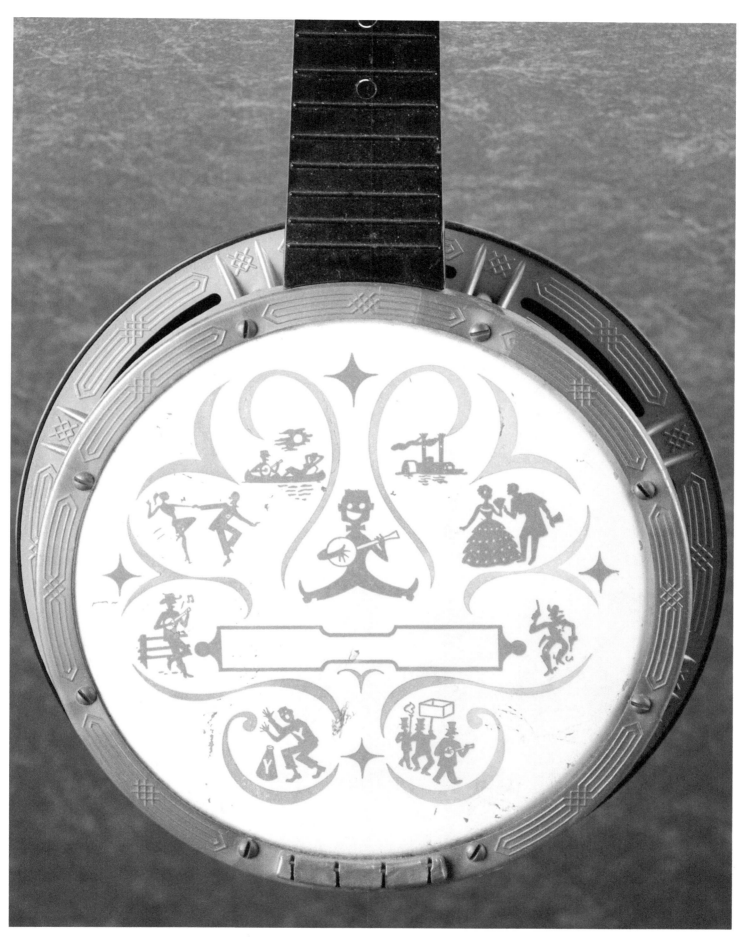

Produced sometime in the early 1960s, the synthetic head of Mastro's banjo uke was stenciled with a host of period images, including cowboys, dancing couples, and more.

ABOVE: Although it's heavily worn and difficult to see, the head of this Valencia brand banjo uke has a pencil drawing of a wedding couple standing before cupid, who is holding an arrow and apparently officiating the marriage.

LEFT: Some decorated banjo heads are signed and dated by the artist, sometimes with a dedication which, in this case, is to "…My Friend Alex Cameron."

This charming image of a tent set up in a mountain meadow is oddly oriented to be right-side-up when the uke is held upside down.

The heads of some banjo ukes were decorated by the company who made them. This Peter Pan uke features hand-painted dancers.

The Art of Vintage Ukuleles • Sandor Nagyszalanczy

ABOVE: A sweet decal of a family camping and canoeing in the country came standard on June Days brand banjo ukes.

their banjo ukes: Instrument manufacturers also saw the value of dressing up a banjo uke's head to make it more appealing to the buyer. Peter Pan brand banjo ukes featured charming hand-painted characters such as dancers, clowns, etc. (see the photo on pg. 158 and Section 3.2). The "June Days" model banjo uke was adorned with a sweet scene of a canoe paddling couple; the same decal applied to their June Days wood-bodied soprano ukuleles. The La Valencia brand "banjuke" sports a large decal depicting a Venetian gondola ride, complete with a female passenger playing a regular ukulele. And in the late 1950s and early 1960s, plastic uke manufacturers Mastro and Carnival each produced several banjo uke models featuring heads sporting colorful decorative images (see the photo on pg. 155 and Section 7.3).

No. 510 "LA VENICIA" 8-inch shell BANJUKE. Finished in black throughout. 12 nickel plated brackets and nickel plated straining hoop. Selected calfskin head with "LA VENICIA" design. Patent pegs; snappy tone. Each..................$11.50
No. 513 Same as above, but equipped with fine celluloid bound wooden resonator. Each......................$13.00

The heads of La Valencia "banjukes" bore a decal depicting a gondola ride in Venice.

Chapter Four
Celebrity Editions;
Signature Ukes of the Early Stars

A few of the signature model ukuleles given to talented performers of the early 20th century. From left to right: Johnny Marvin Professional, Wimbrowla, Bobby Breen and Roy Smeck concert.

How cool would it be to have an instrument manufacturer issue a special signature edition ukulele with your name on it? The reality is, that most of us will never achieve the level of playing ability and public recognition it would take to make this possible.

Given the talent and notoriety of uke-playing celebrities such as Jake Shimabukuro, Dhani Harrison, Grace Vanderwaal and Cynthia Lin, it's no wonder that uke manufacturers Kamaka, Fender and Ohana have honored them by producing their own signature model ukuleles.

But the idea of tying the fame and success of a per-

forming artist with a special-edition instrument isn't exactly new; so-called "signature edition" instruments have been around for at least 100 years. It's likely that they first came into being thanks to some clever marketing person who realized that an instrument maker could capitalize on the success of a well-known performer by creating a special instrument line featuring their name.

The list of 20s era American celebrities who had their own signature model production ukuleles is considerable, including—but certainly not limited to—the ones featured here, in alphabetical order: Bobby Breen, Ray Canfield, the Duncan Sisters, Cliff Edwards, Wendell Hall, Bobby Henshaw, Al Jolson, Johnny Marvin and Roy Smeck. Sadly missing are well-known Hawaiian musicians of the era, including Ernest Ka'ai and Frank Ferara, who were never recognized with their own well-deserved signature models.

Most of the celebrities presented here were born between 1886 and 1900 and represent the first wave of ukulele performers who introduced the American public to the songs, strums and satisfactions that ukulele playing could bring; Al Jolson's the exception here, as we'll see. Given their considerable talents, it's natural that each of these early stars were honored with their own signature model uke, and in some cases, more than one signature model.

4.1 Bobby Breen

This Canadian-born actor and singing prodigy reached the peak of his popularity as a child star in the 1930s. After a professional debut at age four in Toronto, Bobby Breen played in vaudeville before going to Hollywood in 1935. He became RKO's biggest child starring in a string of films including Let's Sing Again (1936), Hawaii Calls (1938) and Escape to Paradise (1939). Unfortunately, Breen's movie career ended

LEFT: Sheet music for one of the popular songs sung by child star Bobby Breen in "Hawaii Calls." the 1938 film Breen stars in.

ABOVE: Regal's Bobby Breen ukulele features Art Deco stenciled decorations and Breen's signature below the bridge.

in the early 40s after his singing voice changed upon reaching puberty. He continued working in nightclubs and as a musical performer in stock theatre, later serving as a guest pianist for the NBC Symphony Orchestra on radio, as well as hosting a local TV show in New York. Fun fact: Breen's profile is on the Beatle's "Sgt. Pepper's Lonely Hearts Club Band" album cover, appearing right behind George Harrison's shoulder.

Although Breen was a vocalist and pianist, his singing performance of "Song of the Islands" in Hawaii Calls as well as his recording of the Harry Owen's song "Down Where the Trade Winds Blow" earned him enough of an association with the Hawaii islands that Regal issued a Bobby Breen signature ukulele in the 1930s. Made from whitewood (likely birch or poplar), the soprano-size uke was entirely painted a dark green metallic color with white painted bindings and Art Deco stenciled decorations atop the body and headstock. His signature appears on the lower bout and, uniquely, an actual printed paper photo of his face is pasted atop the headstock.

Ray Canfield was a talented instrumentalist and vaudeville performer who was known for creating "symphonic" arrangements of popular songs of the era.

4.2 Ray Canfield

Song composer, arranger and musician Ray Canfield, wrote many popular songs in the 1920s and 30s, including "Sailin' On" and "Aloha Beloved." A talented instrumentalist and vaudeville performer, Canfield was once called the "Paderewski of the uke." He was also known for his symphonic ukulele arrangements which appeared in both book form (see the photo above) and in popular sheet music identified by a ukulele shaped logo reading: "This copy contains a Ray Canfield Symphonic uke arrangement."

In performance, Canfield promoted Gibson ukes and usually played a Style 3 Gibson soprano. Around 1930, Los Angeles music store owners Jack and Nathan Schireson (best known for their "Hollywood" line of ukuleles (see section 2.5) produced a Ray Canfield signature model. The soprano-sized Canfield uke fea-

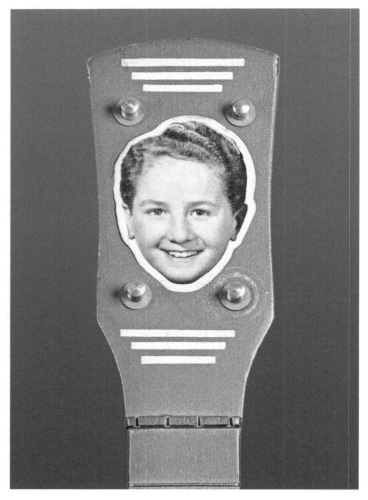

An unusual feature of the Breen uke is an actual paper photo cut out of his face glued atop the headstock.

You have just played through the first volume of
"RAY CANFIELD'S SYMPHONIC UKULELE ARRANGEMENTS"
and we believe you will be interested in knowing that other similar volumes are to follow. You will also find "Ray Canfield's Symphonic Ukulele Arrangements" on the back cover of our song copies—

Look for the Sign of the Uke

This printed logo identified a piece of music as being one of Ray Canfield's ukulele arrangements.

tured a mahogany body with a colorful arabesque decal surrounding a pin-style bridge. A greenish-gold/brown pearloid covered the fingerboard and headstock which bore his signature.

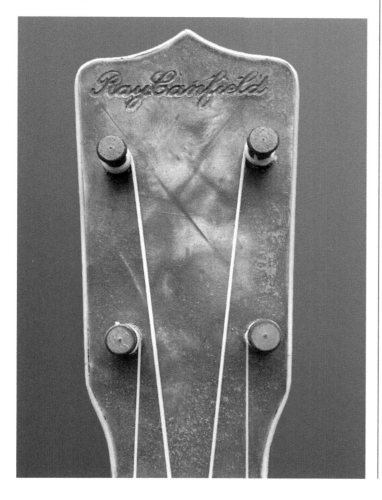

ABOVE: Los Angeles music retailers the Schireson Brothers produced the Ray Canfield Signature ukulele.

LEFT: Overlayed with greenish-gold/brown pearloid, the headstock bears an impression of Canfield's signature.

Los Angeles born sisters Vivian and Rosetta Duncan were attractive blondes who were among the biggest vaudeville stars of the 1910s and 20s.

The sisters appeared in several motion pictures, including MGM's 1929 musical romance "It's a Great Life," based on the sister's own rise to stardom.

A Chicago traffic stop that left Duncan sister Rosetta seriously injured provided the inspiration for "Mean Cicero Blues," a song based on Rosetta's altercation with the cop who stopped her.

4.3 The Duncan Sisters

If you're a baby boomer like me, TV and movie celebrities like Bob Hope, Doris Day and Gregory Peck are very familiar to you. But mention any of those names to a Gen X, Y or Z person and you're likely to get a blank stare. Likewise, unless you're well into your golden years, you're unlikely to know who the Duncan Sisters are. Yet these sisters were once very well-known American stage and screen performers who achieved international stardom.

Sisters Vivian and Rosetta Duncan were born in Los Angeles in the 1890s, the two youngest of five children. Both grew up to be short, attractive blondes with blue eyes. From an early age, they sang, danced and displayed other talents: Rosetta was a natural comic and Vivian played the piano and ukulele. After an early stage career with Rosetta yodeling songs to Vivian's piano accompaniment, they developed their own comedy act. Rosetta played the brash, gruff-voiced comedienne opposite Vivian's straight role as the "dumb blonde." Within a few years, they became seasoned vaudevil-

lians who were in high demand. After a string of engagements in night clubs and on stages in San Francisco, Chicago, New York and London, "the Dunks," as the sisters came to be called, were cast in the 1917 Broadway show "Doing Our Bit" starring Ed Wynn.

In 1923, the sisters, now well-known stars, created their own musical comedy: Topsy and Eva, adapted from Harriet Beecher Stowe's classic novel Uncle Tom's Cabin. Unlike the original story which explored relations between black slaves and their white owners in the early south, the Duncan's version focused on the relationship between slave girl Topsy, played by Rosetta (performing in blackface; something that was common in that era but is highly improper today) and Vivian as Eva, the angelic blond slave owner's daughter. The light-hearted comedy which featured musical numbers written by the sisters themselves was a huge hit. After long engagements in Chicago and on Broadway, the show toured the country for several years, was revived several times and was even adapted into a silent movie.

The Dunks went on to appear in several motion pic-

Richter's Duncan Sisters "Cicero Blues" model soprano ukuleles came in two models: one with a dark-stained mahogany body and one with a blond birch body.

The Art of Vintage Ukuleles • Sandor Nagyszalanczy

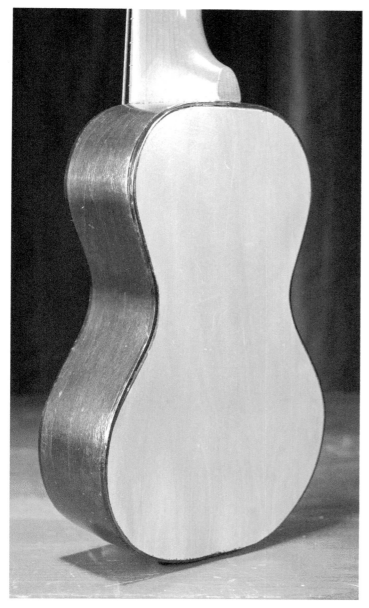

The body sides of both Cicero Blues model ukes were stained bright purple.

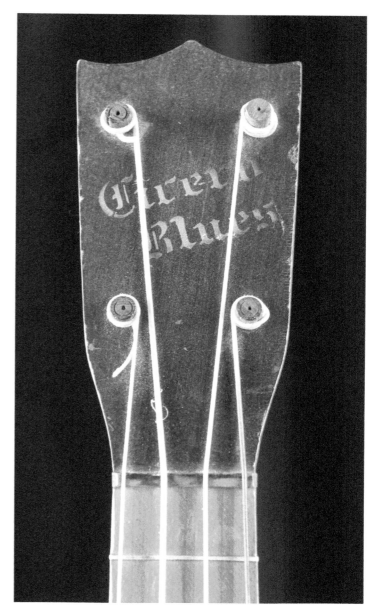

The uke's headstocks were stenciled with the model's name "Cicero Blues."

tures, including an early "talkie": 1929's It's a Great Life, a story based on the sister's own rise to stardom. They continued performing, mostly in night clubs, for several more decades and even appeared on Liberace's television show in 1956. They also recorded quite a few novelty songs, often with wacky titles including "Um-um-da-da," "Bull Frog Patrol," "The Kinky Kid's Parade" and "Baby Feet Go Pitter Patter." Some recordings featured Vivian playing ukulele. But one song they recorded much earlier in their career has a very special story behind it…one that actually resulted in the creation of the "Cicero Blues" ukuleles you see here.

Soon after the Dunk's Topsy and Eva musical premiered, the sisters were driving through Cicero, Illinois, a suburb of Chicago. With Rosetta at the wheel,

the car ran a stop sign and was promptly stopped by a traffic policeman. An altercation ensued in which Rosetta evidently struck the 6'2" cop, who subsequently beat the 4'11" Rosetta rather severely. The incident received lots of publicity and the Chicago Daily News reported on Rosetta's progress as she convalesced. In court, the cop ended up facing attempted murder charges while Rosetta's charges were dismissed; she only paid a $1 fine for the traffic violation. To capitalize on all the press they had received, the sisters recorded "Mean Cicero Blues," a song whose lyrics explicitly described the entire fiasco!

Some years later, Chicago instrument manufacturer Richter came out with a special Duncan Sisters "Cicero Blues" soprano ukulele. The uke came in two models, one with a blond birch body, and the other with a dark-stained mahogany body. Both have birch necks and are fitted with wood friction tuning pegs. Each has black celluloid bindings around the top and back of its narrow-waisted body and a single ring around the sound hole. Uniquely, the sides of both ukes are stained "eggplant" purple. Their headstocks are stenciled with "Cicero Blues" in gold letters and both sport "Duncan Sisters" decals, with images of the sisters as their signature characters Topsy and Eva.

There's a sad but ironic epilog to the Duncan Sisters story: In 1959, long after their fame had faded, the sisters reunited for a nostalgia-themed floor show at a nightclub in Chicago. One night as Rosetta was driving home, she lost control of her car and crashed, resulting in fatal injuries. The crash took place in Cicero, not far from where she'd fought with that cop decades earlier.

This MGM "celebrity" series card features Cliff Edwards, one of the best known and most talented of all vaudevillian performers.

4.4 Cliff Edwards

One of the most talented and best known of all vaudevillian performers is Cliff Edwards. Born in Hannibal, Missouri, Edwards left school at age 14, moved to St. Louis where he started working as a singer in saloons which were often run-down with pianos that were poorly maintained. In order to accompany himself while he performed, Edwards bought a cheap ukulele in a local music shop and taught himself to play. It's rumored that Edwards got his well-known nickname, "Ukelele Ike", from a club owner who simply couldn't remember his name.

Edwards toured as a vaudeville performer and was ultimately featured at the Palace Theatre in New York City. He went on to frequently appear on Broadway, including performances in the Ziegfeld Follies and in George and Ira Gershwin's 1924 Broadway musical: Lady Be Good, alongside Fred and Adele Astaire. After signing with Pathé Records, Edwards recorded jazzy renditions of many pop standards and novelty tunes, including "Hard Hearted Hannah" and "Paddlin' Madelin' Home."

Sometime around 1925, P'mico (the brand name of the Progressive Musical Instrument Corp.) distributed a "Cliff Edwards Ukulele Ike" soprano uke (P'mico

A decal on the front of the ukes features images of the Duncan Sisters in their title roles in the Broadway musical "Topsy and Eva."

PADDLIN' MADELIN' HOME

by Harry Woods

Introduced by
CLIFF EDWARDS
(UKELELE IKE)
in Mr. Chas. B. Dillingham's
Musical Comedy Success
"SUNNY"
at the
NEW AMSTERDAM THEATRE
NEW YORK
MADE IN U.S.A.

MUSIC
PUBLISHERS

ABOVE: Edwards recorded jazzy renditions of many popular songs of the era, including the 1925 novelty song "Paddlin' Madelin' Home."

RIGHT: Cliff Edwards' signature "Ukulele Ike" soprano uke sold by P'mico is a rather plain instrument with a stained birch body and a black painted finger board.

was only a wholesaler; the uke's original producer is unknown). Although it's said to have been offered in two different models, the only one I've ever seen is a rather plain instrument made of birch and stained mahogany brown, with its finger board painted black and a narrow white/black ring around the sound hole. An orange, white and black decal on the headstock bears Edward's name and likeness apparently wearing blackface makeup (blackface was common in vaudeville performances of the time, but is unthinkably and totally inappropriate today). This portrayal is ironic, as Edwards' only performed in blackface with partner Lou Clayton for a brief time sometime around 1922.

Thanks to his natural charm and colorful style of singing and ukulele playing, MGM studios hired Edwards to perform in many early "talkies," including The

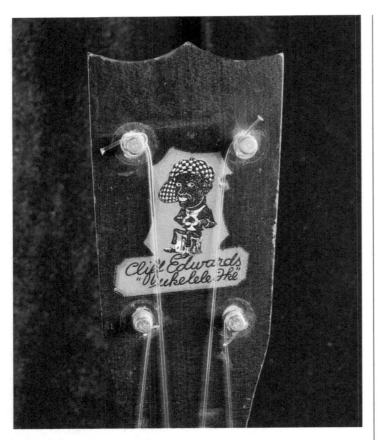

The uke's headstock decal depicts Cliff Edwards in blackface makeup, which is odd as Edwards was only known to have performed in blackface for a short time in the early 1920s.

Hollywood Revue of 1929, in which he sang "Singin' in the Rain" on screen for the first time, accompanied by the Brox Sisters and a team of raincoat-wearing dancers prancing around on a stage soaked by artificial rain. It was the first time this popular tune was featured in film.

Also a talented character actor, Edwards went on to appear in dozens of shorts and full-length features all the way into the 1950s, occasionally belting out a tune in his unique tenor voice accompanied by his signature Martin uke. My favorite of his performances is in the 1930 WWI film Dough Boys, a movie set mostly in war-torn Europe. In a scene that takes place in an army barracks, Edwards uses a pair of wooden drum sticks to tap out a tune on the strings of a taro patch (8-string) ukulele that's held and fretted by co-star Buster Keaton. Another noteworthy Edwards musical performance is in 1933's Take a Chance where he plays and sings "I Did it With My Little Ukulele," a song in which he fantasizes about charming a savage jungle tribe with his uke playing. The scene is complete with a dream-like sequence in which Edward's character is made king of the tribe, but then escapes and sails away in a boat shaped like a giant ukulele!

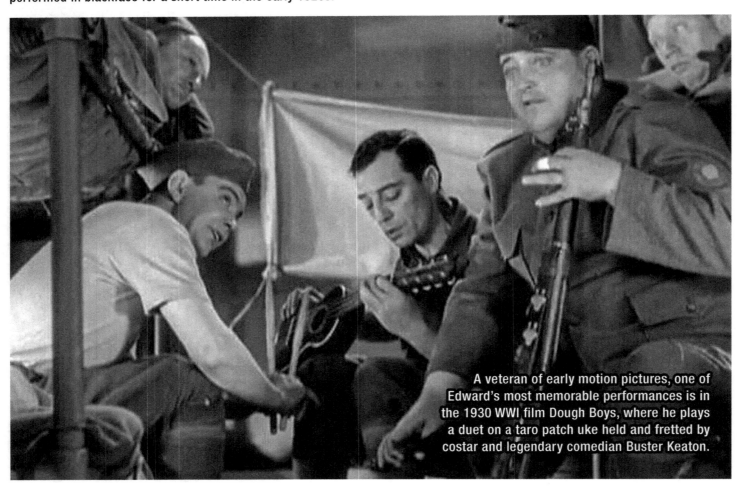

A veteran of early motion pictures, one of Edward's most memorable performances is in the 1930 WWI film Dough Boys, where he plays a duet on a taro patch uke held and fretted by costar and legendary comedian Buster Keaton.

ABOVE: Multi-talented performer, singer and composer Wendell Hall wrote more than 1500 songs, including 1923s "It Ain't Gonna Rain No Mo'," the sheet music for which sold more than a million copies.

RIGHT: A popular radio celebrity and broadcasting director for the CBS "Majestic Theatre of the Air," Hall also performed in musical short films in the 1930s.

4.5 Wendell Hall

Few ukulele players of the vaudeville era were as prolific or as well known in their time as Wendell Hall. A man of many talents, Hall was not only a country singer and multi-instrumentalist, but was also a recording artist, composer, author and a pioneering early radio performer. His career began in the early 1920s, when he worked for Forster Music as a "song plugger," travelling around the country promoting the sale of Forster's songs in music stores, theaters, and on local radio stations. In vaudeville, Hall initially accompanied himself on xylophone, but quickly switched to the much-more-portable ukulele, which he quickly mastered.

A prolific songwriter, Hall wrote more than 1500

Wendell Hall had not one but three different signature ukuleles all made by Regal: The concert-size "Master" and "TV" models (left and right), and the "Red Head" soprano (front).

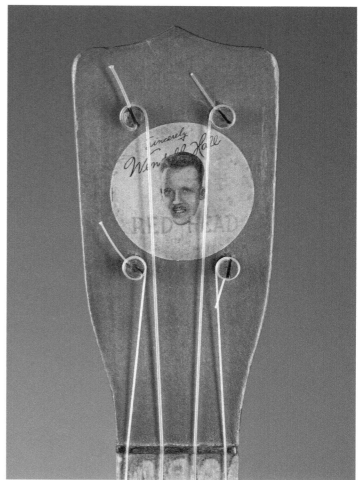

LEFT: Regal's "Red Head" soprano uke is built from figured Cuban mahogany with a multi-color wood rosette around the sound hole.

ABOVE: Hall's flaming red hair earned him his "Red-haired Music Maker" nickname, which is reflected in the red painted headstock of his signature soprano uke.

songs, including lesser-known tunes, such as "Spank it Frank," Whoop De Dooden Do" and "Elevator Man's Ball" His biggest hit, released in 1923, was "It Ain't Gonna Rain No Mo'," which sold over three million copies. Hall performed on countless radio programs around the US and the world and served as broadcasting director for the CBS "Majestic Theatre of the Air" in 1929. His success—and his full head of flaming red hair—earned Hall the nickname: "Red-haired Music Maker."

Hall was a big fan C.F. Martin & Company ukuleles, often performing with a Martin taropatch, but was unsuccessful in obtaining an endorsement deal with Martin. The Regal Musical Instrument Company was much more responsive, producing a line of Wendell Hall signature ukes in the mid 1920s. Their "Red

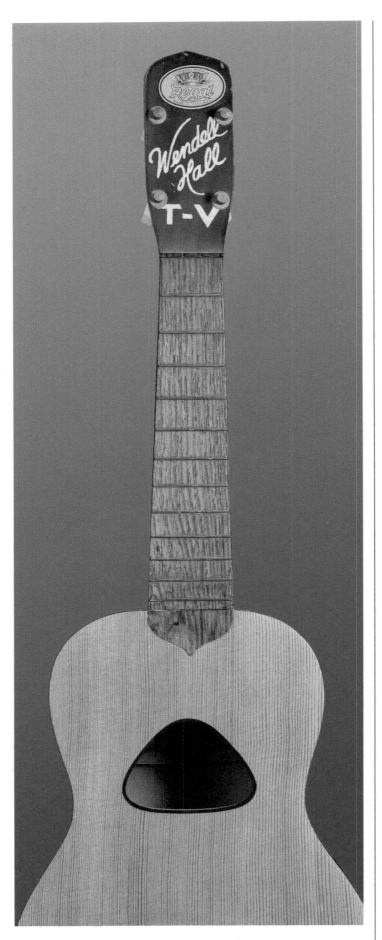

Head" soprano and banjolele had red painted headstocks and rosewood tuning pegs. The soprano was a quality instrument, built from beautiful figured Cuban mahogany with a multi-color wood rosette around the sound hole. Its yellow headstock decal featured Hall's face and signature. Regal also produced a "Wendell Hall MASTER ukulele" with a reddish-stained birch body surmounted by a spruce top. This concert-size instrument featured white and black bindings around the top and a simple white binding around the back of the body. Its most unique attribute was its crown-shaped three-peaked sound hole.

In 1951, at age 55, Hall came out of retirement to host a show on Chicago's WBKB Channel 4 television station. Drawing from his extensive catalog of past songs, Hall sang and played with what was described as "a voice right out of the razzmatazz, ragtime worshiping days of the 20s."

Likely to capitalize on Hall's show, Regal created a pair of new ukuleles: The Wendell Hall "TV" and "Teeviola" models. Both of these concert-sized ukes had spruce tops, whitewood bodies stained dark red, and Brazilian rosewood finger boards. The difference between models is the shape of their sound holes: The TVs is a rounded triangle, the Teeviolas is round.

The concert-size Wendell Hall TV ukulele sports a spruce top with a distinctive rounded triangular sound hole.

A noted vaudeville entertainer of the 1920s known for his prowess on the ukulele, Bobby Henshaw appeared in films and early television, including the 1940 British movie Cavalcade of Variety.

4.6 Bobby Henshaw

Bobby "Uke" Henshaw was a noted vaudeville entertainer of the 1920s that Variety Magazine once said was "…known for his prowess on the ukulele." The New York Clipper entertainment newspaper dubbed him "The Human Ukulele." Starting in the 1930s, Henshaw traveled the world, performing in Greenland, England and throughout Europe. He eventually spent more than a dozen years in Australia. He is said to have introduced the ukulele to England when he performed comedy songs on early BBC Television programs. During WWII, Henshaw and his troupe of USO performers toured far-flung military outposts. In a letter published in 1943, he said: "Sometimes we play

This Bobby Henshaw soprano uke is part of a line of soprano and baritone ukuleles produced by either Vega or Harmony.

LEFT: The box that Henshaw's signature ukulele came in claimed that the instrument is made from "violin toned woods," primarily mahogany. **RIGHT:** A thin pressed metal badge applied to the headstock of a Henshaw ukulele includes mention of Sorkin, NY, a music store that carried the ukes.

where they (GIs) are isolated for six and eight months, and it is a pleasure to hear them laugh." Henshaw also appeared in a number of obscure Hollywood films between 1935 and 1950. Later in his career, he began using the nickname "Uncle Ukie" when performing with his wife Deane in musical shows.

Henshaw endorsed a line of soprano and baritone ukuleles and tenor guitars that bore his name. The all-mahogany "Bobby Henshaw" soprano had a rosewood finger boards and a delicate parquet rosette around the sound hole (the box it came in claimed that the uke was made of "violin toned woods"). In lieu of binding, both the front and back edges of the body

were lightly rounded over where they meet the sides, making the uke quite comfortable to hold. While it's unclear whether these instruments were made by Harmony or Vega, it is known that they were sourced through the Sorkin music stores: Sorkin, NY is printed in small letters at the bottom of the ukes' metal headstock badge. Baritone ukes came with a "Hints by Bobby 'Uke' Henshaw for the Baritone Ukulele" booklet. The booklet stated that: "If any artist is qualified to say what a good instrument should be, it can only be Bobby -- and his choice is the Henshaw Uke. He knows it's made of the finest quality woods and is true in every respect."

THE GREATEST OF ALL SONG FOLIOS

IRVING BERLIN INC.
presents
AL JOLSON'S
Favorite Collection of
COMEDY SONG HITS
(WITH UKULELE ARRANGEMENT)

The first folio of AL JOLSON song hits
ever published, containing 10 Complete
songs with words and music; every one a gem

PRICE 50¢ NET

IRVING BERLIN, INC.
New York

This book is a collection of comedy song hits by Al Jolson,
the most famous and the highest paid performer
of the 1920s.

4.7 Al Jolson

Perhaps the most famous and recognizable name
among the celebrities presented in this article, American singer, comedian and film actor Al Jolson was the
highest paid performer of the 1920s, often billed as
"The World's Greatest Entertainer." Born Asa Yoelson,
Jolson is best remembered as the star of the first full-
length talking motion picture, The Jazz Singer (1927).
However, his career started well before that, in the early
1900s working as a singer in burlesque and vaudeville
shows and theater. Between 1911 and 1928, Jolson
had nine sell-out shows in a row on Broadway, recorded more than 80 hit records, and had 16 national and
international tours.

Despite Jolson's brash and extroverted performing
style, which was melodramatic and shamelessly senti-
mental, he's considered to be the first popular singer
to make a spectacular "event" out of singing. He was
known for running across the stage and up and down
its runway while teasing, cajoling, and thrilling the

Though Jolson was not known as a ukulele player,
the J.R. Stewart company produced an Al Jolson
signature ukulele in the mid 1920s.

audience. Quoting from the Encyclopedia of Popular Culture, "Jolson was to jazz, blues, and ragtime what Elvis Presley was to rock 'n' roll." Modern day singers who acknowledge Jolson's influence include Bing Crosby, David Bowie, Rod Stewart and Bob Dylan.

Although it's unlikely that Jolson was much of a ukulele player, an "Al Jolson" model soprano uke was produced by the J.R. Stewart company of Chicago sometime around the mid-1920s, no doubt to take advantage of Jolson's enormous popularity. The uke's whitewood body and neck are painted black, with white bindings around the top, back and sound hole. Its extended ebonized maple fingerboard features a celluloid stripe down the center and three double pairs of pearl dot position markers. The top is adorned with a shield-shaped white celluloid ornament attached just beneath the bridge. A decal on the headstock and paper label inside the body both display a black-and-white photographic image of Jolson.

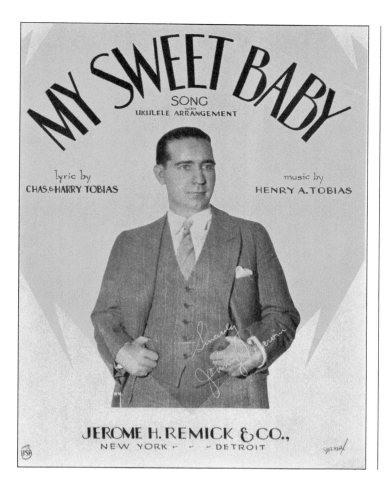

4.8 Johnny Marvin

During the ukulele's great heyday in the "Roaring 20s" one of the instruments' premier players was Johnny Marvin. Born in the Oklahoma Territory, Marvin's smooth voice and stylish ukulele accompaniment were unsurpassed as he performed on vaudeville stages throughout America. Marvin was an accomplished early recording artist who recorded dozens of 78 records between 1924 and 1930, including many songs he composed himself. Marvin performed and recorded both under his own name and under various aliases, such as "Honey Duke and his Uke" and "The Ukulele Ace." His many hits included "Oh How She Could Play a Ukulele," "Show Me the Way to Go Home" and "My Sweet Baby." These records featured not only his

LEFT: Premier vaudevillian and ukulele ace Johnny Marvin recorded dozens of songs on 78 records, including the 1928 hit "My Sweet Baby."

BELOW: A still photo of Johnny Marvin performing in the 1929 short film, Metro Movietone Revue.

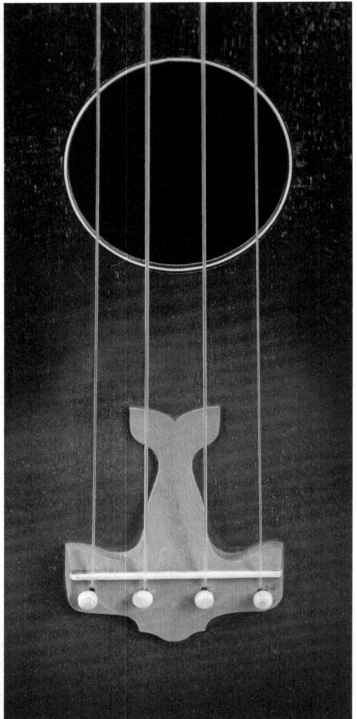

LEFT: Harmony's signature model Johnny Marvin "Professional" tenor ukulele was actually a concert-sized instrument.

ABOVE: The Marvin uke's airplane-shape bridge is said to have been inspired by Lindbergh's solo flight across the Atlantic.

The Art of Vintage Ukuleles • Sandor Nagyszalanczy

In 1928, Johnny Marvin presented a special koa wood "Prince of Wales" model of his signature uke to King Edward VIII, who was the Prince of Wales at the time.

smooth crooning and complex uke strumming, but jazzy vocal effects that often imitated other instruments.

Marvin signed with Harmony Company of Chicago to promote a signature model Johnny Marvin "Professional" tenor ukulele (which was actually concert-sized). Like Wendell Hall, Marvin's endorsement of the Harmony company was a result of being unable to work out a deal with C. F. Martin & Company. Premiering in 1932, the Marvin Professional has a body built from fiddleback figured mahogany with white-black-white bindings on top and white only binding around the back. The uke features an airplane-shape pin-style bridge, said to have been inspired by Charles Lindbergh's solo flight across the Atlantic. The headstock is topped with off-white pearloid with a silver and red decal bearing Marvin's signature.

To promote Marvin's 1928 performance engagement in London, Harmony supplied 10,000 miniature ukuleles to give away as souvenirs. While in England, Marvin met Edward, the Prince of Wales (later to be crowned King Edward VIII) and presented him with a specially-made Johnny Marvin ukulele. To commem-

orate the occasion, Harmony came out with a Johnny Marvin "Prince of Wales model." While the mahogany Harmony G-340 "standard" Professional uke sold for $15., their G-350 "Prince of Wales" model, made of figured Hawaiian koa and fitted with deluxe gold-plated tuners with ivoroid buttons, went for the princely sum of $25. (the equivalent of $436. today).

"Wizard of the Strings" Roy Smeck truly deserved his moniker as he was a virtuoso player of several instruments, including the guitar, banjo and ukulele.

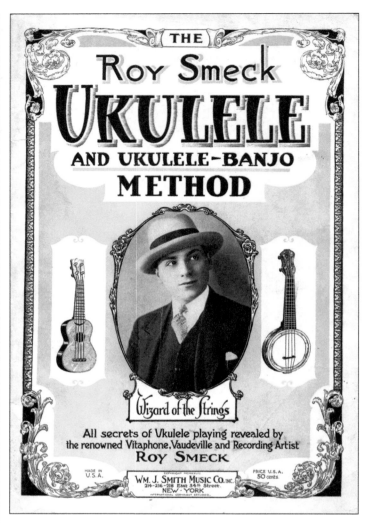

Smeck gave his performances pizazz by employing a variety of novel playing techniques which are described in his 1928 instruction booklet shown here.

4.9 Roy Smeck

Just how good do you have to be to earn the name "Wizard of the Strings?" Well in the case of ace performer, recording artist, author, teacher and film, radio and TV star Roy Smeck, he earned that moniker by achieving unparalleled virtuosity on no less than six instruments: guitar, tenor banjo, octachorda (an ob-

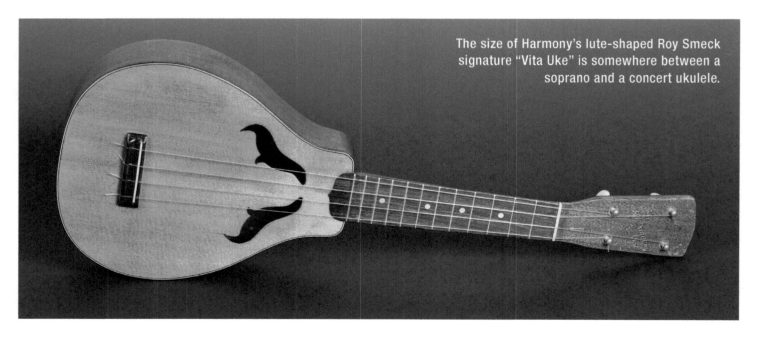

The size of Harmony's lute-shaped Roy Smeck signature "Vita Uke" is somewhere between a soprano and a concert ukulele.

THE ART OF VINTAGE UKULELES • SANDOR NAGYSZALANCZY

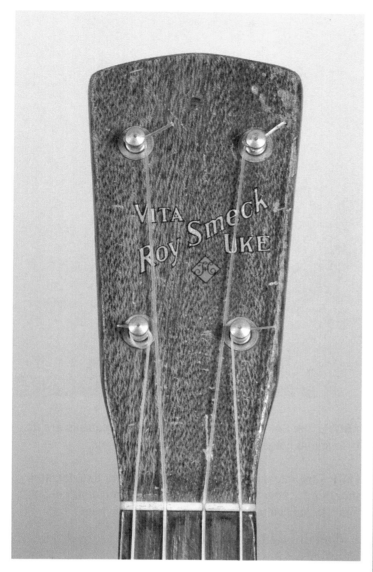

The Vita Uke's headstock decal includes a small red diamond with an "H" which stands for its producer, the Harmony Company.

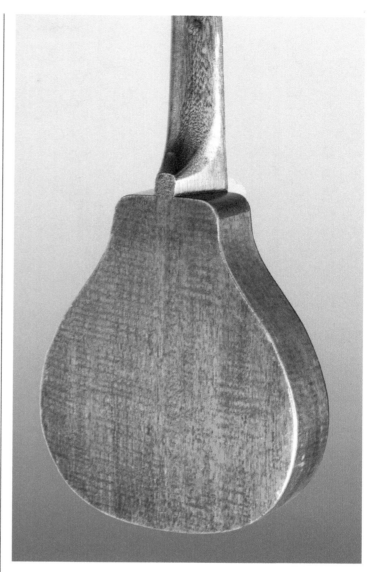

The back and sides of the Vita Uke were constructed from highly prized flame-figured Cuban mahogany.

scure kind of 8-string guitar), lap steel guitar, mandolin and ukulele—the instrument for which he became best known. Lacking vocal talent, Smeck dazzled audiences with playing chops that were nothing short of spell binding. Not only could he pluck or strum with blinding speed, he'd swing and twirl his uke, play it upside down or like a violin, strum it with his leg, blow tones across the sound hole and more.

A respected vaudeville performer who shared the stage with the likes of Al Jolson and George Jessel, Smeck's career skyrocketed in 1926 with his amazing ukulele performance in "His Pastimes," a short film that accompanied "Don Juan," Warner Brother's first feature-length talking picture. Released nearly a year before Jolson's landmark film "The Jazz Singer," Warner's movie employed their novel Vitaphone process which used a projector/sound machine to synchronize the moving film image with audio from a 16-inch-diameter 33 1/3 RPM record.

Smeck's growing celebrity yielded unexpected dividends. After a performance in Chicago, he was approached by Jay Krause, President of the Harmony Company—at the time, the largest manufacturer of string instruments in America. Krause asked Smeck to endorse a new line of instruments based on the success of his Vitaphone films and recordings. Smeck agreed, but when Warner refused to let them use the Vitaphone name, Harmony came up with a clever workaround. The new instruments were called the Vita-guitar, Vita-tenor guitar, Vita-mandolin, and the instrument that introduced the series, the Vita-Uke.

First sold in June of 1927, the Roy Smeck Vita-Uke

ABOVE: The Smeck Vita Uke's most unique features are its twin sound holes, which are the shape of seals.

LEFT: This magazine ad for Roy Smeck's Vita Uke declares that this "...new and original variant of the popular ukuele" has "Greater volume (and) Greater, Sweeter Tone."

had an unusual lute-like shape that was somewhere between a soprano and a concert ukulele in size. Selling initially for around $12. (about $165. in today's dollars), the Vita-Uke's sides and back were crafted from gorgeous flame-figured Cuban mahogany, with a top made of close-grained spruce, all finished in hand-rubbed lacquer. Its' oddest feature was twin sound holes that Harmony described as being "...cut in the shape of seals, which we have found aid materially in producing the [uke's] unusual volume and quality of tone." Despite Harmony's claims that Smeck had designed the Vita instruments himself, Smeck later said he didn't: "They would show me the models that they wanted to use my name on, and I would show them the kind of [playing] action that I liked."

To promote sales of his new Vita-Uke, Smeck embarked on a national tour in the summer and fall of 1927. Appearing in towns and cities across the midwest and south, he performed in theaters as well as informally at local music stores. One newspaper said of him: "He can make the ukulele sound like a whole band." To boost sales, Harmony arranged public uku-

ABOVE AND RIGHT: The more conventional-uke-shaped, soprano-sized Roy Smeck "Concert Uke" has a mahogany back and sides, a spruce top and a sunburst finish.

lele contests which were held when Smeck appeared. By the end of the tour, sales of Vita-Ukes had increased dramatically and Smeck was the highest paid instrumentalist in vaudeville.

By the time production of Vita-series instruments ceased sometime in the mid-to-late 1930s, Harmony had sold tens of thousands of Roy Smeck Vita-Ukes, far outselling their Vita guitars and mandolins. Harmony Vita-Ukes are still highly prized today for their good sound and cool looks.

Owing to the success of the Vita Uke, Harmony produced a new Smeck signature uke in the 1940s. The Roy Smeck "Concert Uke" was another well-built instrument with a spruce top and solid mahogany back and sides. The entire uke was finished in a brown shaded sunburst finish and featured double white bindings around both top and back and 6 pairs of position marker dots along its rosewood fingerboard. Despite its "Concert" designation, this uke was actually soprano sized, with a scale length just under 13 inches.

Yet another Harmony Smeck uke, produced in the 1950s, was the model No. 555, built entirely from mahogany with an eggshell (dull luster) lacquer finish. Part of Harmony's lower-priced line of ukes, it featured an "accurately molded" polystyrene fingerboard, complete with its frets molded in place. In the late 50s, it sold for an affordable $13.50.

Delaware radio personality Dale Wimbrow recorded many of the songs he composed and played on his radio shows for the Del-Mar-Va label.

4.10 Dale Wimbrow

How do you get your own signature model ukulele when manufacturers aren't beating a path to your door? One way is to design and build your own instrument and then convince a noted stringed instrument manufacturer to produce it. That's what Dale Wimbrow did back in the early 1930s. Although it's unlikely you've ever heard of him, part of his legacy lies in the unique ukulele he created, whose name his own inspired: the Wimbrola.

Born in 1895 in Whaleyville, near the eastern shore of Maryland, Peter Dale Wimbrow was a talented guy. He was a vaudeville-era performer and songwriter, a popular radio personality and recording artist, and a poet best remembered for his moralistic poem: "The Guy in the Glass." He was also a painter and an amateur woodworker.

In the 1930s, he hosted several popular programs on the CBS radio network in the New York City area.

Nicknamed "the Del-Mar-Va Songster," Dale Wimbrow designed his own unusually shaped six-string ukulele which he called a "Wimbrola."

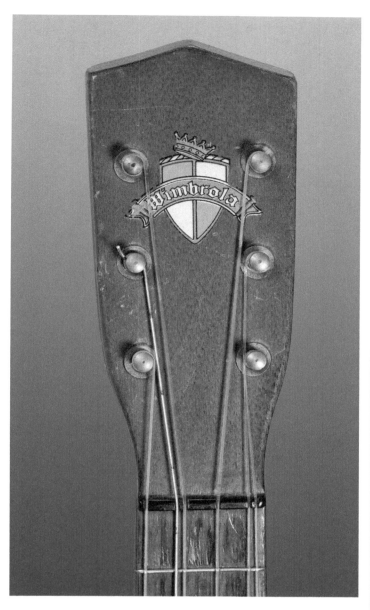

ABOVE: New York City instrument makers the Favilla Brothers produced a limited number of Wimbrola ukuleles sometime around 1932.

RIGHT: Some say that the Wimbrola's body, with its faceted sides, looks rather coffin shaped.

For the Del-Mar-Va Hour on station WJZ, Wimbrow played country bumpkin "Old Pete Daley" and did sketches laced with corny southern-style humor. (Del-Mar-Va is the nickname for the peninsula that's part Delaware, part Maryland and Virginia, where Wimbrow was born). Many of the songs he performed on radio he composed himself, including "The Good Old Eastern Shore" he recorded for the Del-Mar-Va label. In 1928, Wimbrow wrote "Think of Me Thinking of You" with ukulele luminary Johnny Marvin and penned the lyrics for crooner Rudy Vallee's hit "Every Moon's a Honeymoon (With You)."

One of the fanciest **Wimbrola** ukes produced by **Favilla** features extensive pearl inlays and purflings.

But evidently Wimbrow wasn't satisfied with the standard ukuleles he played. So he decided to use his woodworking talents and build his own instrument, which he's holding it in a press photo shown on page 186. This instrument has an octagonal sound hole, ivoroid bindings around the body, neck and headstock, pearl purfling and elaborate fretboard & headstock inlays. According to a 1931 CBS radio press release, Dale "… invented a new instrument called 'the Wimbrola'… a cross between an American ukulele and a Russian balalaika…a little larger than a ukulele but [with] six strings." Dale strung his concert-sized Wimbrola like a Hawaiian Lili'u six-string ukulele, with a single high G string, two C strings, one an octave above the other, a single E string, and two A strings tuned in unison. What made his instrument different is the way he arranged the strings: The doubled strings were grouped in tight pairs at the nut (Lili'u style), but then fanned out and were evenly spaced at the saddle. Despite this unique arrangement, it's unclear what advantages the fanned strings may have offered. The low C string did give the instrument a rich, full-bodied tone that Dale said "sounded like a pipe organ."

Not only did Wimbrow make a Wimbrola for himself, but he made them for others as well. During his radio years, Dale had often made and given away small wood projects to his colleagues, including batons for his fellow composers and carved walking sticks for such notables as orchestra leader Paul Whiteman and CBS president William E. Paley. Dale built at least nine Wimbrolas, but this time, he didn't give them away, selling each for the price of the materials. As he put it: "This thing cost money to make…it's no cane or baton, [but] an honest to goodness instrument."

Despite his enthusiasm, the new Wimbrolas weren't exactly a big hit. As recounted in a 1931 edition of The Brooklyn Daily Eagle: "When the C. B. S. folk got their Wimbrolas, they discovered, much to their consternation, that they couldn't play the things. Wimbrow, as a result, announced that he'd formed a class… when all have mastered the instrument, he will make them play in his Wimbrola band."

Eventually, Dale gave up on building the Wimbrolas himself, saying that "It's too much work to make these darn things." That's when he turned to the Favilla Brothers, Giovanni and Joseph, who founded their stringed instrument company in New York City in 1894. Favilla had built thousands of high-quality ukuleles in the 1920s, including regular sopranos and teardrop-shape ukes, some with colorful paintjobs. According to Thomas Favilla (grandson of Giovanni and son of Herk Favilla, a man who is often credited with the invention of the baritone ukulele), the green-and-silver-labeled Wimbrolas were only made for a couple of years, sometime around 1932.

Favilla built both soprano and concert sized Wimbrolas. The soprano version shown here is 21 inches long and 6 ½ inches wide, with a 13 9/16 in. scale. With a mahogany top and back, its body has ten faceted sides bent from two mahogany strips lightly kerfed on their inside surfaces. Topped with a thin rosewood fret board with 12 frets, the mahogany neck joins the body with a stylish "ice cream cone" heel. The back of the headstock is imprinted: "Made by Favilla Bros. New York. N.Y. U.S.A. PAT. APP'D FOR." The nut and saddle are ebony, the latter set into a mahogany bridge.

Most of the Favilla-manufactured Wimbrolas are relatively plain—no binding around the top or back and only a simple rosette decal with a thin ivoroid ring around the inside of the sound hole. Dale gave most of them away as gifts, always autographing them on the back. Unfortunately, when Dale couldn't come up with the cash to pay off the Wimbrolas production run, Favilla sold the remainder of the ukes to the public.

Before ceasing production, Favilla did produce a fancy Wimbrola for Dale, shown on page 188. It featured Brazilian rosewood sides and back, a mahogany top with a triangular sound hole, both trimmed with abalone purfling, and an abalone lyre inlay in the headstock.

Chapter Five
From Innovative to Weird and Wacky

Although the majority of ukuleles are made of wood and have a standard Spanish "figure of eight" body shape, there's no shortage of vintage ukes with oddly shaped bodies, unique features, and/or non-conventional construction materials.

Maybe it's because of its diminutive size or playful nature, but it seems that the ukulele has been the subject of more innovation and experimentation than any just about any other stringed instrument. This may be, at least in part, explained by the fact that the uke itself is the product of innovation, having evolved from small Portuguese instruments into the Hawaiian four-stringed "flea" that we know today (see Section 1.1).

Once the uke became popular on the mainland in the early 1900s, ingenious inventors, instrument makers and backyard tinkerers directed considerable ener-gy to create ukes that were better in some way: better sounding; more versatile; easier to tune and play. Some of their efforts were met with great success and were awarded U.S. Patents. For an example, consider the banjo uke patented by John Bolander in 1921. By combining the compact size and playability of a regular ukulele with a loudness and snappy tone of a tenor banjo, he created a very popular hybrid instrument. Other innovative efforts fell well short of success. Just consider Altpeter's bizarre double harp Uke or the odd looking "Polk-a-ley-lee," which was one of the wacki-est promotional items ever! (both are described in Section 5.3).

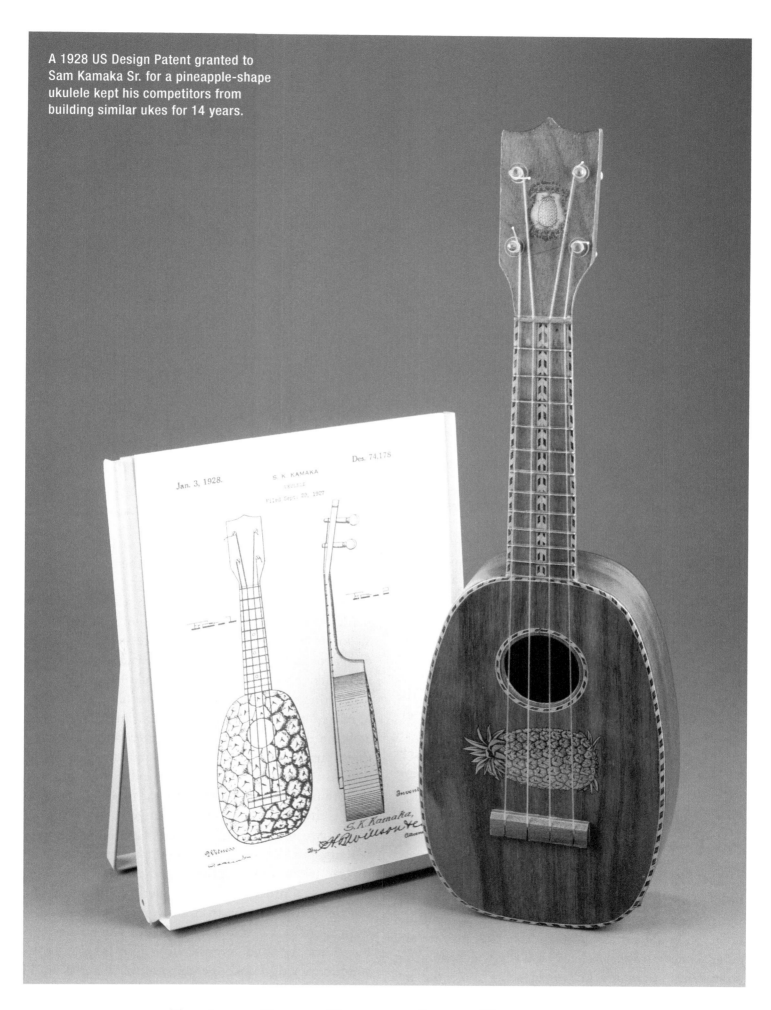

A 1928 US Design Patent granted to Sam Kamaka Sr. for a pineapple-shape ukulele kept his competitors from building similar ukes for 14 years.

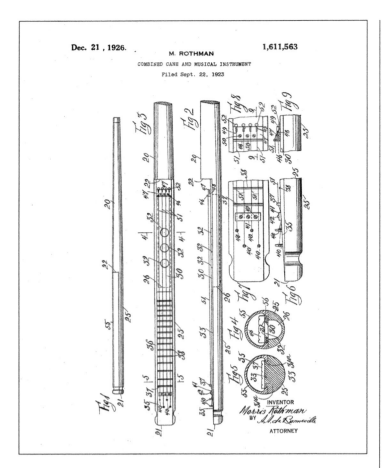

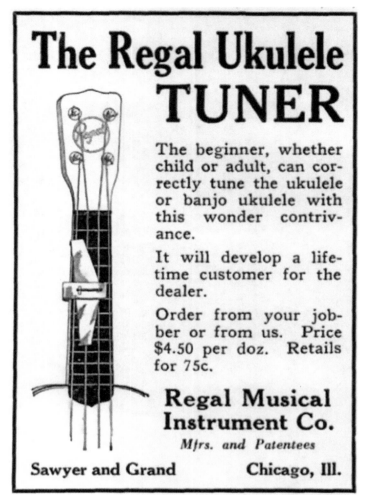

Although it could have been the handiest travel uke ever, Morris Rothman's patented ukulele walking stick was likely poor sounding due to its skinny, shallow body.

Whether or not they were successful commercially, decades of inventive design have left us with a treasure trove of ukuleles that are anything but ordinary. Some of these ukes sport unorthodox body shapes while others are made of odd materials, like cardboard and coconut. There are ukuleles featured in this chapter that don't look—or really sound—like ukuleles at all. Take, for example, a uke-shaped metal tin with the primary function of being a box for chocolate candy. At the end of this chapter, you'll read about an instrument that really isn't a ukulele at all, but likely was created to take advantage of America's fascination with the uke in the 1920s.

5.1 Patented Ukuleles

Did you ever have an idea that was so unique, so brilliant that you thought it might have real financial value? If so, then it's likely that your next thought was how you could protect your idea so that no one else could benefit from it. That's basically what patenting an invention does; it acknowledges that you're the one who came up with the idea and provides you with some degree of protection against others stealing your intellectual property for financial gain.

Founded in July of 1790, the U.S. Patent & Trademark Office has granted many millions of patents to all kinds of inventors: serious professional engineers, designers and scientists, as well as backyard tinkerers, mechanics and luthiers, including ukulele makers. For four-string strummers, exploring the history of ukulele-related patents provides both an entertaining look at some of the more unusual, clever, and sometimes questionable ideas that instrument builders have come up with. Patents can also lend a keen bit of insight into the origins of certain manufactured ukulele models as well as the evolution of ukuleles in general.

The two most common types of patents are utility patents and design patents. Utility patents cover all sorts of inventions: a device or gadget, like a new ukulele tuner; a process, such as a method for molding a plastic instrument; or an improvement to an existing device, such as a bridge that makes uke strings easier to attach. Whatever the invention is, it must be unique, practical and operable and have a real-world

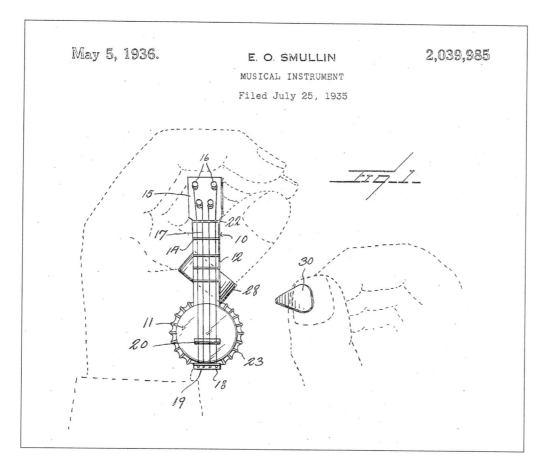

May 5, 1936. E. O. SMULLIN 2,039,985
MUSICAL INSTRUMENT
Filed July 25, 1935

The term "infinitely impractical" comes to mind when pondering E.O. Smullin's US Patent for a miniature uke meant to be worn on the finger.

use. Design patents are granted for original ornamental designs for articles: an ultra-modern jet ski, a fancy kitchen ladle or a uniquely-shaped ukulele. Both kinds of patents are good only in the United States; agencies in Europe, Japan, Korea and China handle foreign patents.

Why would a ukulele maker go to the trouble and expense of applying for a patent? One significant advantage is that it prevents a competitor from copying their idea for the duration of the patent—14 years for design patents, 20 years for utility patents. Ukulele manufacturing legend Samuel Kamaka gained an edge over other uke makers when he created a unique soprano uke with a pineapple-shaped body. His instrument not only looked cool, but had a fuller, more resonant sound and was easier to manufacture than a traditional uke. His 1928 design patent (# D 74,178) assured that Kamaka was the only company producing pineapple ukes at a time when competition was high due to the uke's ever increasing popularity. By the time Kamaka's patent ran out in 1940, he was the only Hawaiian ukulele maker still in business.

Utility Patents

In order to be awarded a utility patent, an invention must be totally unique or offer innovative improvements to an existing design. A good example of the latter is Nichol Pedersen's 1929 patent (#1,721,710) for "An improved form of the ukulele." The text of his patent claimed that "the forms of the ukulele heretofore produced are comparatively crude instruments and do not give a volume or quality of tone which is comparable with that of other musical instruments, such as the violin or the cello." His improvement was to fit four pairs of doubled strings to an otherwise standard uke. The instrument differed from a traditional taro patch because Pedersen paired a silk string and a steel string for each doubled string pair.

Sometimes, patentable ideas merged elements that had never been combined before. Probably the most impressive example is Nicola Turturro's "Turnover," (1929 patent # 1,723,751), a thin-bodied instrument featuring a ukulele on one side and a mandolin on the other (see section 5.4). Morris Rothman obtained a patent in 1926 (#1,611,563) for his novel integration of a ukulele and a walking stick. He might have created the handiest travel uke ever, but it couldn't have been very loud or sounded very good, thanks to its incredibly skinny, shallow body.

Some uke-related patents are based on less practical ideas. Take for example Johnston's 1927 capo device

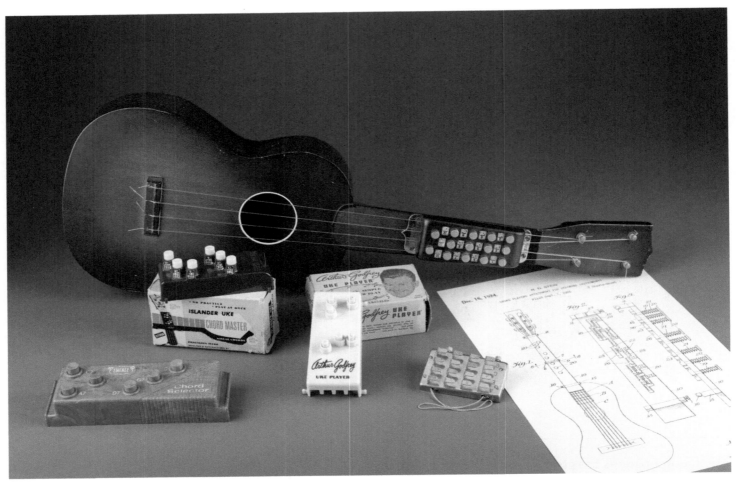

Whether they're designed as detachable accessories or integrated into the ukulele itself, most auto chording devices allow players to form standard chords with the press of a button.

(# 1,616,859). In lieu of the kind of clip-on, removable capos we use today, the device Johnston called a "capo tasto" had to be permanently mounted to a uke's headstock and could only reach up to the 3rd fret (would you screw one to your prized Martin?). Even less impressive was Kordick's uke tuner (1929 patent #1,697,508), which clamped to the neck of a uke and made all the strings play the same note; a relatively cumbersome way to do a simple tuning. Regardless of this, the Regal Instrument Company chose to license Kordick's patent and offer his tuner for sale.

My choice for the most dubiously useful uke patent is Edmund Smullen's 1936 utility patent (#2,039,985) for a miniature ukulele mounted to a ring worn on the user's thumb. All four of the diminutive instrument's strings were supposed to be fretted with one finger while strummed with a tiny pick! How a patent examiner thought this was a "real world" device is beyond me.

Utility patents often provide an interesting glimpse into the development of instrument-related inventions over time. One of the first automatic chord playing devices was patented by Nicholas D. Stein in 1924

(#1,519,881). Originally designed for guitar, the device was then adapted and fitted to a most unusual uke, seen at the rear in the photo above. As it lacks frets, this instrument could only be played by pushing one of the 12 buttons on the device. Two extra buttons on the Stein auto chord player were used for tuning the uke. The next five decades saw a slew of patents granted for removeable chord playing devices, including Reed's metal "Noteless" player (#1,374,388) and Maccaferri's 6-button plastic "Chord Master" (#2,669,151) (see Section 8.4).

One of the most interesting—and complicated— chord players was an integrated part of the "Juka Autoplay" ukulele. This chord device, patented in 1928 by German engineer Theodor Schmidt (U.S. Patent #1,687,849) features seven aluminum levers, numbered 1 to 7. These may be depressed in either of two directions, each playing a different chord. For example, pressing lever 3 forward plays a "C" chord; pressing it backwards creates a "G7." Another unique and interesting feature of the Juka uke was its metal "strumming arm." Pivoting from a mounting point

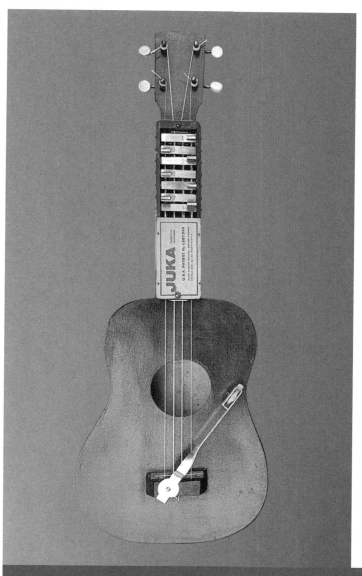

on the bridge, the business-end of the arm holds a felt pick. Juka's claim was that the arm kept the pick at a proper orientation and distance from the strings to make strumming "skill-less," which I guess meant easier and more consistent.

Design Patents

Most design patents granted for ukuleles involve the instrument's overall body shape. Most such patents diverge considerably from a standard uke's figure-8 body shape based on the Spanish guitar or banjo uke's round skin-covered body. Edward N. Guckert's 1923 design for a banjo uke (#D 62,235) featured a horse-shoe-shaped body with an unusual wooden lower portion. Guckert (best known for his 1917 instructional booklet "Guckert's Chords for the Ukulele") called his instrument a "Jazuke; the instrument of enchantment." In addition to Kamaka's pineapple uke (discussed above), early ukulele design patents included

LEFT: Patented in 1928 by German engineer Theodor Schmidt, his "Juka Autoplay" ukulele featured an integrated chord player as well as metal "strumming arm."

BELOW: The Juka's chord player has seven levers that can be depressed in either of two directions, each playing a different chord.

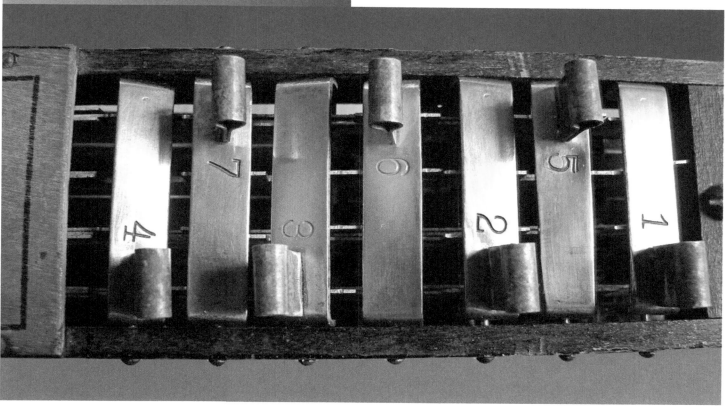

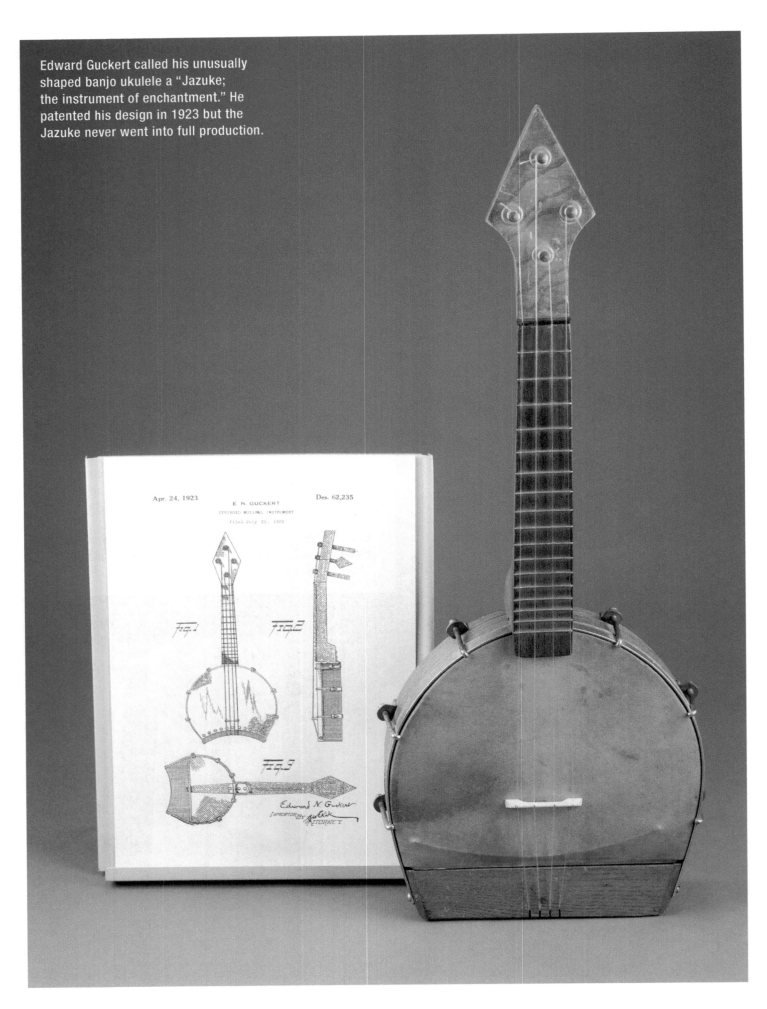

Edward Guckert called his unusually shaped banjo ukulele a "Jazuke; the instrument of enchantment." He patented his design in 1923 but the Jazuke never went into full production.

Design patents protected unique ukes, such as Turturro's peanut (left), Harmony's Valencia banjo uke (top right) and Lyon & Healy's Venetian uke (bottom right).

Turturro's "peanut" uke (#D74,766), Lyon & Healy's canoe-paddle-shaped "Venetian" uke (#D75,494), and Harmony's Valencia brand banjo uke (#D71,589). In the case of these last two patents, both were filed by the presidents of the companies that manufactured them: Marquette Healy of Lyon & Healy and Jay Kraus, Harmony's president from 1916-1940.

The Patent Process

Applying for a design patent requires only the submission of an accurate drawing and description of the item. But obtaining a utility patent is a complicated and often a lengthy and costly process. Applications must include a summary describing the invention, accurate drawings that include all relevant details and a list of claims that specify the various unique and dis-

tinct elements or properties of the invention. Claims can be simple or extensive, specifying one or a dozen or more particular elements. For example, Anthony Cox's 1937 patent (# 2,098,701) contains only two claims, both related to the process of joining a pair of coconuts with a wooden ring to form the body of his Coco-lele uke.

A significant part of the patent application process requires the inventor (and/or their attorney) to search through patent records to assure that no identical (or very similar) inventions have already been patented or had a patent applied for. But there's a catch: To search through patents granted before 1976, you have to know the right classification number and subclass. Unfortunately for jumping-flea enthusiasts, ukuleles don't have their own class number; most fall under the guitar's classification (class number 84, subclass 267). However, many ukulele-related patents fall under other clas-

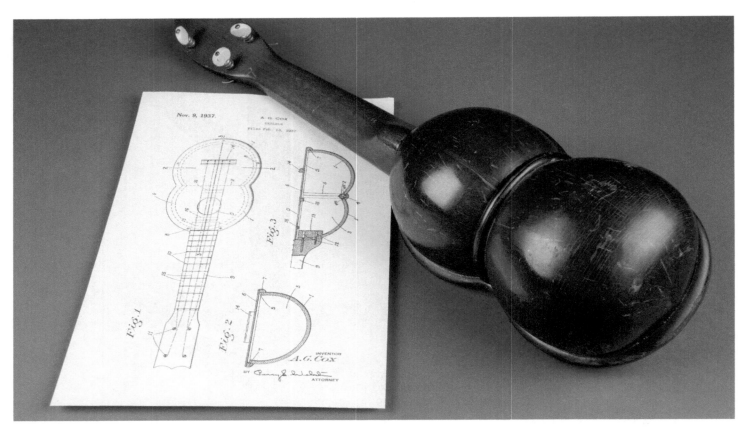

Utility patents could be complicated or simple, the latter illustrated by Cox's 1937 patent for the process of joining a pair of coconuts with a wooden ring.

sifications, and as there are literally thousands of class/subclass combinations, searches can be tedious indeed!

All patent applications are reviewed by a patent examiner who determines if the idea is worthy of being granted its own patent. This process can take years and most inventors don't wait until they actually have a patent in-hand before manufacturing and marketing their inventions. In order to inform would-be competitors that an application has been filed, inventors are allowed to label their items "patent applied for" (usually abbreviated "pat. app'd. for") or, in some cases, "Patent Pending." Such labels are often seen on ukuleles, either printed on a paper label inside the body or stamped on the back of the headstock or on the patentable part itself: The "Tivolette" banjo uke's pressed metal "Music Steps" fretboard says "PAT. APP'D.FOR" just above the nut. Once a patent is actually granted, uke makers usually label the instrument with the actual patent number.

The length of time it takes to obtain a patent can

LEFT: The words "Patent Applied For," such as seen on the Tivolette banjo uke's pressed metal "Music Steps" fretboard, were meant to protect a design from copycats before the patent was actually granted.

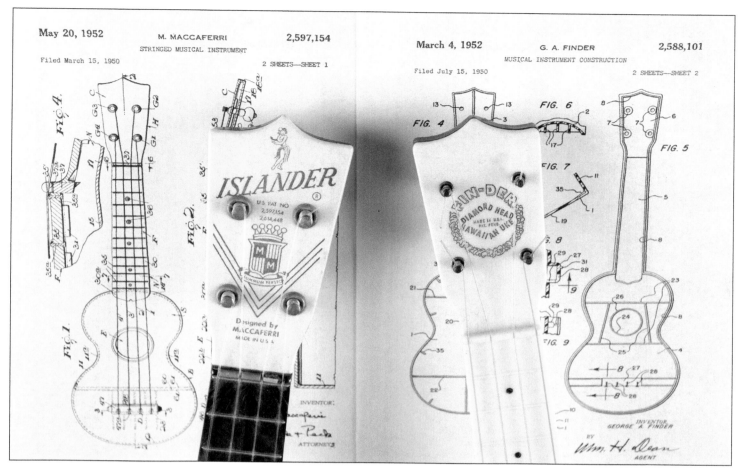

May 20, 1952   M. MACCAFERRI   2,597,154
                    STRINGED MUSICAL INSTRUMENT
Filed March 15, 1950   2 SHEETS—SHEET 1

March 4, 1952   G. A. FINDER   2,588,101
                    MUSICAL INSTRUMENT CONSTRUCTION
Filed July 15, 1950   2 SHEETS—SHEET 2

Occasionally the patent process leads to contention and court cases, as when Mario Maccaferri and George Finder filed applications for similarly constructed plastic ukuleles.

create problems if two (or more) people file applications for similar inventions around the same time. Technically, the person who files first should receive priority. But that doesn't always happen, due to the complicated nature of both the patenting process and overlapping claims in the patents themselves. Consider the case of Mario Maccaferri and George Finder, both ingenious luthiers who applied for patents for the construction of injection-molded plastic instruments. Even though Maccaferri applied for his patent (#2.597.154) first, Finder's patent (#2,588,101) was awarded first. Both men went on to manufacture their own brands of plastic ukes: Diamond Head and Mauna Loa for Finder; Islander and TV Pal for Maccaferri. In 1950, Maccaferri filed a lawsuit against the manufacturers of the Emenee Flamingo uke, alleging that the design of the Flamingo infringed on his plastic uke patent (it's up to a patent holder to identify cases of infringement and defend their patent in court). Although Maccaferri lost his case and subsequent appeal, he still went on to manufacture 9 million plastic ukuleles before selling his patents to Carnival in 1969.

Assigning patent rights

Once a patent is granted, an inventor may choose to produce the patented item themselves, or assign (transfer the ownership of the patent) or license it to another party. For instance, Walter Kirk's patent for a sound-hole reinforcing ring (1925 patent #1,559,108) was employed by Lyon & Healy on a great many of their Washburn brand ukuleles (For more on Lyon & Healy, see Section 2.4, pg. 60). The raised rings made of celluloid, gave these ukes a distinctive appearance, although any advantage regarding the ring's sound-hole-reinforcing properties are somewhat questionable. Lyon & Healy also licensed a design patent for a triangular-bodied banjo uke granted to Paul Arthur in 1927 (# D74,133), but instead of building the instrument as is, they employed the rounded triangular body shape for their classy Shrine model ukes. Coincidentally, another triangular-bodied ukulele was developed by Canadian music educator J. Chalmers Doan as an inexpensive "teaching ukuele" for his students. Doan's 1977 utility patent (#4,041,830) was assigned to a couple of different instrument manufacturers who built Northern brand ukes for Canadian school music programs.

Inventors who obtained patents often licensed them for a price. Such was the case with these two designs, one for a raised sound hole ring, the other for a triangular bodied uke, both licensed and produced by Lyon & Healy.

THE ART OF VINTAGE UKULELES • SANDOR NAGYSZALANCZY

5.2 Tru Fret's Novel Fingerboard

If you asked a room full of luthiers what the most tedious part of building a ukulele is, I bet that most would say it's installing the frets, the thin metal bars on the fingerboard that allow notes and chords to be played accurately. Fretting a ukulele involves cutting a series of narrow, accurately spaced slots along the length of a wooden fingerboard, then, pressing or pounding metal frets into the slots (on some early ukes, frets were installed directly into the neck). Either way, a fret job is a fussy, time-consuming task.

But way back during the uke's first heyday in the 1920s, a clever Chicago instrument maker and inventor named Harry E. Hall endeavored to simplify uke construction by eliminating the need to install a dozen or more separate frets. Hall came up with a process of

LEFT: The name of Tru-Fret ukuleles derives from their innovative fingerboards which are made entirely of metal, frets and all.

BELOW: Unlike the Tivolette banjo ukes ramped fretted metal fingerboard, Harry Hall's fingerboard has regular raised metal frets pressed into a thin metal fretboard.

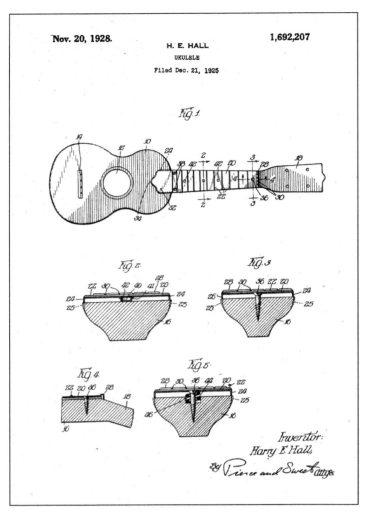

Nov. 20, 1928.

H. E. HALL
UKULELE
Filed Dec. 21, 1925

1,692,207

Fig.1

Fig.2   Fig.3

Fig.4   Fig.5

Inventor:
Harry E. Hall
By Pierce and Sweet attys

pressing a single piece of thin metal into a complete fingerboard, frets and all. His design differed from the ramped fretted metal fingerboards found on Tivolette banjo ukes (see page 201) in that Hall's had regular raised metal frets atop a thin metal fretboard. Hall applied for a U.S. patent #1,692,207 for his pressed fingerboard design in 1925.

Even before being granted a final patent in 1928, Hall licensed his fingerboard to the Globe Music Company of St. Charles, Illinois. Globe specialized in producing all manner of fretted instruments, including guitars, mandolins, banjos, ukuleles and banjoleles. Like other musical instrument manufacturers such as Harmony and Washburn, Globe was primarily an original equipment manufacturer (OEM), for companies which sold the instruments under their own brand names. Globe did make and market some of its own instrument brands, including La Pacific banjoleles and "Tru-Fret" soprano ukuleles that featured Harry Hall's ingenious metal fingerboard.

In period advertisements for the Tru-Fret ukes,

LEFT: Hall's 1925 US Patent for his unique metal fingerboard.

BELOW: An ad for Tru-Fret ukuleles, made by the Globe Music Company which licensed Hall's fingerboard design.

One Tru-Fret model uke has a
black-painted body adorned with
a colorful floral decal.

The mahogany-bodied model Tru-Fret ukulele features ivoroid bindings and unique wood mosaic purflings and sound hole rosette.

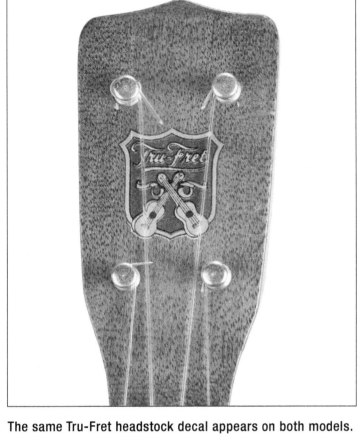

The same Tru-Fret headstock decal appears on both models.

Globe proclaimed that buyers would have "No more fingerboard troubles...our exclusive new patented metal fingerboard, produced at great cost after a year of experimenting, provides you with ukuleles that are guaranteed to be absolutely perfect in tone." They claimed that: "Through the use of a special die, "TRU-FRET" Ukuleles are guaranteed to be fretted accurately to 1000th of an inch." The same die that stamped the frets also formed the nut—the raised bar that supports and spaces the strings at the top of the fingerboard. Globe's advertising boasted that "the nut is always in the exactly correct relation to the frets—neither too high nor too low. This eliminates all buzzing and rattling of the strings."

The Tru-Fret line included six different models which, in the mid-late 1920s, sold for between $4.50 and $12.00. (see photo on page 201). The metal fingerboards on Tru-Fret ukes came in one of two finishes, which Globe called "silver and ebony." The less expensive models had black painted white-wood (typically birch) bodies and necks and sported contrasting bright silver fingerboards. Many of these featured white ivoroid bindings and colorful floral decals atop

the body, below the bridge. The more expensive models were built from mahogany stained a deep brown and featured the black ebonized fingerboards, ivoroid bindings and decorative wood mosaic rosettes and purflings. Both models sported a "Tru Fret" decal on their headstocks. All fingerboards were attached to the necks with three short nails located at the 5th, 7th and 9th frets. The top of each nail was allowed to show, and thus serving as a position marker; pretty darn clever!

As evidenced by the text of his 1925 patent application, Harry Hall believed that by simplifying the job of making a uke's fingerboard, a manufacturer could save enough time and money to allow them to build a better-sounding ukulele without increasing its overall cost. Personally, I don't think the Globe Company got the message. The two Tru-Fret ukes pictured here both sound about the same as other ukuleles built during the same period using the same basic body construction and materials. The patented fingerboards do provide the ukes with very good intonation and playability, the only downside being that in cold weather, playing on that pressed metal makes for some frosty fingertips!

This assortment of ukuleles with non-standard-shape bodies includes (left, bottom to top): Washburn shrine, Wabash deluxe, Tut Taylor "Hee Haw," Turturro peanut, Wimbrola (right, bottom to top): David Mahelona violin, Washburn bell and Regal F-hole.

5.3 Ukulele Oddities

Everyone knows what a ukulele is supposed to look like: a tiny guitar with four "my-dog-has-fleas" strings. But just because that's the norm doesn't mean there aren't a whole lot of ukes out there that don't much look like, well, ukes.

Perhaps it's the ukulele's diminutive size or relative ease of construction or economy of materials that's made it so susceptible to experimentation. For a hundred years, luthiers have re-imaged the basic shape of the uke, resulting in instruments with bodies that look like bells, peanuts, violins, coffins and more. Some models took their shape directly from other instru-

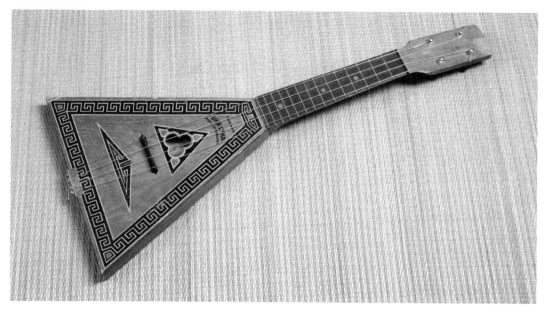

The English-made Uka Lyka has a thin triangular-shape body that emulates a traditional Russian balalaika.

Over the decades, instrument makers have used a variety of materials besides wood to build ukuleles, including plastic, metal, cardboard and even coconuts.

ments, such as the English-made, balalaika-shaped "Uka Lyka." They've also explored a variety of different uke-building materials, including plastic, metal, cardboard and even coconut shell.

But novel materials and body shapes are just the tip of the altered instrument iceberg. Spanning all the way back to the early 1900s, there's no shortage of examples of ukuleles that embody the inventive cleverness of their builders. In this section, I've focused on several of what I consider to be the best examples of vintage uke-building weirdness (several ukes that fit this category, including Turturro's Turnover and Peanut, the Aero uke, Regal's Jungle Uke and the Cocoleles have stories that warrant their own sections later in this chapter) Most of the instruments here are rare today, likely because their strange configurations and features made them less than popular when first produced and marketed (the luthiers who made them were often as

strange as their instruments). Although the majority of these ukes aren't practical and don't sound particularly good, they're still delightful curiosities worth exploring and admiring.

Knutsen Harp ukes

Quite popular around the turn of the last century, harp guitars feature a number of open strings that can be plucked to accompany the strings played on the instrument's regular fretted neck. Typically, these guitars have an arm-like extension of the body's upper bout which serves as an auxiliary resonating chamber for the open strings, which span between an oversized bridge and tuners at the end of the bout extension.

At some point around 1914, Port Townsend, Washington harp instrument maker Chris Knutsen decid-

ABOVE: When Chris Knutsen created a harp ukulele, he shaped the soprano uke's body much like the harp guitars he built, however he omitted the instrument's characteristic harp strings.

RIGHT: Thanks to a pair of custom brass brackets, the angle of the Knutsen harp ukes neck can be easily adjusted.

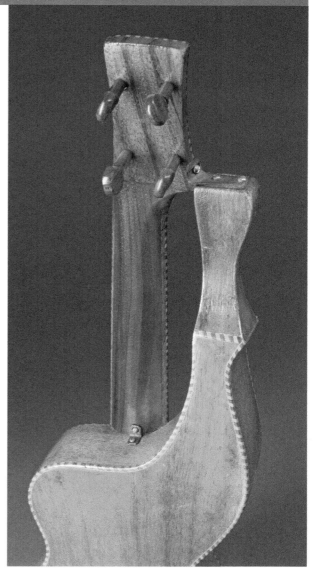

ed he'd create a harp ukulele. The soprano-sized uke's body is shaped much like the harp guitars he built. However, he left off one little thing: the open strings. Hence, the instrument looks like a regular uke with a weird appendage that's grown out of its upper body. Despite this omission, Knutsen harp ukes are really cool little instruments which have a rich sound, were well built and are rare and highly collectible today. The ukes came in several styles ranging from plain (a gumwood body and neck; no ornamentation outside of a simple sound hole rosette) to fancy (figured koa wood body with rope binding around the body, neck and headstock). Knutsen even made a few taro patch harp ukes. One unique detail of these odd-looking instruments is a pair of metal brackets: One attaches the neck to the body, the other connects the headstock to the arm extension. Together, they allow the user to adjust the angle of the neck in order to raise or lower the playing action.

Altpeter's Double Harp Uke

If there was one uke that I could vote "wackiest of the bunch," it would be this one: The "double harp uke" designed and built

by German immigrant Franz Walter Altpeter sometime in the late 1920s. While the uke's basic soprano-sized body shape is familiar, the asymmetrical yoke attached to the top of the headstock, the second headstock and tuners at the bottom of the body, and WAY too many strings make this instrument anything but normal (I think it looks like a ukulele with its own built-in TV antenna!). Besides four standard uke strings, the dark-stained mahogany instrument's top yoke anchors four auxiliary strings, two on either side of the neck. Tuned from the uke's bottom headstock, these strings pass over two small bridges on the body and are played open, like those of a harp. The design was patented by Altpeter in 1927, who not only endeavored to invent a new kind of instrument, but a new method of playing as well: In addition to playing chords on the regular neck, the auxiliary strings on one side were to be played with a metal thumbpick, while the other two were plucked with the fingers. As Innovative as the double harp uke was, the fact that there are very few existing examples is a sure sign that it never caught on with the public.

Stroh Horn Ukulele

It wasn't a luthier, but an electrical engineer in London named John Matthias Augustus Stroh, who, sometime around 1900, developed one of the strangest stringed instruments of all time: the Stroh Violin. His mechanically amplified violin works similar to the way an old-fashioned gramophones does: Instead of a needle mounted to a diaphragm and horn that amplifies the vibration from the grooves of a record, the Stroh's bridge attaches to a diaphragm connected to a horn, thus amplifying the vibration of the strings. This novel construction presented a couple of advantages: it made the Stroh violins louder than regular violins, so they could be heard in orchestras featuring brass instruments. Further, the horn gave the Stroh a more directional sound, which worked well for early recordings which relied on megaphones which concentrated the sound at the stylus of a record cutting machine.

After developing his violins, Stroh branched out to manufacture guitars, cellos, mandolins, ukuleles and even double basses. His soprano-scale ukes have a mahogany neck, an ebony fretboard, an aluminum

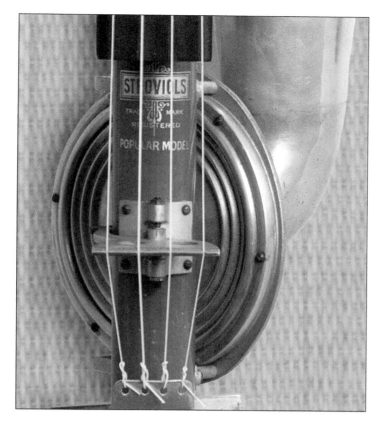

LEFT: The Stroh horn uke's unique bridge attaches to a gramophone-like diaphragm which is connected to a horn that amplifies the vibration of the strings.

LEFT BELOW: The large diaphragm and metal horn on the Stroh ukulele made its sound louder and more directional than regular ukes.

BELOW: To make the oddly-shaped instrument easier to hold, Stroh ukes were fitted with an adjustable arm rest at the bottom of the body.

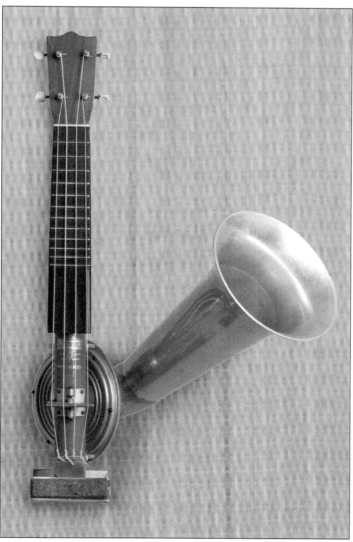

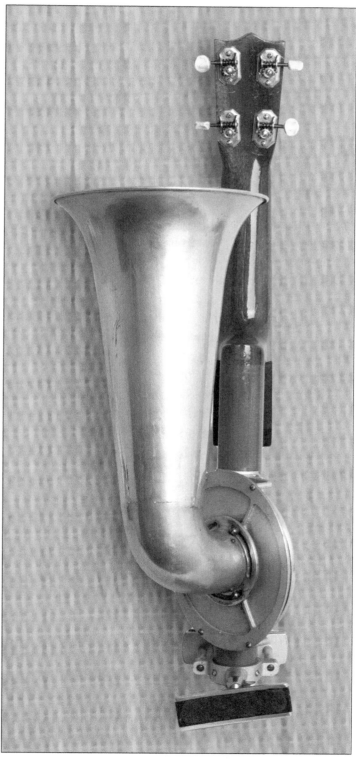

This English advertisement for Strohs No. 50 "The Popular" ukulele claims that its horn "…accentuates the sweetness of the natural tone of the Ukulele."

resonator and sound box and a nickel horn and adjustable arm rest. The latter is necessary to make the oddly-shaped Stroh easier to hold. The Model No. 50 Stroh ukulele was referred to in advertisements as "The Popular" and was touted as an instrument that "Makes the dark nights bright." Stroh claimed that the uke's horn "accentuates the sweetness of the natural tone of the ukulele, and there is an added richness to the notes as they flow from the Stroh."

Although they never became very popular, Stroh wasn't the only one who made horn-amplified string instruments: A.T. Howson of London started building horn resonator fiddles in 1906 and went on to produce at least one ukulele model.

The Polk-A-Lay-Lee

The Polk Brothers department store chain was Chicago's most prominent appliance and electronics retailer from the mid 1940s through the 1980s. Brothers Sol, Sam, Harry, David, Morris and sister, Ghisella pioneered the art of retail discounting, their motto being: "No customer walks out of the store without at least buying something." Master pitchman Sol Polk ran regular in-store promotions for televisions, microwave ovens and even Christmas trees. But one promo in the mid 1960s is surely one of the

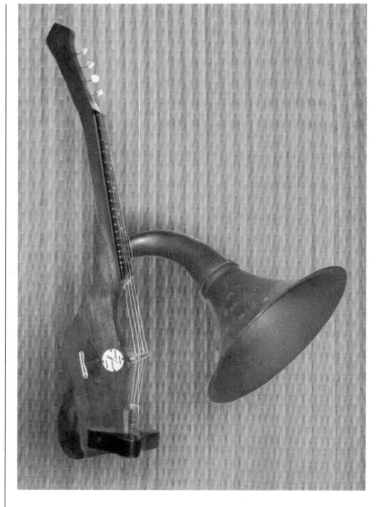

Yet another horn-amplified ukulele made by A.T. Howson of London sometime in the very early 1900s.

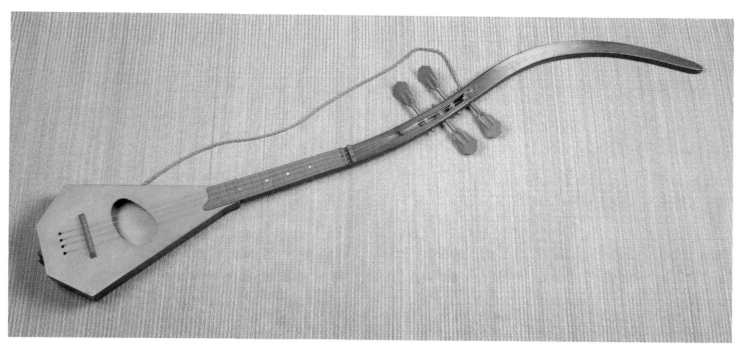

ABOVE: Made by Peterson Instruments in Ohio for the Polk Brothers department store chain in Chicago, the Polk-A-Lay-Lee uke was touted as being "America's newest, most unique musical fun instrument."

LEFT: In what had to be one of the strangest promotions in department store history, if you bought a Webcor tape recorder from the Polk Brothers, you could then buy a Polk-A-Lay-Lee for only $5 more.

BELOW: Swagerty's line of Kooky-Ukes with their plastic fretboards, large tuning pegs and narrow, extended headstocks likely provided the inspiration for the Polk Brothers Polk-A-Lay-Lee.

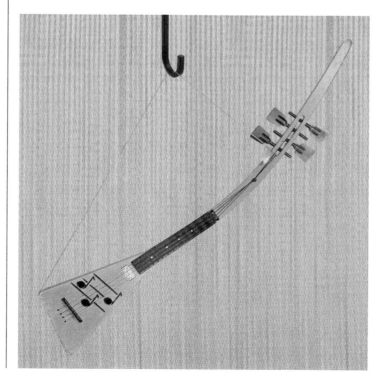

strangest ever: Buy a $70. Webcor reel-to-reel tape recorder and get a Polk-A-Lay-Lee uke for only $5! These odd ukulele-based instruments, made by Peterson Instruments in Ohio, were clearly modeled after Swagerty's Kooky-Ukes (See Section 7.5, pg. 307). They featured plastic fretboards, paddle tuning pegs and narrow, extended S-curved headstocks. A Polk Bros. ad for the instrument said it was "America's newest, most unique musical fun instrument" and

ABOVE: Resembling a child's toy rather than a real musical instrument, New York confectioner Barricini sold their Kosher chocolates in a metal tin fitted with a plastic neck, which could be played as a ukulele.

RIGHT: Each Barri-uke came with a small booklet titled "Serenade in Sweets" that provided basic playing instructions as well as few songs to strum.

that "It's made of fine quality woods handcrafted in America for home folks from 2 to 92." Polk-A-Lay-Lees came in walnut finish, "gleaming black," or "gay black and red" packed in hot-pink cardboard boxes that reflected Polk Bros. penchant for hyperbolic advertising, claiming that they were made of "solid wood" (the bodies are actually plywood) and produced a "quality tone" (it's generous to say that they sound horrible).

The Barricini Candy Box Uke

At first inspection, this strange looking concert-scale ukulele appears to be nothing more than a child's toy, its cheap-look-

The top of Barricini's "Barri-uke" tin featured colorful graphics of 50s-era people playing various sports.

ing one-piece plastic neck/fretboard/headstock attached to a round metal body that's barely an inch deep. Designed in the 1950s by Robert M. Karoff, a well-known creator of all kinds of novelty items, the uke's black-painted body is adorned with stencils of colorful 50s-era characters, as well as the name "Barri-uke." But wait, there's more: the Barri-uke's metal body opens like a cookie tin to reveal its dual purpose: The tin originally came packed with Barricini Kosher chocolates. The idea was, that after you consumed the confections, you could close the body back up and play it like a regular uke. A small instruction and song booklet, titled "Serenade in Sweets," that came with the Barri-uke proudly announced: "Be the center of attraction and the life of the party. You can have happy and wholesome fun when the gang gathers with the two-purpose Barri-uke—serve the candy, then entertain your friends with their favorite melodies." The uke was part of a promotional campaign that Barricini waged against their staunchest competitor: Barton's. The fierce competition between these two confection companies for their share of the Jewish confections market came to be known as "the Kosher chocolate wars."

This fancy lyre-shaped mandolin known as a "mandolira," was built by Italian luthier Nicola Turturro after he immigrated to America in the early 1900s.

THE ART OF VINTAGE UKULELES • SANDOR NAGYSZALANCZY

Turturro opened a shop in New York City in the mid-1920s, where he not only built instruments, including ukuleles, but also repaired them and offered playing lessons.

5.4 The Turturro Turnover and Peanut

Once apprenticed to a cabinetmaker in Rome, Italian-American inventor and luthier Nicola Turturro immigrated to America in the early 1900s and started building musical instruments in the Italian enclave of Mount Vernon, just north of New York City. It was a time when mandolin music was extremely popular in America, and most Italian luthiers focused on mandolin construction. But they faced stiff competition from large American factories that supplied companies such as Sears Roebuck & Company and Montgomery Ward, whose mail-order catalogs offered dozens of different models. Since most mail-order models were cheap (in 1905, a nice nine-rib round-back mandolin cost just $1.95), small-shop Italian luthiers had to offer extraordinary instruments in order to compete. Turturro's answer was to create an impressive looking double-armed "mandolira," a fancy lyre-shaped mandolin. He even patented his design in 1904 (U.S. Design Patent #767,023)

When the American ukulele craze hit its full stride in the mid-1920s, Turturro opened a shop in New York City and turned his creative talents to building four-string instruments. He soon developed and patented designs for two truly unique models: a round-backed "Peanut" uke and a very unusual combination ukulele/mandolin, which Nichola dubbed "The Turnover."

The Peanut uke was built in much the same way as traditional bowl-back mandolins, where individual strips of thin wood are formed over a mold and glued edge-to-edge to form the instrument's curved back. In

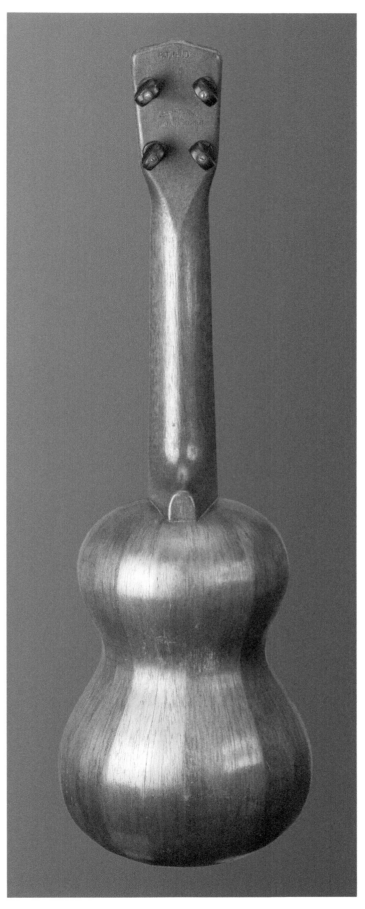

The back of Turturro's "Peanut" ukulele reveals its double-humped shape, created from separate strips glued together much the way a bowl-back mandolin is constructed.

Standard Peanut ukes were made of mahogany and clear finished; the back of the uke in the foreground was specially covered in golden pyralin, a nitrocellulose plastic akin to celluloid.

LEFT:
Nichola Turturro's ingenious "Turnover" ukulele features a ukulele on one side and a mandolin on the other.

The Art of Vintage Ukuleles • Sandor Nagyszalanczy

The Turnover's headstock with mandolin tuners protruding at the edges and, as seen reflected in a mirror, chess-piece-style uke tuners in the center.

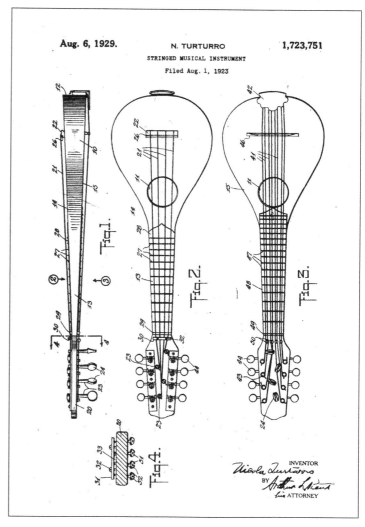

The 1929 patent for Turturro's Turnover uke shows that its thin body has strings, fingerboards and bridges on both sides.

the case of the Peanut uke's body, Turturro bent the strips into a sort of double-humped shape. This not only gave the back a peanut shape, but allowed the top to have the familiar Spanish figure-eight shape as a typical ukulele.

The first two things you'll notice about the Turturro Turnover is that the instrument has way too many tuning keys, as well as a sound hole that goes all the way through its body. Flipping the instrument front-to-back reveals that it's a four-string uke on one side and an 8-string mandolin on the other.

Besides the Turnover's unique double sound hole and dual set of tuners (friction pegs with Bakelite knobs and four-in-row geared mandolin tuners), its other unique—and patented—feature is the nut: To

RIGHT: A Massachusetts music shop's ad for the Turnover uke, which came in three different styles.

Turturro Turnovers were played by two sisters who were members of a well-known vaudeville and circus act called "The Doll Family."

make the Turnover's design work, the body is very thin (which also accounts for its weak sound), the peghead has only a slight break angle relative to the rosewood fretboard. Hence, a screwed-on brass bar holds the uke strings engaged in the nut, and four screws do the same for the mandolin strings. For all these innovative features, Turturro was awarded U.S. utility patent #1,723,751 in 1929.

Promoted in a 1924 advertisement as "the newest musical convenience," Turturro's Turnover was described as "…A perfectly practical mandolin on one side and—turn it over—a fine ukulele on the other." It came in three styles: The all-mahogany #1, the mahogany and spruce topped #2, and the deluxe style #3 that featured an extra-fine spruce top and a pick guard. They sold for $13.00, $14.50 and $16.00 respectively. By far, the greatest number of Turnovers that survive today are plain style #1 instruments, adorned only with a sound hole ring and no body bindings, fret-

board position markers or headstock inlays.

In addition to his unique patented models, Turturro also produced a number of more conventional instruments, including soprano and concert ukes, taro patches, tiples, and even guitars. Some of these were sold under his own name, while others bear the labels of companies he manufactured for, including Stadlmair (Miami brand), C. Bruno & Sons, S. S. Stewart and B&J (Buegeleisen and Jacobson).

Although Turturro's ukes never achieved great popularity, they did gain some notoriety: A pair of his Turnovers were played by two sisters in a well-known vaudeville and circus act called "The Doll Family." This quartet of little people consisted of four German siblings: Gracie, Tiny, Harry and Daisy. Various "Family" members appeared in popular movies, including the 1932 Todd Browning cult classic Freaks. All four played munchkins in 1939's The Wizard of Oz, with Harry a singing member of the "Lollypop Guild."

THE ART OF VINTAGE UKULELES • SANDOR NAGYSZALANCZY

Capitalizing on America's fascination with Charles Lindberg's trans-Atlantic flight, the Stromberg-Voisinet Company produced a unique airplane-shaped ukulele called the "Aero Uke."

5.5 The Aero Uke Takes Flight

The 50th anniversary of the first moon landing seemed to have everyone thinking about America's great accomplishments in flight. And right up there with the names of well-known aviation heroes like Neil Armstrong and Chuck Yeager is Charles Lindbergh, the first man to make a solo, non-stop flight across the Atlantic in 1927. At a time when long-distance flight was relatively sketchy, Lindbergh flew his single-engine "Spirit of St. Louis" airplane from New York to Paris in a mere 33 ½ hours covering approximately 3500 miles, mostly over open water. Only 25 years old at the time, Lindbergh collected the $25,000 prize offered by New York hotelier Raymond Orteig for completing the flight. His remarkable feat instantly propelled him to mega celebrity status and worldwide acclaim and renown.

Predictably, merchandisers were quick to cash in on the enormous popularity of Lindbergh's accomplishment. Up for sale were Lindbergh Postage stamps, commemorative coins, buttons, pins, plaques, plates & medals, picture puzzles, souvenir beanies, fans and flyswatters, spoons and ashtrays, gum dispensers, and tin toy reproductions of the Spirit of St. Louis plane. His flight was also celebrated in song and sheet music with

Lindbergh's solo flight was commemorated by numerous songs, the most popular of which was the 1927 tune: "Lucky Lindy."

The Aero Uke's airplane-like appointments include a wing-shaped body, a neck serving as the fuselage, and a tail rudder headstock.

A turned wood propellor provides the tailpiece that the uke's strings attach to.

THE ART OF VINTAGE UKULELES • SANDOR NAGYSZALANCZY

titles including: "Lucky Lindy," "Lindy Did It," "Lindbergh the Hero of Our Heart," "Oh, Charlie is My Darling" and "Like an Angel You Flew Into Everyone's Heart." Most of these sheets included ukulele chords.

As the Lindbergh flight perfectly coincided with the peak of America's first ukulele craze, it's not surprising that uke makers were also eager to capitalize on it. There was a soprano-sized "Lindy" uke (likely made by Regal), its top stenciled with an image of the Spirit of St. Louis and the words: "New York - - - - - Paris." Harmony also got in on the action with a new airplane-shaped bridge that they fitted to their Johnny Marvin signature model ukuleles (see photo on page 180 in Section 4.8)

But the most interesting and unusual Lindbergh-related instrument was undoubtedly the "Aero Uke," a concert-sized ukulele designed to look as much like an airplane as practically possible. It's wide, slightly trapezoidal body (14 1/2" wide, 5 5/8" long and 2 ½" deep at the center, tapering down to just 9/16" at the narrow ends) resembles the wings of a plane, while its mahogany neck acts as the fuselage. The uke's headstock, surmounted by a shapely center vain, simulates a plane's horizontal stabilizer and rudder. A turned-mahogany

propeller is mounted on the bottom edge of the body with a center spinner that extends beyond the prop to serve as an anchor for the strings (see photo).

The sides of the Aero's body are made from solid mahogany, while thin mahogany plywood covers its curved back. The top is solid spruce adorned with three decorative transfer decals (the center one says "Aero Uke" in small letters). The stylish mahogany bridge has a small screwed-on metal bar that holds the strings down against the saddle and increases their break angle. The uke's twin 1 ½" dia. sound holes are located on the neck-side of the body, one on either side of the neck. On deluxe Aero models, these sound holes featured semi-circular trim pieces marked to simulate aeronautical air speed and altitude gauges.

The construction of the Aero Uke is as unusual as its overall shape. Instead of the neck attaching to the body via a traditional neck block, there's a thick wood dowel that extends from the base of the neck to the bottom end of the body—construction more commonly used in banjo ukes.

Often mis-identified as a Harmony-made instrument (possibly because of Harmony's airplane bridge Johnny Marvin), the Aero Uke was actually produced

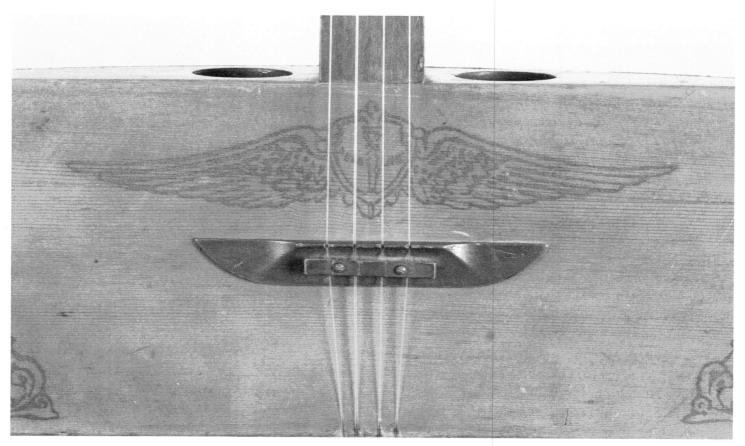

The uke's solid spruce top is decorated with three decorative transfer decals, including a large center wing shaped one with the words "Aero Uke" in small letters.

The Stromberg-Voisinet AERO UKE

Handy to hold, it cuddles naturally into the crook of the arm, leaving the wrist free for all styles of stroking. This AERO UKE sets a new standard in volume and depth of tone. It is entirely new and novel in appearance.

WE INVITE TONE COMPARISON

Order from your Jobber

Stromberg-Voisinet Company
316 Union Park Court
Chicago, Ill.

Stromberg-Voisinet's ad for the Aero Uke states that the instrument "...sets a new standard in volume and tone."

by the Stromberg-Voisinet Company (SVC) of Chicago Illinois. Like uke manufacturers Regal and Harmony, SVC made relatively inexpensive instruments that were mostly sold through mail order catalogs. Although to my knowledge, no instruments have been found bearing company stamps or identifying paper labels, the origins of the Aero are easily confirmed by SVC's vintage print advertisements. The Aero's fanciful headstock further confirms its maker as it's top edge exactly the same shape as the headstocks found on the many banjo ukes SVC produced. This distinctive headstock shape was not used by any other ukulele manufacturer.

Despite the Aero Uke's odd appearance, it's remarkably comfortable to play. As its vintage ad states, the Aero is: "Handy to hold, it cuddles naturally into the crook of the arm, leaving the wrist free for all styles of strumming." Given its relatively small body size, it's also impressively loud, with a tone that's pleasantly warm and well balanced.

Lindbergh's "Spirit of Saint Louis" in flight.

LEFT: Regal's Jungle Uke is covered in faux leopard fur, which deadens the sound of the instrument considerably.

ABOVE: The edges of the faux fur on back of the Jungle Uke show just how thick the fur material is.

5.6 Regals' Jungle Uke

While researching the section on ukulele patents (Section 5.1), I was impressed by the number of different inventions that luthiers came up with to make their ukuleles unique looking and/or better sounding. Ironically, the uke discussed here is a model that not only eschews any sort of structural or sonic innovations, its very design makes it one of the poorest-sounding ukes ever made. But the same thing that makes it short on tone also makes it one of the coolest ukes ever: The aptly named Jungle Uke has a body that's completely covered in fake leopard fur fabric!

As you might guess, the glued-on fake-fur fabric has a significant damping effect on the vibration of the uke's top, making it sound soft and lifeless. Not helping matters is the uke's top, made of solid white wood (possibly birch) that's all of 1/8 in. thick; a typical so-

A leopard head is featured on the decal atop the Jungle Uke's headstock.

Films with Jungle themes, including "Tarzan, King of the Apes," were very popular in the 1940s and 50s.

prano uke's top is only about 5/64 in. thick. The sides and back are also made of similarly stout stock—no fear of breaking this uke, should you take a tumble while riding your elephant. One thing that the fuzzy fabric has going for it is that it's soft to the touch, which makes this uke very comfortable to hold and play.

The soprano-sized Jungle Uke has a 13 1/8 in. scale and a birch neck with 12 frets set directly into it—no separate fingerboard here. A pair of gold and black decals mark the 5th and 7th frets and a headstock decal shows "Jungle Uke" written in an exotic green bamboo font with a colorful image of a leopard just below it. The instrument lacks any sort of manufacturer's label or markings (there may have been a paper label inside the body, but if so, it's missing on mine). It was almost certainly produced by the Regal Musical Instrument Company of Chicago, the prime clue being the shape of the Jungle Uke's headstock which is identical to those found on the majority of Regal ukes made in the 20s through the early 50s.

Although I could find no advertising or catalog references for the Jungle Uke, it's a fair guess that it was produced sometime between the late 1940s and the mid 1950s. This timeframe coincides with the rise in popularity of jungle-themed adventure movies, which I'm sure Regal was eager to capitalize on. Jungle thrillers had been a staple for Hollywood studios as far back as the 1920s. By the 1940s, African-themed movies abounded with danger and romance, for example 1942's White Cargo, starring Hedy Lamarr who played the capricious native beauty "Tondelayo." Johnny Weissmuller starred in no less than 15 movies in the 40s based on Edgar Rice Burroughs' Tarzan character. By the 1950s, jungle themed films were box-office gold with enduring classics like The African Queen (1951), starring Humprey Bogart and Katherine Hepburn, and 1953's Mogambo, starring Clark Gable, Grace Kelly and Ava Gardner. Unfortunately, nary a single ukulele appeared in any of these films, leopard-fur covered or otherwise.

ABOVE: Island artisans have long used coconut shell for making all manner of tourist trinkets, such as this covered bowl

RIGHT: Both the better quality Niu Kani uke (left) and inexpensive souvenir uke (right) feature bodies made from a single large coconut surmounted with a thin wood top.

5.7 Crazy Cocoleles

If you've ever built a ukulele from scratch, you know there are several tricky bits to tackle, including shaping the neck, laying out and installing the frets, and the most time-consuming process of all: building the body from scads of separate parts. In the 1970s, instrument manufacturer Ovation simplified guitar and uke body construction by developing the one-piece body cast from ABS plastic.

But long before Ovation made plastic-bodied instruments, Pacific Island luthiers came up with another time-saving innovation: They made the bodies of their ukuleles and other small instruments from coconuts. Abundant on the majority of Pacific islands, including Hawaii, coconuts have strong shells that can be cut, shaped and polished much like wood. Island artisans and entrepreneurs have long used coconut shell for making all manner of tourist trinkets, from earrings and keychain fobs to dishes and bowls to souvenir spoons and kitschy decorative items.

No one knows when the first ukulele with a coconut shell body was made, but Hawaiian examples of such instruments from the 1910s and 20s are plentiful. These include higher quality ukes, like the Niu Kani

shown at left (above) as well as cheaper souvenir ukes made specifically for the tourist trade. The construction of these ukes is straightforward: about a third of a large dried coconut is cut off and the remaining part of the shell is used for the instrument's body. A thin wood top is glued over the shell's open side and a simple fretted neck is attached, usually via screws, to the coconut. The rest of the instrument—tuning pegs, bridge, frets—is done much like a regular ukulele.

By the mid 1930s, an enterprising man born on the island of Maui named Anthony G. Cox developed his own unique twist on the coconut-bodied ukulele concept: Cox mated two medium-sized coconuts together to form a body with a figure-8 shape. This not only expanded the size of the uke's body cavity (resulting in a modest increase in volume), but it allowed Cox to fit a koa wood top with a shape like a regular Spanish-style-bodied ukulele. He initially called his instrument a "Kokolele," but later changed the name to "Cocolele."

A pair of coconuts cut and joined together were used to create ukuleles with the familiar Spanish "figure of eight" body shape.

LEFT: The twin-coconut-bodied Cox Coconut Ukuleles were manufactured by a most unusual maker: the Automotive Service Company of Honolulu.

BELOW: Examples of coconut ukuleles sporting bodies made from one, two and three coconuts.

Coconut ukes weren't just made in Hawaii: These two were made on the South Pacific island of Rarotonga.

Cox's design was unique enough that he was granted U.S. patent #2,098,701 in November of 1937 (see the photo on page 198). In the patent's text, Cox states: "...the principle object of my invention [was] to produce a ukelele (Cox's spelling) having fine tone, and I accomplish this by constructing a substantial portion of the main body... from cocoanut [sic] shells." The patent points out some interesting constructions used in Cox's uke, including a wooden "connecting bead" that covers the mating seam between the two coconut shells and a ¼ in. wide wood rim that secures the uke's top to the shells which, Cox claimed, allowed the top to vibrate more freely.

Around the time his patent was granted, August Cox and his brother formed the "Cox Brothers Cocolele & Curio Mfgrs" in Honolulu, which made Cocoleles for only three or four years before the business disbanded. Production of the instruments continued, as Cox licensed his patent rights to two other firms: The Pacific Mfg. & Sales Co. Ltd. and the Automotive Service Company, both located in Honolulu. (yes, it seems odd that an automotive company made ukes, but who knows, maybe they did it to pass the time between oil changes?) Automotive Service Co. made their own version of the twin-shell Cocolele, as did Pacific Mfg., which also made a three-shell Cocolele with a top shaped much like a Roy Smeck Vita Uke (Cox's patent covered uke bodies built with two or more coconuts). The larger body cavity formed by the three truncated shells gave this uke more volume and tone than a one- and two-shell Cocolele. All Cox patent ukes were produced in limited numbers, and since production all but ceased with the advent of WWII, these instruments are fairly rare.

You can still buy single-coconut-bodied ukuleles today, although most of these are cheap, souvenir-quality instruments manufactured in the Far East. Coconut ukes were also produced on several South Pacific islands, including Rarotonga, where they were made by both local artisans and the inmates of the local prison in Arorangi. The tops of these crudely made ukes are often painted with picturesque island scenes.

Ukulele banjos are basically like four-stringed tenor banjos with smaller bodies and fretted soprano or concert scale ukulele necks.

5.8 American and British Banjo Ukes

The banjo ukulele, also known as the banjolele, banjulele or banjuke, is based on the four-stringed tenor banjo, but with a smaller body and a fretted ukulele neck. This innovative instrument came to life in the early 1900s, when the Hawaiian ukelele was first becoming popular. People loved the uke's sound, but didn't always appreciate its relatively soft volume. Vaudeville performers in particular needed an instrument that played with the ease of a regular soprano ukelele but had a lot more volume. The banjo uke fit that need perfectly.

The earliest known banjoleles were conceived in the mid-1910s by both Californian John A. Bolander and Honolulu-born brothers Kelvin and Alvin Keech. While it's not known which person actually invented the instrument or built the first one, Bolander received U.S. patent #1,378,212 for his basic banjo uke design in 1921 and was an early pioneer in their manufacture. Heedless of Bolander's patent, the Keech brothers designed and built their own line of banjo ukes.

Both brothers were musicians and entrepreneurs who lived in San Francisco, Los Angeles, London and Paris at various times in their lives. Their high-quality instruments were manufactured in the UK from around 1918 until 1939.

The banjo uke's short scale, familiar "my-dog-has-fleas" tuning, and playing style of a regular ukulele combined with the construction and distinctive tone of a banjo led to the instrument's great popularity in the 1920s and 1930s. In the U.S., banjo ukes were particularly favored by ukulele players who performed with jazz or Dixieland bands, as they were loud enough to be heard over a band's horn section. American companies that produced regular banjos also made banjo ukes, including Bacon, Ludwig and Slingerland as well as Gretsch (see the photos on pg. 58 and 59) Some of the nicest playing and most coveted banjo ukes were made by guitar and ukulele maker Gibson (see Section 2.2). Lyon & Healy also produced some very nice banjo ukes, including the attractive "Hanalei" brand models. Banjo ukes were—and still are—particularly popular in England; see the Sidebar (page 235).

Construction wise, most banjo ukes are built like

LEFT ABOVE: Keech brothers banjo ukes were manufactured in the UK sometime between 1918 and 1939.

LEFT BELOW: Although John Bolander patented the basic design for his banjo ukulele in 1921, both Bolander and brothers Kelvin and Alvin Keech are said to have first built banjo ukes in the late 1910s.

ABOVE: The back of a Keech banjo ukulele showing its unusual resonator plate, which is scalloped to provide access to the uke's head tensioning fasteners.

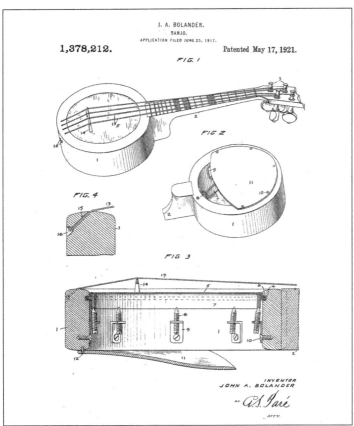

regular tenor banjos but on a smaller scale (but there are exceptions, like Guckert's "Jazuke" ; see the photo on page 196. A banjo ukulele's neck typically has sixteen frets set to the same scale length as a soprano uke or, less commonly, a concert-sized uke. Bodies, known as "shells" may be made entirely of metal or consist of a wood ring, either lathe-turned or built up from layers of wood laminated together. Some of the more unusual banjo ukes feature non-circular bodies made of solid wood or plywood. There are also a handful of models, including the Werco and Dixie, made mostly (the Werco) or entirely (the Dixie) of metal. Regardless of body type, each banjo uke has a metal ring or "hoop" that supports and

LEFT: A few of the better-know American companies that produced regular banjos as well as banjo ukes are (left to right) Bacon, Ludwig and Slingerland, who made the Premier model.

BELOW, LEFT: This Lyon & Healy catalog page shows eight different banjo uke models that they produced, including Mauna Loa and Hanalei branded instruments.

BELOW: The rope-binding trimmed headstock and neck of a Hanalei brand banjo uke, manufactured by Lyon & Healy.

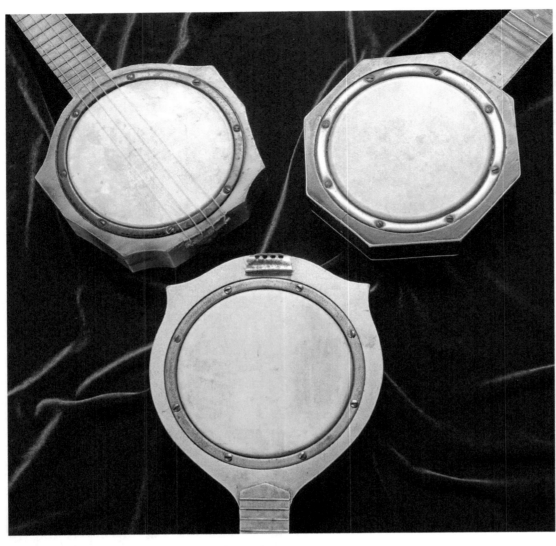

LEFT: These three unusual banjo ukes feature non-circular bodies. The instrument brands are, clockwise from upper left: Valencia, Peach and La Pacifica.

BELOW: The Dixie banjo uke (top) is made entirely of metal while the Werco uke below it has a wooden body shell and the same all-metal neck as the Dixie.

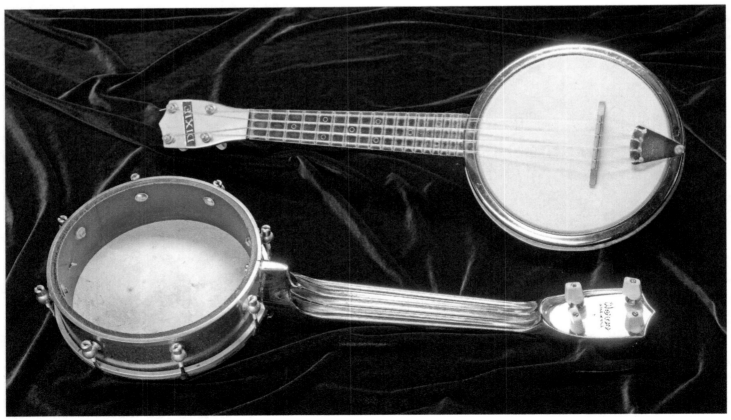

THE ART OF VINTAGE UKULELES • SANDOR NAGYSZALANCZY

ABOVE: The traditional method of tensioning the skin head of a banjo with a metal hoop secured by hooks can be seen on the banjo uke at left, while the uke at right uses an internal hoop for tensioning the head.

RIGHT: The thin wood resonator back on this no-name banjo uke is perforated by a pair of f-holes.

ABOVE: A trio of banjo ukuleles that all feature metal shells and resonators made from sheet metal

BELOW: A pair of large wood resonators featuring decorative details: a ring of hearts decal on the "Sweetheart" model, left, and floral marquetry on the Maxitone model at right.

THE ART OF VINTAGE UKULELES • SANDOR NAGYSZALANCZY

tensions the instrument's drum-like head, traditionally made of calf skin. A loose wood bridge set atop the skin head supports and maintains proper spacing between the strings. Vintage ukes were often strung with steel strings, although some players preferred to use gut strings instead.

The diameter of a banjo uke's head varies quite a bit depending on the particular model, ranging from 6 in. to around 8 in. in diameter. Less expensive instruments with small-diameter heads often have simple metal rings that secure and tension the skin head. Bet-ter banjo ukes (typically with larger-diameter shells) have tensioning hooks or similar devices fitted around the body that adjust the tension of the head. Firmer tension creates a tight, bright sound while looser tension yields a softer tone.

Some banjo ukuleles are open-backed while others have a round rear resonator made of wood or metal which serves to direct more of the instrument's sound forward. Wood resonators are often decorated, sometimes with decals, sometimes with inlays or colorful wood marquetry.

SIDEBAR: English Banjo Ukes & The Faerie Queen

I know there are a lot of ukulele players out there who cringe a bit at the mere mention of the banjo ukulele. But don't say that to a banjo uke fan, especially if they hail from across the pond. All over the UK, scads of strummers embrace that small, skin-headed four string in a big way. Well before George Formby popularized the instrument while singing and expertly strumming his way through a string of comical movies released during WWII (see Section 6.1) the Brits had been in love with the banjo ukulele. Some of the finest of these instruments were made in England by a handful of manufacturers, most prominently A.O. Windsor, George Houghton & Sons, Barnett Samuel & Sons and John E. Dallas & Sons, who produced a George Formby signature uke English instruments carried a dizzying array of brand names, including Jedson, Whirle, Swanee, Merry Bright, Jolli-Joe, Fitzroy, Tonella, Melody, Marvel and John Grey & Sons.

Now "John Grey & Sons" may sound like the name of a manufacturer, but it was actually a brand name created by Barnett Samuel & Sons (BS&S) of London, who began building banjos in 1901. This was purely a marketing ploy for selling their instruments; there was no John Grey... or his sons. To make matters even more confusing, John Grey & Sons branded banjos and banjo ukes weren't actually made by BS&S, but by Francis Beddard who had once worked for S.S. Stewart in American.

Regardless of what they're called and who built them, the majority of John Grey banjo ukes were

Some of the best vintage banjo ukes were made in England by a handful of manufacturers, including John E. Dallas & Sons, who produced the George Formby signature model that George is playing in the photo.

well made, good sounding instruments. The line included a basic model with a 7-in. diameter head, a mahogany neck and round plywood body capped with a pressed-plywood "resonator" back as well as more deluxe models featuring larger 8 in. dia. heads

ABOVE AND RIGHT:
Manufactured in London, the John Grey & Sons brand line included some really great banjo ukes, including this basic model with a 7-in. diameter head and plywood body capped with a pressed-plywood "resonator" back

and full resonator backs covered in figured wood veneers. They also produced several Roy Smeck signature banjo ukes, ranging from a cheaply made, green-painted "Junior" model to the fancier "Deluxe" which featured extensive pearl fretboard inlays and a fancy resonator.

But John Grey & Sons' top-of-the-line banjolele was the charmingly named "Faerie Queen." First produced in the 1920s, this attractive instrument has a short 13 ¼ in. scale and a body, fretboard and resonator all covered in glistening ivory pearloid. It's 8 in. dia. head is mounted to a thick plywood body with a tone ring, tensioning hooks and harp-like tailpiece all made from yellow brass. The outer-front edge of the

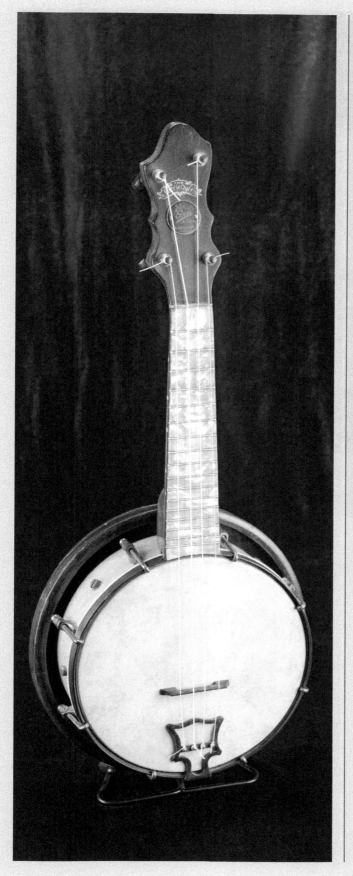

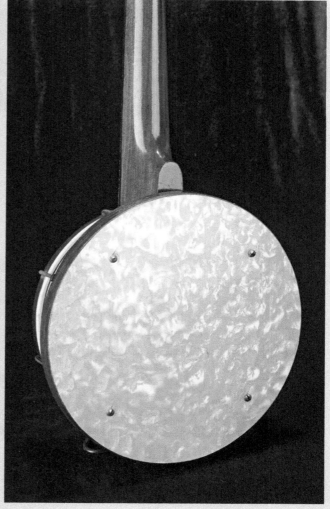

ABOVE AND LEFT:
John Grey & Sons' flagship model was the "Faerie Queen" which featured a body, fretboard and resonator all covered in flashy ivory pearloid.

9 ½ in. dia. resonator is reinforced by a thick ring of laminated walnut. Its stout walnut neck is surmounted by a shapely elongated headstock fitted with large patent friction tuners—much like a full-sized tenor banjo. The top of the headstock is covered in ebony veneer and bears the "Faerie Queen" decal and metal John Grey & Sons logo badge. [KEY PHOTO 5.8 #18] Sound wise, the Faerie Queen has a tone that's uncharacteristically rich and warm for a banjo uke. In fact, it's one of the best-sounding banjoleles I've ever played.

ABOVE: The Faerie Queen model's hoop rings, hooks and brackets and tailpiece are all made of yellow brass.

RIGHT: An irregular shaped headstock bearing a Faerie Queen decal and metal John Grey & Sons medallion tops this attractive ukulele.

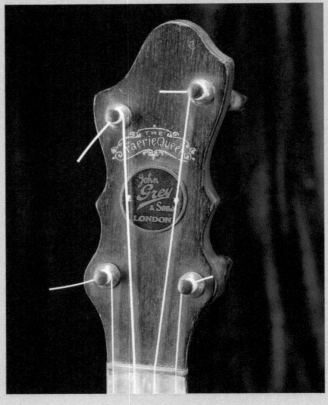

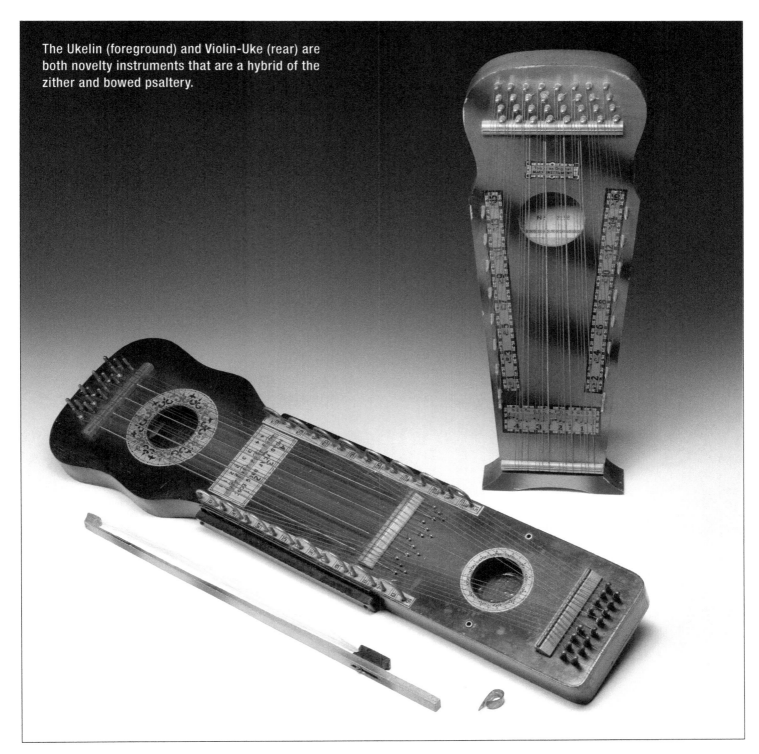

The Ukelin (foreground) and Violin-Uke (rear) are both novelty instruments that are a hybrid of the zither and bowed psaltery.

5.9 The Ukelin & Violin-Uke

If you're a frequent visitor to flea markets and/or junk shops, there's a good chance you've seen an odd-looking vintage instrument called a "Ukelin." The strange thing is that besides having strings, a sound hole and "uke" in its name, this instrument has nothing at all to do with ukuleles. Ukelin (pronounced "u-ke-lin") is the trade name of an instrument that's a hybrid of the zither and bowed psaltery. It's part of a small family of patented novelty instruments that include the "Violin-Uke" and "Hawaiian Art Violin," two instruments that are basically identical but manufactured by different companies. It's very likely that the names of all three instruments were concocted to take advantage of America's fascination with ukuleles and all things Hawaiian in the early 20th century.

Ukelins and Violin-Ukes each have 16 melody strings as well as 16 bass strings divided into four groups of four, each tuned to a different chord. With the instrument set on a table or stand, the melody strings are played with a short violin-like bow while the bass strings are plucked or strummed with the fingers.

The Ukelin and Violin-Uke both came to life around the mid-1920s. The identity of their original inventor is uncertain, as three different men—Paul F. Richter, John Large and Walter Schmidt—all filed US Patents for very similar bowed-and-plucked instruments. The Marx Colony Music Company of New Troy Michigan was one of the first to manufacture the instruments, which they branded as Violin-Ukes. Instead of the usual practice of distributing these poorly-made instruments for sale though music shops and emporiums, they took a more novel approach, selling them directly to the public through traveling door-to-door salesmen who often preyed on poor rural families. Ukelins, made by both the International Music Company and Oscar Schmidt International Inc., were sold the same way.

This is how the scam worked: The salesmen began by skillfully playing a tune or two on the Violin-Uke/Ukelin, then claiming that it was the perfect instrument for a beginner, as one could learn to play it in just a day. They would then tell the unsuspecting customer that they could buy the instrument for half of what it would cost them at a music store—a flat-out lie, as they were not sold in music stores! The average retail price for these instruments in the depression-era was $12.95, although huckster salesmen could sell them

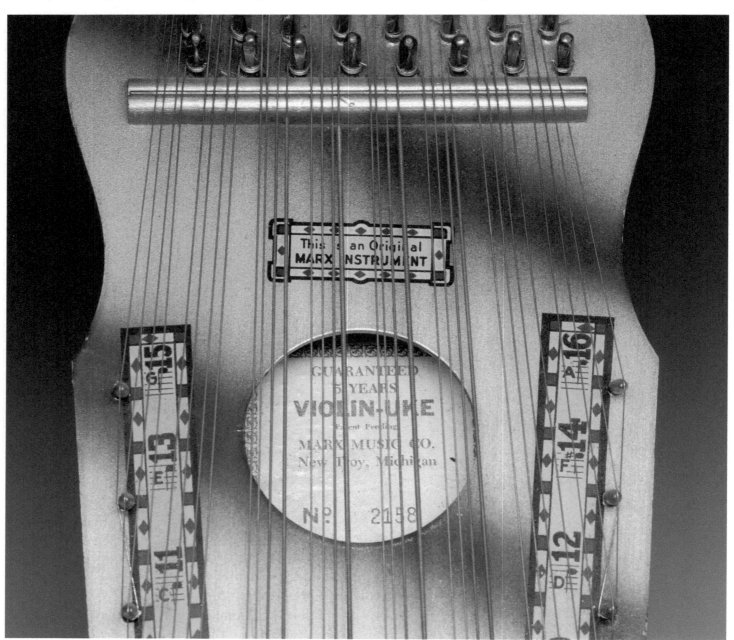

Marx Violin-Ukes were sold directly to the public through traveling door-to-door salesmen who often used unscrupulous tactics to secure a sale.

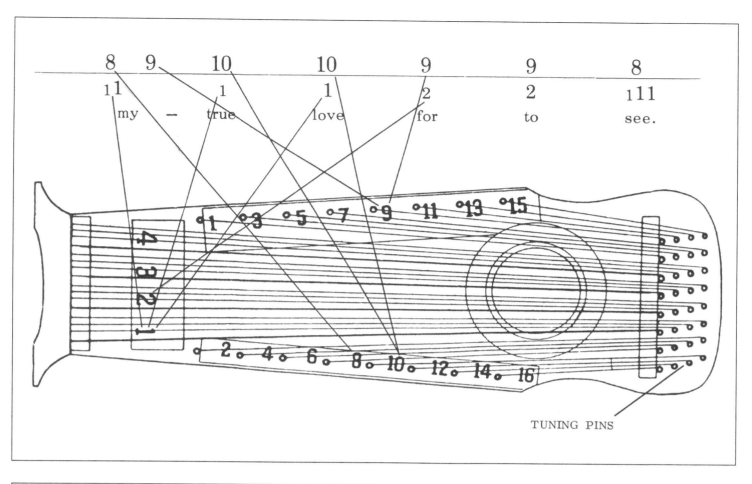

This diagram from the Violin-Uke booklet shows how to play a song using both the bow to strum the outer strings and fingers to pluck/strum the inner four-string groups.

PLAYING POSITION

Sit down at a table and place the instrument diagonally in front of you as shown in illustration. In this position the melody strings are easily played with the bow and the left hand is in correct position for playing the chords.

This page from the instruction booklet that came with a Violin-Uke shows the correct playing position.

for whatever they could get. Those who did fall for the pitch and buy the instruments quickly discovered that even simple tunes were difficult play, as one had to follow a complex numbered string/chord system outlined in the booklets that came with them. Not only that, but the instruments' diatonic scale tunings severely limited the songs one could play. Another problem was keeping those 32 strings in tune, especially difficult as these instruments didn't come with tuning keys. The Marx Company even went as far as suggesting that their Violin-Ukes be shipped back to the company for tuning! A great many folks did indeed ship their instruments back to their manufacturers, often complaining that they had been duped into buying an essentially worthless instrument.

Despite the sales chicanery, Ukelins and Violin-Ukes continued to be peddled door-to-door all the way up to the mid 1960s. In 1964, Oscar Schmidt owner Glen Peterson discontinued making Ukelins after learning of his salesman's shady sales practices.

Chapter Six
The Uke Goes to War

Four ukuleles from the WWII era and beyond. From left to right: Gretsch Army Uke, Harmony Wings model, soldier-made mess kit uke, Regal "Victory" uke.

Last November 11th on Veteran's Day, I was curious about how interest in the ukulele had revived both during and after World War Two (WWII). But I realized that all I knew about this was from the few brief paragraphs I'd read in books and magazines. The abbreviated story goes like this: GI's stationed in Hawaii learned to play ukuleles and brought them home after the war. Considering that more than half a million American service men and women served in the South Pacific during WWII with Hawaii as a center of operations, it's no wonder that military personnel were exposed to Hawaiian music and culture, including the uke. But as it turns out, there's a lot more to the story, both on the home front and in the war zones—in the Pacific, Europe and across the globe.

US Army Air Corps insignia: 1919 - 1941

ABOVE: A 1942 booklet with humorous cartoon drawings of GIs in the Hawaiian Islands (okole maluna means "bottoms up").

RIGHT: Many soldiers picked up the ukulele during their time in Hawaii during WWII, including a member of this group of Navy soldiers photographed in Honolulu.

WE'LL ALWAYS
REMEMBER PEARL HARBOR

Words and Music by
ALFRED BRYAN
WILLIE RASKIN
and
GERALD MARKS

MILLS MUSIC
Music Publishers

Musical instrument makers faced many new challenges when the U.S. entered WWII in December of 1941 after Japan's bombing of Pearl Harbor.

6.1 Ukuleles in WWII

By the time the war was in full swing in Europe in the late 1930s, the huge ukulele craze of the 1920s was well over. Although C.F. Martin & Company did experience a bit of a resurgence in uke sales during the late 30s and early 40s, most manufacturers saw declining sales during that time. By the time the United States officially entered WWII in December of 1941, after Japan's infamous bombing of Pearl Harbor, instrument makers faced many new challenges. Essential supplies required by the war effort, including wood and metal, became hard to come by. Even gut strings were in short supply, as most were made in Italy or Germany—both Axis countries at war with U.S. and its Allied forces. Wartime restrictions limited the number of musical instruments that manufacturers were allowed to produce. As a result, many manufacturers switched to building supplies for the war effort. For instance, Gibson spent the better part of the war making radar assemblies and parts for submachine guns. In Hawaii,

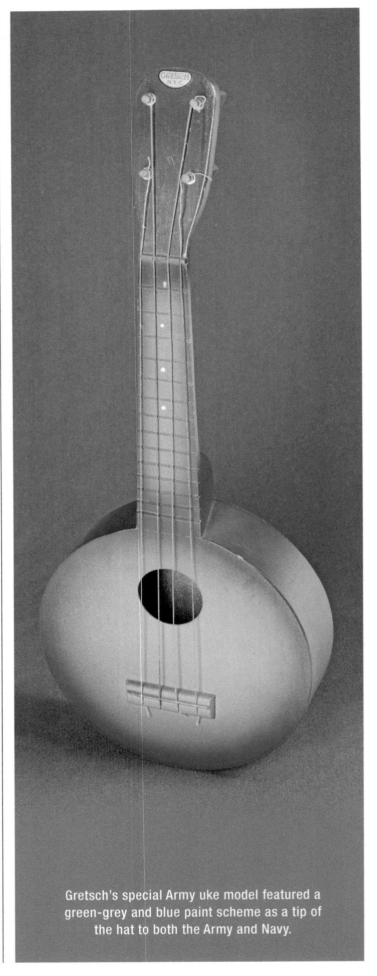

Gretsch's special Army uke model featured a green-grey and blue paint scheme as a tip of the hat to both the Army and Navy.

Made to be hung up in a barracks or a USO club, Gretsch's "Easy Play Ukulele" charts featured lessons in holding, strumming and tuning the uke.

Sam Kamaka Sr., who had first begun building ukuleles in 1916, found it necessary to supplement his uke businesses reduced income by renting out his Honolulu shop, as well as taking on part time work and even growing mangoes.

The Gretsch Musical Instrument Company also ceased most instrument building during the war and company president Fred Gretsch Jr. left to serve in WWII as a Navy commander, leaving his brother Bill to run the business. Gretsch did, however, produce one special instrument during this time: the so-called "Army Uke" which was sold to soldiers going off to war between 1939 And 1945. Retailers advertised these ukuleles as "...the perfect gift for the troops." (These same ukes were also distributed to refugees escaping the 1956 Hungarian Revolution as part of then-president Eisenhower's "Operation Safe Haven" humanitarian airlift) The round-bodied ukes featured a green-grey and blue paint scheme, a tip of the hat to both the Army and Navy. Their banjo-like shape and plywood construction closely resembled the "Camp Ukes" made by both Gretsch and Lyon & Healy in the 1920s.

To help soldiers learn to play their ukes, Gretsch published large (38"x25") "Easy Play Ukulele" charts that could be hung up in a barracks or a USO club. The chart's 14 pages featured lessons in holding, strumming and tuning the uke, as well as chord diagrams and music for several popular songs including Red River Valley, I've Been Working on the Railroad and The Marine Hymn.

Another mainland manufacturer that continued to build ukuleles during the war was The Regal Musical Instrument Company in Chicago. But the special model they made wasn't for the troops, but mostly for folks back home.

To boost moral on the home front and provide much-needed supplies of vegetables at a time when many food items were rationed, the Department of Agriculture encouraged civilians to plant "Victory Gardens." To get young people involved, American seed companies had special "premium" catalogs. A red, white and blue painted "Victory Uke" was among the premiums offered by the Paradise Seed Company (see Section 6.2).

Shipping ukes to the troops

In parallel with raising spirits back home, the U.S. government wisely recognized the need to bring relief to combat weary servicemen and women. Hence, the War Department created a "Special Services Division" of the military. Headquartered at Fort Meade in Maryland, this organization was responsible for training entertainers, including famous swing band leader Glenn Miller, to prepare them for traveling to war zones to perform for the troops. Another significant project they undertook was the creation of portable entertainment kits which were shipped to Allied bases in war zones. Each kit, packed in its own large crate, was specialized: Athletics kits provided equipment for baseball, football, boxing, horseshoes, basketball, volleyball, etc. Theatrical kits had supplies to allow GIs to stage their own skits and shows. Movie kits enabled the GIs to watch first run Hollywood movies. Music kits contained a phonograph and records, a radio, and the latest sheet music, including songs written specifically for the war effort, such as G.I. Blues, Bell Bottom Trousers and Der Fuehrer's Face. The crate contained a

Regal's "Victory" uke was available as a premium for selling packets of Paradise Seed Company seed packets.

THE ART OF VINTAGE UKULELES • SANDOR NAGYSZALANCZY

Written specifically for the war effort, the novelty song Der Fuehrer's Face's sheet music shows Disney character Donald Duck throwing a tomato at Adolf Hitler's face.

special small-sized "Victory Vertical" piano, specifically crafted by the Steinway Piano Company for the war effort. There were also dozens of small instruments: harmonicas, ocarinas, flute-like tonettes and…ukuleles! To help soldiers learn to play these instruments, music kits were stocked with "10 Minute Self Instructor" booklets. These provided basic lessons for playing each of the kit's four instruments as well as a providing few dozen songs to play. A section at the end of the booklet even provided instructions on how soldiers could make their own ukuleles using either a cigar box or a No. 10 tin can as a body, straightened paper clips for frets and telephone wire for strings!

GIs make their own ukuleles

Although I've never seen a WWII era uke that looks anything like it might have been made following the sparse directions provided in the Special Services' Self Instructor booklets described in the last paragraph, it's clear that some soldiers did build their own ukes during the war. You can see two examples in the photo on page 250. The uke on the left was ingeniously built using the phenolic headliner from an army helmet as a body and pieces of acrylic plastic, likely scavenged from a broken aircraft windshield, as a bridge. The red

Music kits packed in special crates shipped to GIs in the field contained a small-sized "Victory Vertical" piano, made by the Steinway.

THE ART OF VINTAGE UKULELES • SANDOR NAGYSZALANCZY

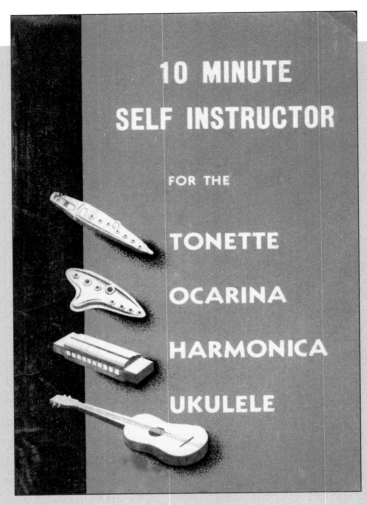

10 MINUTE SELF INSTRUCTOR

FOR THE

TONETTE

OCARINA

HARMONICA

UKULELE

"10 Minute Self Instructor" booklets helped soldiers learn to play the instruments packed in the music kits, including ukuleles.

IT'S EASIER THAN YOU THINK

THE thousands of amateur and professional musicians in the armed forces need no book of instruction. But there are thousands of others—perhaps you are one of them—who enjoy music, can "carry a tune," and wish that they could play some kind of a musical instrument for their own amusement. It is for them that this book was written.

Obviously, you must first choose an instrument that is easy to carry around and one that is easy to play. That is why this book deals with the tonette, ocarina, harmonica, and ukulele. They are just about the easiest of all instruments to learn. You probably played around with one of them when you were a kid.

You will quickly see that this book is very different from the usual volume of instruction. It dispenses with what might be called the normal approach to music reading. It's whole purpose is to help you play some tunes in the least possible time. However, your proficiency will be limited only by your own ambition. This method will not only develop the feeling of playing by ear, but will also make the transition to music notation an easy one.

As in everything else, it's practice that makes perfect. Don't be discouraged if your first efforts sound thin and wavery. And don't be embarrassed if your pals kid you a bit at the beginning. Stick at it and it won't be long before they'll be *asking* you to play.

1

HOW TO MAKE A UKULELE

THE diagrams are self-explanatory and show how instruments can be made from materials at hand.

To build the ukulele shown in top diagram, the only material required is a No. 10 can, cut in half; a piece of wood, the strands of a telephone wire and a few nails. The ukulele shown in lower diagram substitutes a cigar box for the No. 10 can. Otherwise the procedure for building is the same.

Frets are made by using wire approximately the thickness of paper clips, in fact paper clips when opened up and fastened to the neck of the ukulele make excellent ones. It is important that they be properly spaced in order that they will produce the correct pitch when the strings are pressed down.

A good pattern to follow is to place the first fret three fourths of an inch below the top bridge as shown in the diagram. The distance between the first and second should then be ¹⁄₃₂ of an inch less than the distance between the bridge and the first fret. As each successive one is added, the distance between it and the preceding should be ¹⁄₃₂ of an inch less, until there are 12 frets. There should be ⅜ inch interval between the last two frets. This difference between frets will compensate for change in the vibration frequency of the strings.

Lower Bridge—Small piece of wood used to raise the strings above the surface of the instrument permitting them to vibrate.

51

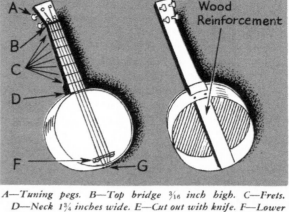

A—*Tuning pegs.* B—*Top bridge ³⁄₁₆ inch high.* C—*Frets.* D—*Neck 1¾ inches wide.* E—*Cut out with knife.* F—*Lower bridge ⅝ inch high.* G—*Tacks ½ inch apart. Length from lower bridge to top bridge 14 inches.*

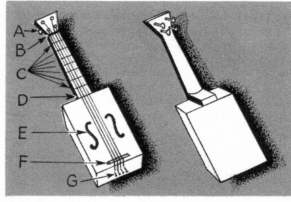

52

A section at the end of the Self Instructor booklet provided instructions on a soldier could make his own ukuleles using either a cigar box or a No. 10 tin can as a body.

painted uke at right was more precisely crafted from a standard-issue soldier's mess kit and a few pieces of sheet metal. The frets of this uke were pressed directly into its metal fingerboard/neck.

Two of the most incredible stories of soldiers making their own ukuleles during WWII comes not from an Allied military base or battlefield, but from a Japanese prisoner of war camp. British army volunteer Tom Boardman was captured by the Japanese during fall of Singapore in February, 1942. He was taken to the Changi Prisoner of War Camp where he remained a captive until the end of the war. Despite being forced to work at a labor camp on the Burma Railway, Boardman managed to cobble together a makeshift ukulele, piecing it together from any odd scraps of materials he could find, including old Red Cross boxes and tuning gears scrounged from a mandolin-like Chinese instrument. Wood parts were joined by nails he hammered with a rock. Once finished, he entertained his fellow captives with George Formby tunes he'd learned before the war.

Another Changi prisoner, Australian soldier Les O'Connell, coped with boredom at the camp by making a ukulele from pieces of coconut shell and wood from tea chests whittled with a knife. After his liberation in 1945, O'Connell decided to start his own the instrument business, JMG Industries in Jolimont Western Australia, building ukuleles and guitars sold not only throughout Australia, but also in Britain, American, Ceylon and even Singapore.

Performing for the soldiers

Another way the U.S. Army supported their troops and lifted their spirits was to entertain them, both at home and in Europe and the Pacific. Founded in February of 1941, the USO (United Service Orga-

Two examples of ukuleles made by US soldiers during WWII, the one at right from a mess kit, the left one from scrap wood with a helmet liner for the body.

British army volunteer Tom Boardman made his own ukulele from Red Cross boxes and odd scraps of materials during the years he was held captive at Japan's Changi Prisoner of War Camp.

One of the USO's most popular "Camp Shows" during WWII was Bob Hope's "Hope's Gypsies" troupe, which included guitarist Tony Romano and tap dancer Patricia Thomas.

nizations) first created a network of club locations stateside and abroad where service members could go to relax, socialize, and partake in recreational activities (ping pong, dancing, reading, music, etc.). Within 8 months, the USO organized an extensive series of "Camp Shows" arranged in four branches: The Victory Circuit and Blue Circuit, which entertained military personnel stateside; the Hospital Circuit, whose troupes visited the wounded, and the Foxhole Circuit responsible for performing for active troops overseas. The Foxhole circuit troupes included dozens of big-name Hollywood celebrities, including Bing Crosby, Mickey Rooney, Judy Garland, Dinah Shore, Laurel & Hardy, The Andrews Sisters, Edward G. Robinson and Marlene Dietrich. Among the 7000 performers that toured with the Camp Shows, few brought GIs more laughter and joy than Bob Hope, whose "Hope's Gypsies" troupe, which included guitarist Tony Romano and tap dancer Patricia Thomas, performed hundreds of shows throughout Europe and the Pacific. Although very few troupe members played the ukulele, there were a handful, including a colorful female strummer who went by the name of "Sis Silly." In Hawaii,

It's likely that many talented ukulele players entertained GIs at USO clubs in the Hawaiian Islands, including this club in Hanapepe on the south shore of Kauai.

British comedian and movie star George Formby serenaded the troops as he toured the front lines from North Africa to Normandy France.

Formby stummed his way through a series of British war time movies, including this 1938 comedy musical "It's in the Air."

Camp Shows often featured local talent, including virtuoso uke player Bill Tapia, who entertained GIs at USO clubs throughout the islands.

The British army had its own version of the Camp Shows, featuring popular entertainers from around the U.K. The most famous of these was undoubtedly George Formby, a British comedian and movie star well known for the funny, often double-entendre, novelty songs he sang and played on the banjolele. Formby's flat feet kept him from active military service, but as part of the Blackpool Home Guard, he traveled extensively to deliver a long series of troop concerts. First to visit the British Expeditionary Force in Normandy in 1940, he eventually toured the front lines of North Africa, Malta, Sicily, Gibraltar and Italy, and was in Normandy less than a week after the D-Day invasion. Formby bravely entertained more than three million allied soldiers and was presented the OBE (Order of the British Empire) award by George VI, King of England. He also starred and stummed his way through a series of war time movies, including Bell Bottom George, To Hell with Hitler and It's in the Air.

Ukuleles occasionally appeared in WWII-era movies produced for American audiences, including the 1940 film "Isle of Destiny" starring June Lange and Wallace

Ford. Ukes also appeared in numerous WWII films made in the 1950s, such as "Go for Broke," starring Van Johnson and a mostly Asian cast, portrays Japanese American soldiers as they fought—and played their ukes—in war-torn Europe.

Soldiers entertain themselves

It wasn't just professional musicians who entertained the troops during WWII: Soldiers in all branches of service played their ukuleles to pass the time and entertain themselves and their comrades. Several members of the 442nd Infantry Regiment played the ukulele. This regiment, the most highly decorated unit of its size in U.S. military history, was comprised mostly of Nisei (American citizens born to Japanese immigrant parents) soldiers, many of whom came from Hawaii. In the photo on page 253, an in-

Ukuleles appeared in American WWII-era movies, including the 1940 action-adventure film "Isle of Destiny" starring June Lange and Wallace Ford.

The infantryman playing a Ka-Lae Pineapple uke is part of the US army's highly-decorated 442nd Infantry Regiment comprised mostly of Nisei soldiers, many of whom came from Hawaii.

Ukulele playing soothed frayed nerves of West Australian regiment soldiers during the siege of Tobruk, where Allied forces prevented Axis troops from seizing the port.

During WWII, a young wife sent a ukulele in a care package to her soldier sweetheart as a Valentine's day present.

fantryman is seen playing a Ka-Lae Pineapple ukulele made by Johnny Lai (see Section 1.4).

In combing through military archives, I ran across some wonderful stories about soldiers and their ukes. Evidently, many took their ukes with them, not just overseas but into the battlefield. Corporal Harold Smith, a member of a West Australian battalion, was often called on to play his ukulele and sing at camp concerts. During the Western Desert Campaign in Libya, Corporal Smith's uke playing soothed frayed nerves of his comrades during the 241-day-long-siege of Tobruk, as Allied forces repelled Axis troops from seizing the port. After the war, Smith's ukulele was inscribed with the signatures of more than 200 appreciative men from his battalion.

Allied soldiers weren't the only ones with ukes: A German soldier named Schlunke was captured by American forces in Europe and taken to England where he became a prisoner of war. A watchmaker by profession, Schlunke repaired the GI's watches in the POW camp. An accomplished musician, Schlunke also played ukulele to entertain both his fellow prisoners and the Americans who ran the camp. Years later, that ukulele somehow ended up in a junk shop in Mississippi, bearing not only Schlunke's name, but the names and home states of his American captors.

Evidently, not all soldiers were fond of the ukulele: An American GI named Jimmy had only been married a few weeks when he was sent to fight in the war overseas. For Valentine's Day, his young wife sent him care package containing a ukulele. Soon thereafter, a member of Jimmy's unit wrote his wife a letter of protest, claiming that listening to Jimmy's uke playing was a worse form of harassment than any that the enemy had to offer!

6.2 The Victory Uke

When one thinks of items of memorabilia connected with a past war, ukuleles don't usually come to mind. But there's one very special uke that's directly connected to America's civilian efforts on the home front during World War II.

After the U.S. joined the war following the Japanese attack on Pearl Harbor, the Department of Agriculture encouraged civilians to plant "Victory Gardens." Their intention was to boost morale and to provide much-needed supplies of vegetables during a time when many food items were rationed so that U.S. soldiers abroad could be kept well fed. Throughout America, people plowed up their front and back yards in order to grow their own vegetables. Many public lands were also tilled, including San Francisco's Golden Gate Park which boasted more than 800 Victory Gardens. Former First Lady Eleanor Roosevelt even planted a Victory Garden on the White House lawn!

To promote the sale of seeds for Victory Gardens, as well as to involve more young people in the civilian war effort, several American seed companies employed a clever ploy: They distributed special "premium" catalogs filled with prizes that kids could earn in exchange for selling packs of seeds. One such company, The Paradise Seed Company of Paradise, PA, included a "pledge" postcard with their catalog. Any child who filled out and mailed back the postcard then received

After Japan's infamous attack on Pearl Harbor, the US Department of Agriculture encouraged civilians to plant wartime "victory gardens," promoting the practice with posters like this one.

Offered as a premium by the Paradise Seed Company, a Regal "Victory Uke" could be obtained by selling 24 10-cent seed packets and sending the company the money along with an extra dollar.

The WWII-themed Victory Uke made by the Regal Musical Instrument Company atop a leather bomber jacket and soldier's foot locker.

The red, white and blue Victory Uke was decorated with squadrons of war planes, stars and stripes, an American eagle and a pair of V's promoting Allied victory.

Due to supply shortages during WWII, the entire Victory Uke was made of wood, including the tuning pegs, bridge, nut and frets which were made from thin strips of maple.

24 packets of "Sure Grow" vegetable and flower seeds to sell, at 10 cents each. Once all the packs were sold, the proceeds were sent back to the company, along with the child's prize selection (a small additional charge, which varied with the value of the chosen prize, was usually required). Kids could choose from fun stuff, like roller skates, a "bucking bronco" ring, a catcher's mitt, or model warplanes, or pick a more practical prize, like a home barber outfit, a cuckoo clock, Turkish towels or even live animals: rabbits, guinea pigs, "lively chicks," canaries, etc.

The coolest prize in the Paradise catalog, certainly for readers of this book, had to be the "Victory Uke" made by the Regal Musical Instrument Company of

Chicago. From the 1920s on, Regal had created multitudes of inexpensive, white-wood ukuleles bearing all manner of colorful decorations. But never had they created an instrument with a more thoroughly patriotic theme. Sporting a red, white and blue overall paint scheme, the top of the ukulele's body was stenciled with military iconography: squadrons of war planes, stars and stripes, an American eagle and a pair of V's promoting Allied victory. There are also several "dot dot dot dash" Morse Code symbols representing the letter "V," for "Victory."

But military decorations aren't the only thing that made Regal's Victory Uke unique: In addition to its birch body and neck, the entire rest of the instrument

This ad which ran in a 1942 issue of Popular Mechanics magazine promoted the Victory Uke which could be purchased directly from Regal for only $2.50 postpaid.

was made from wood, including the tuning pegs, bridge, nut and even the frets, which are thin maple strips inlayed into the neck!

Why would Regal choose to build a uke with wooden frets? The answer harkens back to the circumstances on the home front during WWII: Certain raw materials were in seriously short supply during the war, especially metals like brass, nickel and steel, all typically used to make musical instrument parts, including tuners and frets. Whatever small quantities of metal were available for domestic manufacture were very expensive. Whether Regal decided not to use metal frets for economic or purely patriotic reasons, the Victory Uke's maple frets were clearly never destined to deliver lasting performance: The frets on the 75-year-old Victory Uke shown here are significantly worn down,

even though there's hardly any signs of wear on the rest of the uke.

For those who wished to acquire a Victory uke without the trouble of selling seed packets, Regal also sold them via mail order through ads placed in magazines, such as Popular Mechanics. The Victory sold for only $2.50 postpaid. The ads featured an image of a group of soldiers playing and singing together and this sales pitch: "Whether in camp or at home, you can be the LIFE of the PARTY—playing and singing favorite songs and cowboy tunes on a VICTORY UKE."

THE ART OF VINTAGE UKULELES • SANDOR NAGYSZALANCZY

The remarkable increase in ukulele sales in the years after WWII prompted the Harmony Company to produce the air-force-commemorating "Wings" model uke.

6.3 The Uke's Post-War Comeback

A few years after the Second World War ended, as postwar consumer demand fueled unprecedented economic expansion in the U.S., the Honolulu Advertiser newspaper reluctantly printed an "obituary for the ukulele," declaring that, outside of Hawaii, the uke was 'deader than a doornail.' Yet just a week later, the Long Beach Press Telegram reported a remarkable increase in ukulele sales and predicted that millions of instruments would be sold over the following decade. In a 1949 interview for Billboard Magazine, Jay Kraus, president of the Harmony Company, estimated that more than 300,000 would go into consumers' hands that year, including their air-force-commemorating "Wings" model uke.

While it's true that American servicemen who came home with ukuleles they'd picked up while stationed in Hawaii contributed significantly to the resurgence of interest in the uke, there were two things that basically kicked the post war ukulele revival into high gear: modern plastics and television.

During WWII, the U.S. government spurred the chemical industry towards making advancements in plastics technologies, as new plastics were desperately needed to replace natural materials that were in scarce supply. The castable thermoplastic polymers they developed were used to make countless wartime parts, including airplane windshields and helmet liners. The same plastics and casting techniques also provided post-war manufacturers with a way of quickly and cheaply producing all manner of goods, including toys and small instruments like the uke. By 1947, the consumer market was flooded with mostly toy plastic ukes that sold for as little as 59 cents. Better quality full-soprano size ukuleles were soon to follow, with instrument manufacturers, including Mario Maccaferri's Mastro Plastics company, producing millions of inexpensive ukes cast from styrene plastic (see Section 7.3).

The flames of the growing ukulele frenzy were further fanned by its regular appearance on radio and television, most notably in the hands of musical celebrity Arthur Godfrey, who hosted an impressive number of programs between 1945 and the late 1950s. Godfrey not only played the ukulele on his shows, but became its greatest promoter and champion, urging parents to go out and buy their children plastic ukuleles (reassuringly, he told parents: "If a kid has a uke in hand, he's not going to get into much trouble"). On one of his daytime television programs, Godfrey even taught young viewers how to play the uke, thus introducing the entire post-war baby boomer generation to the joys

No. G-104

$2.80

No. G-104. "Wings"—A low priced ukulele, handsomely finished and decorated. Ebony-black finish, with ivory, high lighting around the soundhole. Decorations on body, position markers on fingerboard, and name stencilled in ivory. Semi-gloss lacquer finish.

Each......................................$2.80

6.3 #02 A magazine ad promoted Harmony's $2.80 Wings model ukulele, which featured an ebony-black painted finish and ivory-colored stencil decorations.

of strumming those four strings.

Not everyone greeted renewed interest in the ukulele with enthusiasm. A writer for Salt Lake City's Deseret News wrote: "If you hear the neighbor next door or Arthur Godfrey on the radio strumming a uke to the accompaniment of a song that you can murder better than they can, don't fall prey to the current craze for chord plunking and rush out to buy a ukulele. Don't let appearances and sounds deceive you: Those apparently aimless nylon string pickers are MUSICIANS." And in a piece published in the Toledo Blade newspaper:

U.S. servicemen who came home with ukuleles they'd picked up while stationed in Hawaii contributed significantly to the resurgence of interest in the uke on the mainland.

"A cloud no bigger than a ukulele pick is hanging over the Sierras. According to a news dispatch, the ukulele is coming back. Like the foot-long snails recently discovered in gardens at San Pedro and threatening the nation, the ukulele revival has first appeared in California. May both the giant snails and the uke be halted by pest controllers before they can spread beyond the mountains and crawl eastward." Despite such negative sentiments, the post-WWII uke craze did last for well over a decade and a half, all the way into the early 1960s, when it was supplanted by an even bigger craze for electric guitars and rock n' roll music.

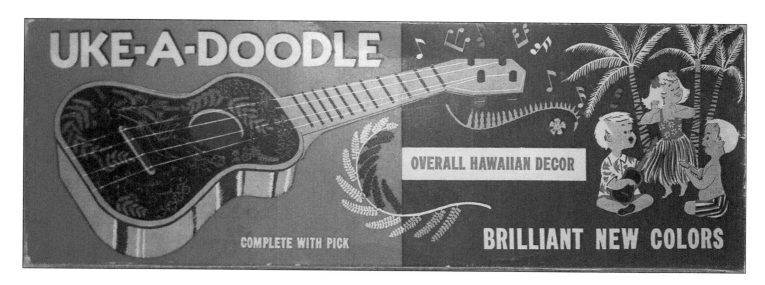

ABOVE: Mattel's "Uke-A-Doodle" toy was one of the plastic toy ukes that flooded the consumer market from the late 1940s through the mid 1960s.

RIGHT: Popular celebrity and ace ukulele player Arthur Godfrey hosted various radio and TV programs between 1945 and the late 1950s which helped to promote the uke's popularity in America.

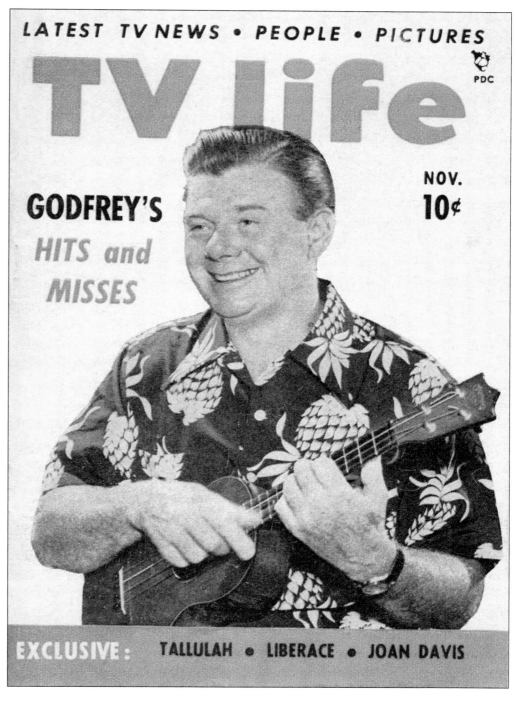

Chapter Seven
The Second Wave

Four ukes that represent America's renewed interest in the ukulele are, from left to right: the Northern uke, Regal cowboy uke, Swagerty Surf-A-Lele and Mastro T.V. Pal.

America's interest in the ukulele which waned significantly in the late 1930s was awakened slightly after WWII, mostly thanks to servicemen who learned to play the uke while stationed in the Pacific (see Section 6.1). But a number of other factors were responsible for catalyzing the uke's second wave of popularity in the 1950s and early 60s. By the late 1940s, Western movies set in the wild west had all but replaced tropical island fantasy pictures and kids were dressing in cowboy outfits rather than doing the hula. The 1950s saw a flood of technological innovations including injection-molded plastics, which made it possible to produce inexpensive ukuleles by the millions. The 50s also saw the birth of the largest member of the ukulele family: the Baritone. In the 1960s, a dedicated Canadian music teacher developed a revolutionary instruction method that taught kids music by teaching them to play the ukulele at an early age. About the same time in Southern California, an eclectic woodworker was building exotic looking ukuleles initially marketed to surfers. And as musical performances got louder, players started electrifying their ukuleles.

THE ART OF VINTAGE UKULELES • SANDOR NAGYSZALANCZY

Western movies and television programs that captivated the imaginations of many young baby boomers no doubt inspired instrument makers to produce western-themed ukuleles.

7.1 Rootin' Tootin' Cowboy Ukuleles

Like so many of us who endured the COVID19 pandemic, I had to come up with ways of keeping myself amused while being cooped up at home. One day, I decided to text/email a bunch of my male friends, all baby boomers, and ask them this question: What were the coolest things you got for Christmas when you were around 10 years old? To my surprise, most had the same answer I did: "a six-shooter cap gun" (that's mine in the photo above) Some were lucky enough to get a whole cowboy outfit, complete with hat, boots, chaps and faux-leather holsters, or perhaps a Red Rider BB gun, Hopalong Cassidy lunchbox, or a Fort Apache play set complete with molded-plastic horses, cowboys and Indians.

It seems that back in those days, my comrades and I had all fallen under the spell of the cowboy western. When we played, we pretended that our backyards were rustic towns or high desert plains as we imitated our favorite cowboy characters from western movies and television shows: The quick-drawing gunfighter; the lariat-twirling bronc rider; the trail-savvy frontiersman; the justice-keeping sheriff…or perhaps the unscrupulous outlaw.

Cowboy history

Short stories and novels about cowboys and the old west became very popular around the turn of the last century when they provided the plots for thousands of silent western movies. When Hollywood ditched cowboy films with the advent of talking pictures, radio picked up the slack to feed the public's western appetite. Musical radio programs featured singing cowboys, such as Gene Autrey and Tex Ritter, performing songs from their latest recordings. Western radio dramas—basically modern morality plays set in the west—became hugely popular with hit serials such as Death Valley Days, The Cisco Kid, and Red Ryder. Cowboy movies were revived in the 1930s with a flowing stream of B-pictures, and scored even greater appeal in the

By the mid-1950s, loads of inexpensive western-themed instruments were produced by big the instrument companies, including Harmony who made the two guitars shown here.

cowboys played them. Dozens of affordable steel-string guitars were produced by the big instrument companies, including Harmony, Regal, and Richter—all of which also made ukuleles.

Cowboy guitars were not high-quality instruments, but rather "beginners' level" guitars mostly intended for younger cowboy fans. Typically made from whitewoods (birch, poplar, etc.) most of these guitars were either painted or stained and decorated with stenciled or silk-screened graphics depicting western themes: Gun-slinging cowboys riding their horses across cactus-strewn deserts, roping cattle, or gathering around campfires drinking and singing. In lieu of fancy inlays or other appointments, body bindings and fretboard markers were usually just painted on. Signature models bore the names of famous cowboy stars and characters of radio, movies, and early television: Buck Jones, Gene Autrey, Ray Whitley, Red Foley, The Lone Ranger, Roy Rogers, etc. Non-celebrity models had names which reflected their colorful graphics, for example: "Buckin' Bronco," "Trail Driver," "Roundup," "Prairie Ramblers" and "Black Stallion."

Of course, many of the same companies that made

1940s and 50s with box office smashes The Ox-Bow Incident (1943), Red River (1948) and High Noon (1952). But nothing did more to spur the passion of boomer-generation cowboy wannabes than television western programs. Many shows, including The Lone Ranger, Have Gun–Will Travel, Gunsmoke, Colt .45 and Broken Arrow, were adapted for TV from earlier films or radio dramas.

By the mid-1950s, America was deep in the throes of an all-out cowboy craze. Store shelves were overflowing with toys, books, comics, apparel, and other goods that capitalized on the popularity of westerns. Instrument manufacturers weren't long in boarding the bandwagon (or should I say stagecoach) by coming out with western-themed instruments. Guitars were the first to get the cowboy treatment; sensible, since many singing

Singing cowboy star Carson Robson was a talented songwriter who penned more than three hundred songs issued as sheet music and also in songbook collections.

One of the first cowboy ukuleles to hit the market, Regal's Carson Robson ukulele was sold by the Montgomery Ward department store chain.

cowboy guitars also ended up making western-themed ukuleles. It's important to remember that, by the mid 1930s, the Hawaiian ukulele craze of the 1920s had pretty much ended and that ukes, in general, had lost their popularity. I believe that companies, like Harmony and Regal, hoped that their new western models could rekindle the public's interest in the uke. Like their 6-stringed counterparts, cowboy ukes were typically inexpensive, cheaply-made instruments. While they were visually appealing and reasonably playable, none were particularly good sounding.

Carson Robson

What better way to excite the buying public than to come out with a new ukulele that's endorsed by a celebrity. One of the first cowboy ukuleles to hit the market bore the name of a genuine singing cowboy star: Carson Robson. A native of Oswego, Kansas, Carson Robson worked for years on railroads and in oil fields until 1920, when he decided to pursue his lifelong love of music. At age 30, he moved to Kansas City where he began performing on radio station WDAF, thus

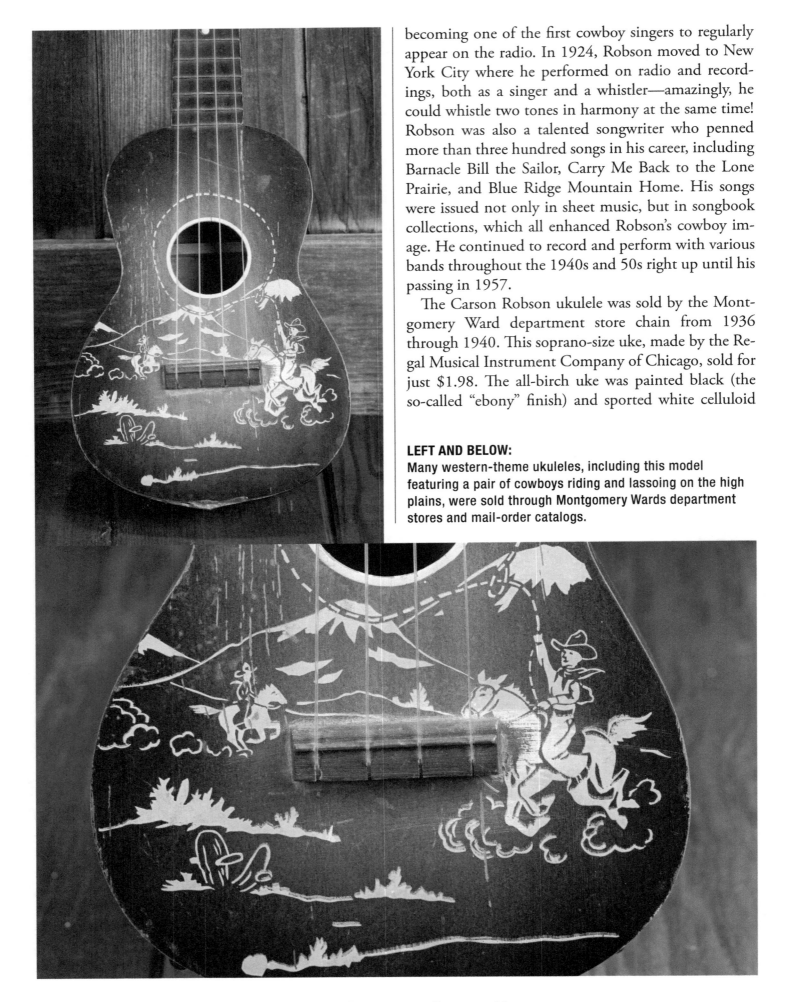

becoming one of the first cowboy singers to regularly appear on the radio. In 1924, Robson moved to New York City where he performed on radio and recordings, both as a singer and a whistler—amazingly, he could whistle two tones in harmony at the same time! Robson was also a talented songwriter who penned more than three hundred songs in his career, including Barnacle Bill the Sailor, Carry Me Back to the Lone Prairie, and Blue Ridge Mountain Home. His songs were issued not only in sheet music, but in songbook collections, which all enhanced Robson's cowboy image. He continued to record and perform with various bands throughout the 1940s and 50s right up until his passing in 1957.

The Carson Robson ukulele was sold by the Montgomery Ward department store chain from 1936 through 1940. This soprano-size uke, made by the Regal Musical Instrument Company of Chicago, sold for just $1.98. The all-birch uke was painted black (the so-called "ebony" finish) and sported white celluloid

LEFT AND BELOW:
Many western-theme ukuleles, including this model featuring a pair of cowboys riding and lassoing on the high plains, were sold through Montgomery Wards department stores and mail-order catalogs.

THE ART OF VINTAGE UKULELES • SANDOR NAGYSZALANCZY

This western model uke made by Regal features stenciled graphics of a cowboy and cowgirl leaning against a split-rail fence.

THE ART OF VINTAGE UKULELES • SANDOR NAGYSZALANCZY

The enormous popularity of the Lone Ranger movies and television series led to the character's own ukulele model, sold at T. Eaton department stores.

binding around the top of the body as well as the sound hole. Its fretboard was covered in snazzy white pearloid (a material that modern luthiers often refer to derogatorily as "mother of toilet seat"). The uke's headstock has an unusual art deco "streamlined" shape. Green and white painted graphics on the top include Robson's signature above an iconic cowboy on his horse at the edge of a cliff, with a log cabin and pine trees across the valley in the distance.

Ukes from Montgomery Wards

Many of the cowboy ukuleles produced in the 1930s and 40s were sold through Montgomery Wards, both through their department stores and mail-order catalogs. The same year that Wards came out with the Carson Robson model, they offered another western-themed uke featuring a shaded brown top stenciled with graphics of a pair of cowboys riding the high plains, one throwing his lasso so that the rope encircles the uke's sound hole. The scene is complete

The Buckeye Brand "Swing High" soprano uke made by the United Company in New Jersey features characters at a western "hoedown" dance party.

with cactus and sagebrush and snow-peaked mountains in the background.

Another of Ward's offerings was a model with stenciled graphics of rope-toting cowboy and a pistol-packing cowgirl leaning against a split-rail fence. Built using the same inexpensive construction used for similar ukes, this soprano was sold only in 1936 and 1937. It came in several different colors, with a body painted either gray, black or dark mahogany. It featured painted-on bindings around the top and sound hole and the same shapely headstock as found on the Carson Robison ukulele, so it's safe to assume they were both manufactured by Regal.

In 1939 and 1940, Wards offered another western model called "The Plainsman." This ukulele had a scaled-down version of the same graphics found on their Plainsman model guitar. Its body is painted in a bronze color topped with a stenciled-on scene of a cowboy on horseback standing opposite a large pine tree. This uke sold for $1.39 ($25.50 in today's money), complete with an instruction book and pick.

Cowboy Ukes of the 1950s

Popularity of all things western continued in the 1950s, likely buoyed by the proliferation of TV western programs. One of the most popular series was "The Lone Ranger," probably the most significant cowboy hero of all time. This fictitious western character was a masked former Texas ranger who fought for truth and justice in the old west, along with his native American sidekick Tonto. First appearing as a radio program in 1933, the popular series spawned several movies, a comic strip as well as the hit television show starring Clayton Moore as the Lone Ranger and Jay Silverheels as Tonto. The series ran from 1949 to 1957.

Among the prodigious ephemera generated by the enormous popularity of the character was a Lone Ranger model ukulele. Sold by the Canadian department store chain T. Eaton, this birch-bodied, black painted uke featured red and white graphics of the masked ranger mounted atop his trusty palomino, proclaiming his trademark phrase: "Hi-Yo-Silver."

Also produced in the 1950s, the Buckeye Brand "Swing High" soprano uke was made by the United Company in Jersey City, New Jersey. It differs from other cowboy ukes in that its theme is based on a "hoedown:" a dance party, often held in a barn, where country music was played and participants typically

square danced. This uke's birch body is stained a dark walnut color with stenciled graphics showing a quaint hoedown scene complete with a seated guitar player, tambourine toting dancer and a cowhand waving his hat. The headstock has a gold painted "Buckeye Brand" logo featuring a deer with a large rack of antlers.

Kenny Roberts

Another singing cowboy who ended up getting his own signature ukulele was Kenny Roberts. A popular entertainer on stage, radio and television, Roberts began his career playing guitar with the "Down Homers" western trio in the 1940s (the trio featured a young Bill Haley, who later formed the pioneering rock 'n roll band the Comets). As a recording artist, Roberts had his first top 10 hit on Billboard's country charts in 1949 with the million-selling novelty song "I Never See Maggie Alone." Thanks to his talented vocalizations and energetic stage antics, Roberts became known as "King of the Yodellers" and "The Jumping Cowboy." He recorded numerous songs that showcased his country-style blue yodeling, including She Taught Me To

A popular 1940s musical entertainer on stage, radio and television, Kenny Roberts was known as "King of the Yodellers" thanks to his talented vocalizations.

Made by Regal and first sold in 1950, Robert's "Little Pal" ukulele featured a spruce top, which gave it a bit more volume and a slightly better tone than other all-whitewood ukes.

Yodel and Yodel Polka. In the early 1950s, Roberts appeared on Arthur Godfrey's CBS television program "Talent Scouts," and later performed a couple of yodeling tunes in the 1991 Richard Pryor/Gene Wilder movie "Another You."

Robert's "Little Pal" ukulele was made by Regal and first offered for sale in 1950. Unlike other inexpensive ukes made entirely from birch or other white woods, the Little Pal featured a spruce top, which gave it a bit more volume and a slightly better tone. At the time this uke was introduced, Roberts had a popular television show on which he performed cowboy songs and showed cartoons. The name of the uke comes from Robert's habit of referring to children in his audience as his "little pals." The headstock bears his name, as well as a stencil of a large cowboy hat.

Two other cowboy ukes: the "TV Western" and the "Pal O' Mine" had virtually the same construction and most of the features of the Little Pal. In fact, the maroon-painted TV Western has exactly the same body graphics, except rendered in white. The "Pal O' Mine" uke's moniker likely references a popular song of the same name written by Bob Nolan, a founding member of the popular western band "The Sons of the Pioneers." Nolan composed many of the best-know western tunes of the era, including Cool Water and Tumbling Tumbleweeds. The Pal O' Mine uke has a natural clear-finished birch body with stenciled graphics of a cowboy atop a rearing horse, waving with his ten-gallon hat to a cowgirl who's waving back. The headstock has "Rancher" stenciled on it and the same cowboy hat on the Kenny Robert's uke.

Plastic, Fiberboard & Tin

When sales of wooden cowboy guitars and ukuleles sputtered out in the 1950s, instruments made from plastic, fiberboard and tin quickly replaced them. The injection-molding process made it highly economical to produce styrene plastic ukuleles in huge numbers. Hence, a plethora of plastic uke models were created, with many featuring cowboy and western themes. Intended mainly for young children, A great many were only 13 ½" to 16 ½" long; much smaller than a standard soprano-sized ukulele. These ukes were often sold as toys rather than serious musical instruments. The Carnival Plastics Company's line of cowboy ukes included the "Home on the Range," "Branding Cattle," "Zorro" and the "Country and Western Banjo Do-Si-

The TV Western model uke has a cheaply-made birch body and neck which was painted maroon and decorated with white painted bindings and stenciled images.

Do," the latter sporting a round body. Plastic ukulele maven Mario Maccaferri's "Mastro" brand ukes, including their "Swing Your Partner" banjo model, was an exception to the many small toy ukes on the market, as he designed his instruments to be acceptable both in terms of playability and sound (see Section 7.3).

Many of the plastic (and fiberboard) ukuleles of this period were named and advertised as "junior guitars" rather than ukes, even though most had four nylon strings and were meant to be tuned and played as ukuleles. My guess is that manufacturers took advantage of the guitar's popularity with singing cowboys (none of whom played the uke). These instruments included Carnival's "Gaucho" and Mastro's "Jr. Guitar". The Mastro is a red-and-ivory-plastic, soprano-uke-sized instrument with 6 strings which could be tuned like a regular uke (doubling two pairs of strings) or as a higher-pitched guitar. Emenee's Gene Autry cowboy guitar was a baritone-uke-sized instrument with cool western elements (a revolver, spurs, cow horns, etc.) as well as Gene's likeness and signature molded directly into the top. It came complete with a push-button chord playing device and a booklet of Autrey's songs all packaged in a hansom faux-alligator cardboard case. My favorite guitar-branded ukulele is the western-style "fun guitar" made by the Harmonic Reed Corp. of West Conshohocken Pennsylvania. Printed cardboard glued to the uke's plastic body gives it the appearance of a horse-

The injection-molding process made it possible for instrument makers, including Mastro, Carnival and Mattel, to produce inexpensive styrene plastic ukuleles in huge numbers.

Carnival's sopranino-sized, western-themed ukettes sold for only 89 cents in the 1950s and early 60s.

THE ART OF VINTAGE UKULELES • SANDOR NAGYSZALANCZY

The round-bodied Carnival "Do-Si-Do" Country Western ukette features boy and girl characters singing, playing and dancing.

To take advantage of the guitar's popularity with singing cowboys, Carnival's "Gaucho" and Mastro's "Jr. Guitar" models were soprano-uke-sized instruments with 6 strings which could be tuned like a higher-pitched guitar.

THE ART OF VINTAGE UKULELES • SANDOR NAGYSZALANCZY

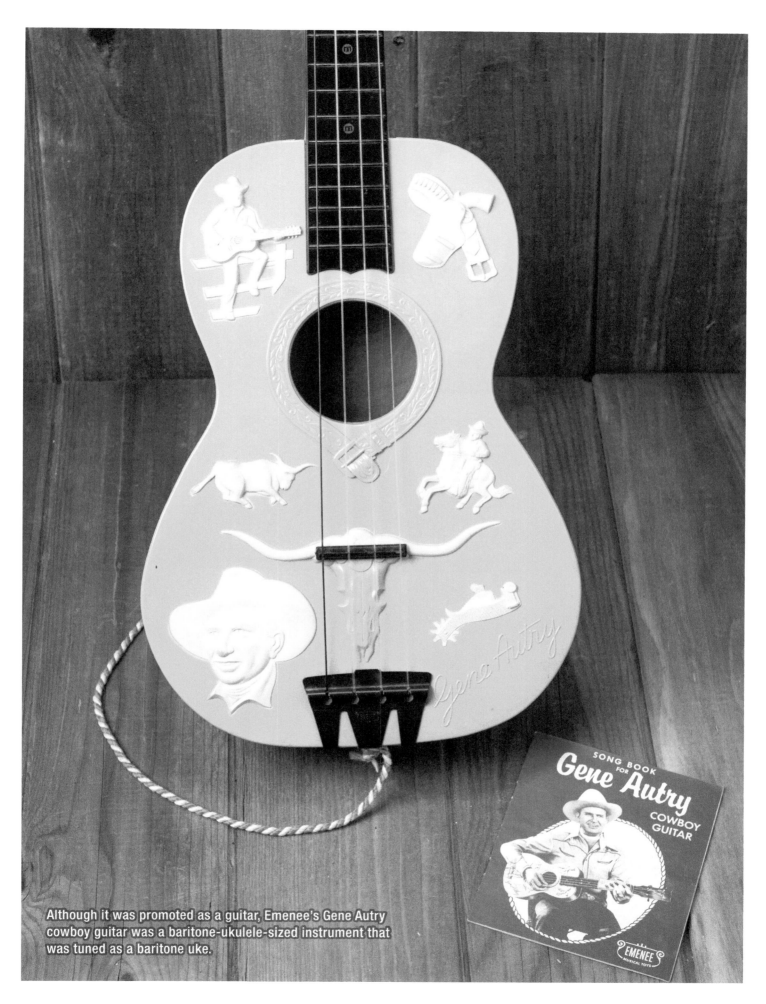

Although it was promoted as a guitar, Emenee's Gene Autry cowboy guitar was a baritone-ukulele-sized instrument that was tuned as a baritone uke.

With a size and scale equal to a soprano banjo ukulele, Mastro's "Swing Your Partner" model sports a large plastic resonator back.

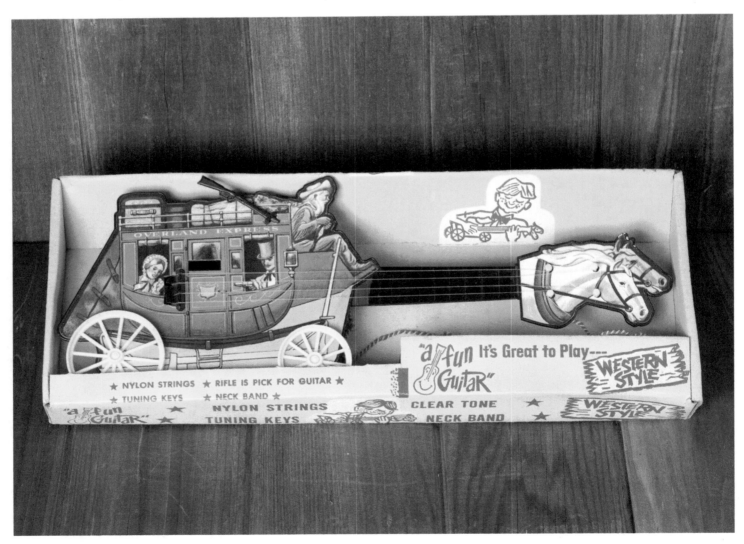

Possibly the coolest cowboy uke ever, Harmonic Reed Corps' plastic "fun guitar" model takes the shape of a horse-drawn western stagecoach.

THE ART OF VINTAGE UKULELES • SANDOR NAGYSZALANCZY

Some of the worst sounding cowboy guitars and ukuleles had bodies made from fiberboard —
a thin, stronger version of cardboard.

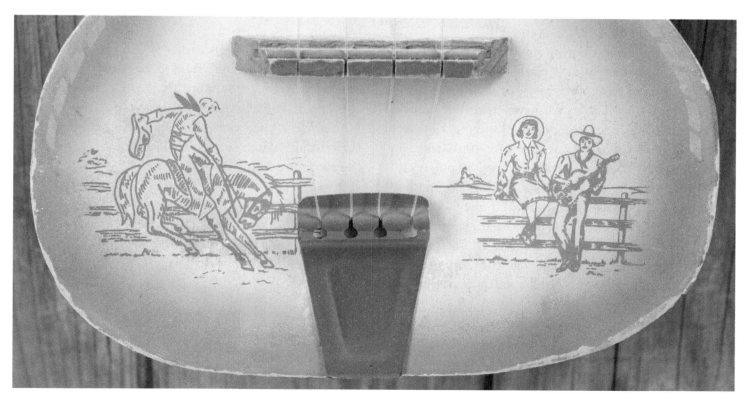

Cowboy western theme stencils decorate the top of this fiberboard uke, made by the Jefferson Manufacturing Company
of Philadelphia, PA.

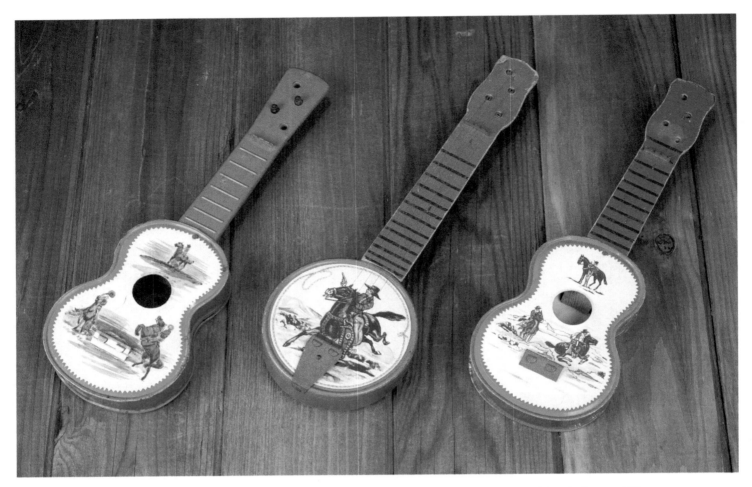

Made in Japan in the 1950s, these uke-like tin instruments sported charming western graphics, but were little more than noisemaking toys.

drawn stagecoach. It features yellow plastic wheels and a removable rifle that serves as a pick!

Some of the oddest cowboy guitars and ukuleles of 1950s and 60s had bodies made from fiberboard—basically, a thin, stronger version of cardboard. These painted and stenciled instruments featured wooden necks and bridges and wood or plastic friction-style tuners. They were very inexpensive, both to manufacture and purchase, making them popular children's toys. The Jefferson Manufacturing Company of Philadelphia, Pennsylvania produced the lion's share of fiberboard instruments, both 6-string guitars and ukuleles. Their cowboy-themed line of ukes ranged from the pint-sized "Rodeo," to the soprano-sized "On the Range" to tenor-sized models including the round-bodied "Roundup Time."

Compared to plastic ukuleles, fiberboard ukes were somewhat more durable; they wouldn't out-and-out break if you sat on one or used it to whack your kid brother. Despite advertising literature which proclaimed: "Not just a toy, but a real ukulele," fiberboard ukes are barely playable and sound just awful.

Made in Japan, tin "toy guitars" had metal bodies (actually made from thin sheet steel), wood necks and, often, cardboard fretboards. Although strung with four thin metal strings, these diminutive uke-like instruments were little more than noisemakers—there were no actual raised frets to press the strings against. Nonetheless, they were beautifully decorated with artistic lithographed scenes, typically of cowboys riding the range on their horses.

THE ART OF VINTAGE UKULELES • SANDOR NAGYSZALANCZY

One of first baritone ukuleles ever may be the cut-away instrument Arthur Godfrey is seen playing in the 1966 movie "Glass Bottom Boat" which co-stars popular singer Doris Day.

7.2 The Birth of the Baritone

Quick quiz: Among the four common sizes of ukuleles—soprano, concert, tenor and baritone—which one is tuned differently? Answer: the baritone. While the first three are tuned in standard "C" tuning: GCEA, the baritone (or "bari") is usually tuned like the top four strings of a guitar: DGBE. So, where did this variant of the ukulele universe come from? As with so many other popular inventions, it turns out that the answer isn't entirely clear.

The two names most closely associated with the origin of the baritone uke are Arthur Godfrey and Herk Favilla. Godfrey was an avid musician, radio personality and early television star of several programs including "Arthur Godfrey and his friends" and "Arthur Godfrey and his Ukulele." Hercules "Herk" Favilla was a 3rd-generation luthier and the son of John Favilla, who in 1890 with brother Joseph, co-founded the Favilla Brothers stringed instrument company in New York City. Herk took over the family business in 1959 and continued to build ukuleles, mandolins, banjos and guitars until he retired in 1980. As to which man is the true father of the baritone uke, we must rely on a

RIGHT: Sometime around 1950, Boston's Vega Company produced three different Arthur Godfrey signature baritone models, including the bottom-of-the-line standard, which Godfrey holds in the photo.

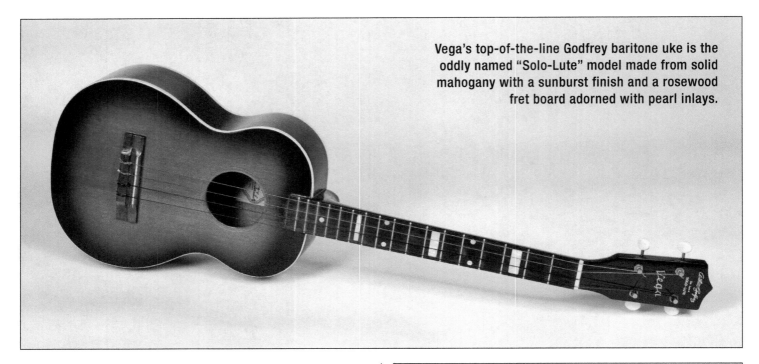

Vega's top-of-the-line Godfrey baritone uke is the oddly named "Solo-Lute" model made from solid mahogany with a sunburst finish and a rosewood fret board adorned with pearl inlays.

pair of oft-repeated stories with only a handful of facts to support either one:

Godfrey's tale begins with a banjo player named Eddie Connors, a musician at CBS (Godfrey's network) who had recorded with such big-band greats as Tommy and Jimmy Dorsey. Evidently Godfrey asked Connors to design a larger-bodied, lower-pitched ukulele. That first instrument is likely the cut-away baritone Godfrey regularly played on his TV shows as well as in the 1966 movie "Glass Bottom Boat." Connor's basic bari design (sans cutaway) was subsequently put into production by the Vega Company of Boston, Massachusetts sometime around 1950. Primarily a guitar, mandolin and banjo manufacturer, Vega made three different baritone models: The Standard (which Godfrey is holding in the photo on page 279), the De Luxe, and the oddly named "Solo-Lute," their fanciest model made from solid mahogany with a sunburst finish and a long neck with a rosewood fret board adorned with pearl inlays and a 21 inch scale with 16 frets clear of the body. Despite the fact that some De Luxe models have paper labels that read: "…created and designed by Eddie Connors…" Vega's promotional booklets clearly stated that the Solo Lute was "personally designed by Arthur Godfrey." This baritone uke does have Godfrey's signature on the headstock, no doubt part of his endorsement deal with Vega.

Herk Favilla's story takes a different tack. His grandfather John and uncle Joseph founded the Favilla Guitar Company in New York City shortly after they immigrated from Italy to America around 1890. Over

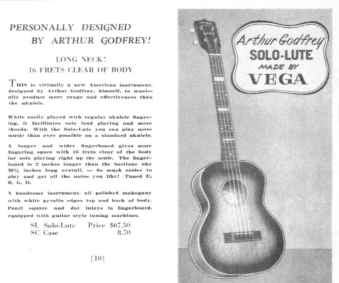

The Solo Lute's promotional booklet announces that the $67.50 baritone uke "…is virtually a new American instrument, designed by Arthur Godfrey, himself,…"

the next few decades, they built all manner of guitars, mandolins, banjos, violins, and ukuleles. Their ukuleles included both regular Spanish figure-8 bodied and teardrop-bodied soprano models, as well as the one-of-a-kind 6-stringed "Wimbrola" (see Section 4.10). Being an accomplished guitar player and teacher, Herk said that he designed the baritone "with the thought in mind of simplifying guitar study for the beginner." Thus, he created a four-stringed instrument tuned to match the first four strings of a guitar. He likely chose to marry his baritone to the ukulele

Godfrey's signature appears on the headstock of his signature Solo Lute model baritone uke.

family both to distinguish it from the tenor guitar, which used a different tuning, and because of Favilla's long history of manufacturing ukes (although, aside from the 1920s, ukuleles never accounted for more than 10% of Favilla's overall production). Herk's son Tom recollects that the first Favilla baritones were built in the late 1940s by grandfather John, but no records exist to substantiate this. (Intriguingly, Tom also claims that Arthur Godfrey's first baritones were actually built by Favilla, but when Godfrey had a dispute with them, he switched to a "Vinci" bari—a Favilla without a label—then later to a Vega.) All Favilla baritones sported solid mahogany bodies and necks and rosewood fret boards with a 19" scale (for comparison sake, Martin baritones, which didn't appeared until 1960, have 20" scales). Like all Favilla instruments, the baritone's headstock features a gold embossed "Favilla" logo, complete with their crown and shield logo. Around 1950, Herk was the first to author a series of instructional booklets specifically for the baritone ukulele player.

Since no known patents exist for the baritone ukulele and Arthur, Herk and Eddie have all long passed, we'll probably never know for sure which birth of the baritone story is true. Perhaps, as with so many inventions, both Godfrey/Connors and Favilla independently developed similar instruments.

But there's something that might cloud the whole is-

Three of the well-made ukuleles produced by the Favilla Guitar Company in New York City (bottom to top): Wimbrola, Teardrop, and U-1 soprano.

Great-sounding Favilla baritones sported solid mahogany bodies and necks and rosewood fret boards with a 19" scale.

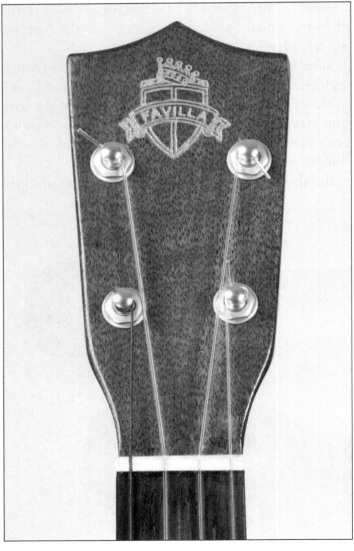

The Favilla baritone's headstock features a gold embossed crest, complete with the company name on a banner on a shield surmounted by a crown.

The first instruction book written specifically for the baritone ukulele, authored by Herk Favilla.

Large Size Ukuleles

No. 98   Tenor Ukulele. Slightly larger than the Concert Size. Entire instrument finished in medium mahogany color, somewhat shaded. Dull finish. Top edge bound with white celluloid. Equipped with patent pegs. Marvelous tone and big seller. Each **$6.00**

No. 91   FULL TENOR SIZE UKULELE. Length over all, 22 inches. Has proven to be a big seller on account of the deep mellow tone. Entire instrument made of carefully selected birch and sides and back are finished in light Koa color with neck finished to match, whereas the top is finished in its natural white color. The fingerboard is of white pearlette and frets are adjusted correctly. Entire instrument finished in high gloss. Each. . . . **$6.80**

No. 108   Bass Ukulele. Somewhat larger than the Tenor Ukulele. Entire instrument finished in dull mahogany, slightly shaded. Both edges bound with white celluloid, ebony finished extension fingerboard. Patent pegs; deep marvelous tone. Each **$10.00**

No. 108 Bass Size

No. 91 Tenor Size

Could the "Bass Ukulele" seen in the Tonk Brothers' 1928 catalog have been the actual first baritone-sized ukulele ever made?

sue of who invented the baritone?" you just read about. One of the pages of the 1928 Tonk Brothers musical wholesale catalog features an instrument called a "Bass Ukulele." Described as being "somewhat larger than a tenor ukulele," and possessing a "deep, marvelous tone," could this instrument—which, to my knowledge, no one has ever seen an example of—have been the actual first incarnation of the baritone uke, appearing more than two decades before the Godfrey or Favilla creations? Perhaps we'll never know.

Italian luthier Mario Maccaferri's Mastro Industries company produced well over a dozen different models of ukuleles, banjo ukes and ukettes.

7.3 Plastic Fantastic Ukuleles

When I had the unexpected pleasure of meeting Mario Maccaferri back in the early 1990s, I knew he was master luthier who had once been a virtuoso guitarist in Europe. But I had no idea that this slight man with bright eyes and a quick wit was also a talented inventor and plastics pioneer responsible for creating millions of instrument-quality plastic ukuleles and introducing a generation of baby boomers to the joys of making music.

Born only a few years after a small four-string Portuguese instrument had evolved into the Hawaiian ukulele, Mario apprenticed at age 11 to the famous Italian luthier, Luigi Monzzani, who taught him stringed instrument construction and how to play classical and harp guitar. By his mid-twenties, Mario was an accomplished classical guitarist performing throughout Europe, considered to be in the same league as Andres Segovia. In the late 1920s, he headed up a new

THE ART OF VINTAGE UKULELES • SANDOR NAGYSZALANCZY

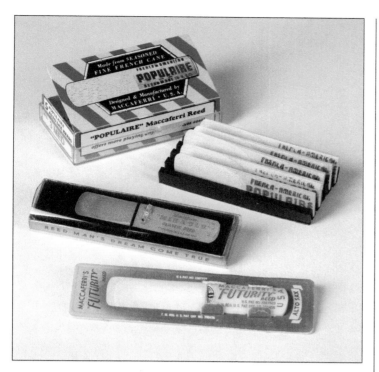

As natural cane became scarce during WWII, Maccaferri's French-American Reed Company made their "Futurity" and "Miracle" saxophone and clarinet reeds from polystyrene plastic.

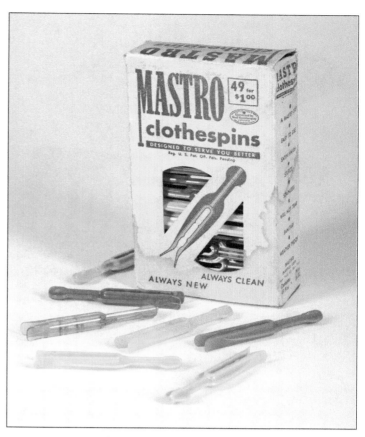

As a plastic products company, Mastro Industries produced everything from colorful plastic, including fishing lures, tape dispensers, toilet seats and clothespins.

guitar production department for the French company Selmer where he created a unique type of jazz guitar championed by gypsy jazz virtuoso Django Reinhardt. Maccaferri went out on his own in the early 1930s, starting a company that made clarinet and saxophone reeds using a manufacturing process he developed.

With WWII on the verge of engulfing Europe, Maccaferri moved his family and "French-American Reed Company" to America in 1939 and set up shop in the Bronx borough of New York City. As raw materials became scarcer during the war—including the natural cane necessary to make his reeds—Mario happened to see a new material on display at the New York World's Fair: synthetic plastic. Modern plastics had come from the government's development of new synthetic materials for the war effort. For his new "Futurity" and "Miracle" plastic reeds, Mario chose polystyrene, a strong, moldable thermoplastic that wasn't affected by moisture or excess humidity. The reeds turned out to sound pretty good, and received endorsements from Benny Goodman and other big-band stars.

Early success encouraged Maccaferri to develop his own molding and manufacturing processes and start his own plastic products company, Mastro Industries. Mastro made everything from clothespins, to fishing lures, clothes hangers, tape dispensers, toilet seats and

more, eventually supplying post-war America with the inexpensive household items they needed. In the mid 1940s, Mastro produced mountains of plastic tiles, used in the effort to quickly build housing for soldiers returning from the war. But by the end of the decade, industry competition had left Mario deep in debt and scanning the horizon for new markets in which to exploit his plastics capabilities and know how.

What happened next is the stuff of legend. On vacation at the Kenilworth Hotel in Miami, Mario had a chance meeting at poolside with the then-popular radio/TV personality Arthur Godfrey. Godfrey, 'The Ole Redhead' as he called himself, was a talented ukulele player and crooner (see Section 7.2). He and Mario had a few drinks and played a few songs together. As Mario tells it, they then chatted about the lack of availability of good, playable ukuleles. "At one point, Godfrey told me that if I could produce an affordable uke that played well and had passable tone, he could sell a million of them." This was no idle boast: Godfrey had a top-rated variety show on television, where he dressed in a Hawaiian shirt, played his custom-made baritone uke and even gave on-the-air uke lessons

Maccaferri chose Dow "Styron," plastic for molding Mastro ukuleles and guitars, as the resilient plastic gave his instruments a nice warm tone.

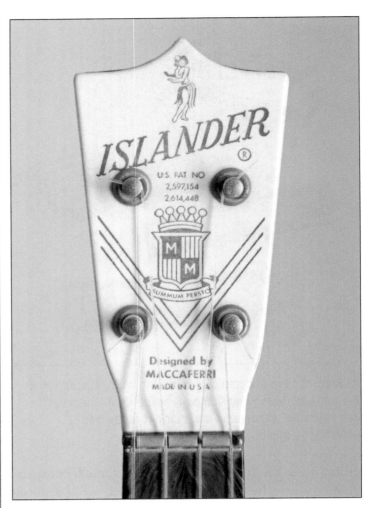

Mastro's first plastic uke was the "Islander" model soprano, which was loosely based on a Martin style #0.

twice a week. He was famously very good at selling products on his shows, and promoted everything from tea and shampoo to paint and aspirin to chicken soup and cigarettes. But his best talent turned out to be selling his viewers on the ukulele itself, introducing them to an instrument that hadn't been widely popular since the Great Depression.

Mario once told me he'd been searching for a way to make plastic stringed instruments years before meeting Godfrey, but he lacked the manufacturing capital and wasn't sure plastic instruments would sell. Inexpensive plastic ukes had been introduced as toys some years earlier; Mattel made a fortune in the mid-1950s selling their "Uke-A-Doodle" toy uke (see the photo on page 293). However, Mario wanted to use his considerable lutherie expertise to create more than a toy. He wanted to produce a serious musical instrument. After Godfrey bolstered his confidence, he quickly set about obtaining funding to tool up for production.

Mario spent months searching for a type of plastic

To demonstrate how impervious Islander ukes were to moisture, Maccaferri would submerge them in a water-filled aquarium.

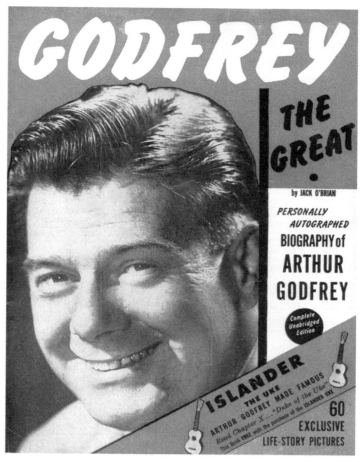

The "Godfrey the Great" booklet included with Islander ukes featured the life story of Arthur Godfrey, who was a major promoter of Mastro ukuleles.

that had the tonal qualities of wood. He ended up choosing Dow "Styron," a versatile, resilient plastic that gave instruments a nice warm tone. His first Styron plastic uke was the "Islander" soprano, which he loosely based on a Martin style #0. Each instrument was assembled from eight separate molded plastic pieces. To ensure good intonation, he molded the frets directly into the fingerboard, adding a zero fret just ahead of the nut—a signature element seen on

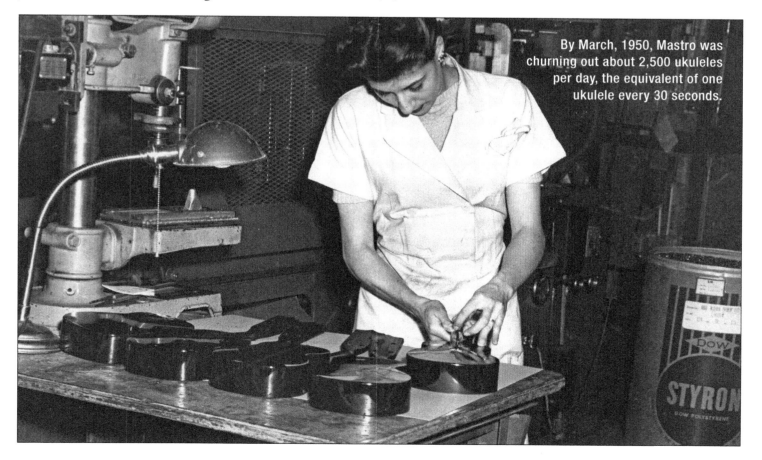

By March, 1950, Mastro was churning out about 2,500 ukuleles per day, the equivalent of one ukulele every 30 seconds.

Mastro's line of Islander ukes expanded from the basic model (left) to include the Islander Semi-deluxe (center) and the Islander Deluxe which featured an extended fingerboard (right).

all Maccaferri's ukuleles and guitars. Islanders were strung with "Nylotone" nylon strings made by Du-Pont and used "Tune Tite" tuners to help them stay on pitch. The first Islanders had cream-colored tops and "simulated rosewood" backs and sides. The ukes came with a felt pick, a tuner adjuster tool, playing instructions and a songbook by "Ukulele Lady" May Singhi Breen. Mario introduced the Islander at a trade show, where he demonstrated how impervious the uke was to moisture by displaying it submerged in a water-filled glass aquarium!

When Godfrey got his hands on the Islander, he

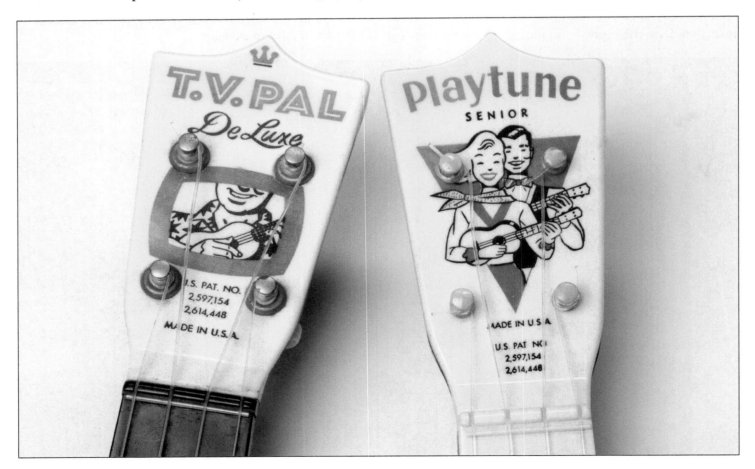

The Mastro plastic uke line grew with the addition of the TV Pal and Playtune® Sr. models.

THE ART OF VINTAGE UKULELES • SANDOR NAGYSZALANCZY

Mastro Styron ukes were produced in a rainbow of swirling colors, including reds, blues, purples, greens, and a yellowish-red plastic Maccaferri called "mustard and ketchup."

Mastro's sopranino-sized Ukettes came in more than half a dozen different models, including the Davy Crockett (front) and (left to right): Sparkle Plenty, PlayTune, Mastro Twins, Islander, and River Queen.

loved it and immediately promoted it on his TV show, telling his viewers that "It frets good, has good tone… and it's only $2.50!" He also cautioned against buying cheap, poorly-made instruments and told parents: "If a kid has a uke in hand, he's not going to get into much trouble." He did all this without asking for any financial compensation from Maccaferri! Mario's charming wife, Maria, did tell me that "for years, he (Mario) tried to pay Godfrey back for the endorsement, but Godfrey never accepted a dime". They did subsequently include a booklet with the ukes, titled "Godfrey the Great: The Life Story of Arthur Godfrey."

It didn't take long for orders to flood in for Islanders. Maria, who ran the Mastro factory, told me that on that first day after Godfrey's TV promo, the phone rang constantly and they ended up taking it off the

hook. By March, 1950, the same month that Mario filed a U.S. patent application for his Islander (see the photo on page 199). Mastro was churning out one ukulele every 30 seconds; about 2,500 a day. As orders backed up to 100,000 ukes and more, they stepped up production to 6,000 ukes a day! Kids wanted them, and the stores could hardly keep them in stock. By the end of that first year, Mastro had produced nearly 350,000. The Islander, which sold for $2.50 cost about $1.50 to make, but Mario said he only made $0.25 on each uke; the balance of the profit went to the dealers and retailers.

With his early success, Maccaferri expanded Mastro's uke line to include the Islander Semi-deluxe (with a decorative sound hole ring and a different bridge) and the Islander Deluxe (with an extended fingerboard).

Pretty blonde-haired Sparkle Plenty was a character in the popular Dick Tracy comic strip series.

The Sparkle Plenty Ukette was promoted through magazine ads, which claimed that the toy-sized instrument has "...a real ukulele tone."

The Mastro TV Pal, both regular and DeLuxe versions (both with a graphic image on the headstock that looks a lot like Godfrey), and the PlayTune® Sr. Models were soon to follow. The instruments were produced in a rainbow of swirling colors—reds, blues, purples, greens, and a yellowish-red plastic Mario called "mustard and ketchup." Because of the unpredictable nature of mixing colors in the injection molding process, each instrument's color pattern was unique.

As the Mastro ukulele line expanded, they introduced cutaway-bodied Islander Baritone ukes (see the photo on page 106), soprano-size banjoleles and sopranino-sized "Ukettes." The Ukettes came in more than half a dozen different models, including the Islander, PlayTune, TV Pal, Davy Crockett, River Queen and Sparkle Plenty. Based on characters from the popular Dick Tracy comic strip, the Sparkle Plenty Ukette was promoted through magazine ads in which the pretty blonde-haired daughter of yokel character "Gravel Gertie" declared that the pint-sized Ukette is "...specially designed for us kids." Her Ukette came with a Sparkle Plenty instructional comic book (see the photo on page 325). Although the Ukettes were usually sold as toys, Mario took great pride in the fact that all his instruments were fully playable. It's said that May Singhi Breen carried a Ukette in the pocket of her fur coat and would occasionally play it at parties.

Maccaferri also created—and patented—the "Chord Master," an automatic chording device which attached to a uke's neck with rubber bands to allow fledgling ukesters to play six basic chords with the simple push of a button, autoharp style (see the photo on page 348). I suspect this device held some special significance for Mario, as his own classical guitar playing career had ended after a swimming accident in 1933 seriously injured his fretting hand.

As public demand for plastic ukuleles began to dwindle in the mid-1960s, Mastro introduced a number of new models including the "Twist and Shout," and a line of "Beatles" instruments, including the soprano-uke-sized "Four Pop". Mastro's instrument product line also grew to include other plastic instruments: castanets, horns, sparkly-red snare drums, child-sized

As interest in ukuleles waned during the mid 1960s, Mastro introduced the Beatles "Four Pop" (left) and "Twist and Shout" (right) models.

violins, bongos and more. They also made a few promotional instruments, the oddest of which has to be a banjo uke for Carling Black Label Beer, with a head that reads: "Put More Flavor in Your Life."

In 1969, after selling more than nine million plastic ukuleles, Mario Maccaferri decided to sell his Mastro plastic instrument business to rival plastic instrument company, Carnival, who continued producing plastic uke up to sometime in the 1970s.

Plastic Competition

Of course, Mastro wasn't the only company to produce plastic ukes. Their main competitors included plastic instrument makers Fin-Der and Carnival, as well as two companies primarily known for manufacturing toys: Mattel and Emenee.

Mattel began in 1945, in a garage workshop owned by Harold Matson and Elliot Handler. Their business name "Mattel" was a combination of the letters of their last and first names, respectively. Mattel Creations (as it was called then) produced their first big-seller, the "Uke-a-doodle" toy ukulele in 1956. It was the first really successful toys they made, helping to transform Harold Matson's small garage-based company into the huge corporation it is today. Mattel made many toy ukuleles over the years including a few licensed by Disney, such as the "Mickey Mouse - getar" model. They also produced a whole series of small crank-box toy ukes featuring popular cartoon characters of the 1950s and 60s, such as Bugs Bunny, Popeye, Yogi the Bear, The Cat in the Hat, and Casper the Friendly Ghost. Mattel also made a more complex music-playing ukulele: Their "Strum Fun" uke which came with interchangeable music discs, each with a different song.

George A. Finder and partner Nino Marcelli set up the Fin-Der Plastic Ukulele manufacturing company in San Diego in 1950 and started manufacturing plastic ukuleles about the same time as Maccaferri. In fact, Finder's patent for plastic uke construction has been granted a couple of months ahead of Maccaferri (see page 199 in Section 5.1) Besides their best-known "Diamond Head" model, which featured multi-colored tuning pegs (see the top photo on pg. 297), Fin-Der produced quite a number of other models, including the "Lisa" "Aloha" "Surf Rider" "Royal Hawaiian" "Mauna Loa" and "Harry Owens" Signature models.

Based in Bridgeport, Connecticut, The Carnival Toy Mfg. Corp. produced a great many decorative uke models, ranging from toy-sized ukettes to sopranos and banjo ukes. Each model in their extensive line of ukettes had its own theme: Cowboys, Rock n' Roll, Hawaiian Aloha, Yankee Doodle, the Romper Room TV show, etc. Carnival also made a ukette that was sold as a souvenir at the 1962 World's Fair in Seattle Washington. Their soprano sized models include the 6-stringed "Gaucho", two different versions of the college-themed "Varsity" uke and the "Davy Crocket" and "Aloha."

Emenee Industries, founded in 1949, manufactured mostly toy organs and other musical toys for children. Their line of ukuleles, produced from the early 50s through the late 1960s, included the "Hootenanny Sing," "Bandstand," "Zorro," "Howdy Doody," and "Flamingo" models. For a time, the Flamingo came in a cool faux-leather box case and included the Arthur Godfrey auto-chord player. Some Flamingo ukes featured a nifty set of tuning pipes attached to the headstock (see the photo on page 133). Molds used to make the Flamingo uke were also used for several other soprano models, including the "Wai Ki Ki," the auto-uke-player-equipped "Automatic Uke" and the Jimmy Durate signature "Hot Cha Cha."

Other plastic uke manufacturers of the period

Mattel produced many different plastic ukuleles in the 1950s, 60s and 70s, including the concert-uke-sized "Mickey Mousegetar" and soprano-scale "Monkees" models.

The Art of Vintage Ukuleles • Sandor Nagyszalanczy

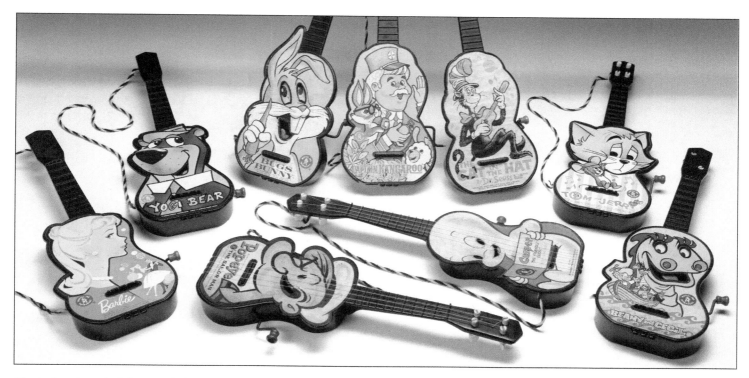

Music box toy ukuleles made by Mattel included more than a dozen models that featured popular cartoon characters of the era.

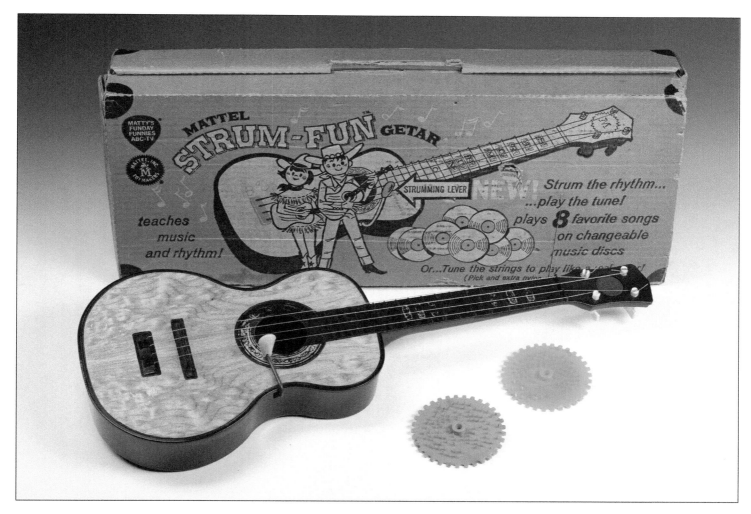

The yellow-tipped lever on the ukulele-based Mattel "Strum Fun Getar" rotated a disc inside the instrument which played a tune. Eight interchangeable discs were included, each of which played a different song.

George Finder's "Fin-Der" company produced more than half a dozen different plastic ukulele models, including (left to right): The Surf Rider, Mauna Loa and Diamond Head.

THE ART OF VINTAGE UKULELES • SANDOR NAGYSZALANCZY

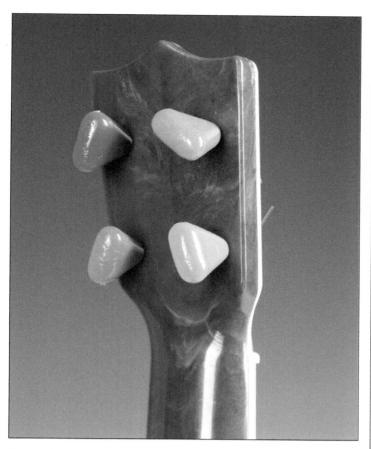

Many Fin-Der Diamond Head ukes featured large, rounded, multi-colored tuning pegs.

include New Jersey based Lapin Products, which made the "Happy Tune" model ukulele and the Canadian plastics company Reliable, which produced the rock n' roll themed "Mod Guitar" and "Davy Crocket" model soprano ukes. English company Selcol, which was the plastics division of the Selmer Company, produced several uke models, including the concert-sized "Skiffle Junior" (it's safe to assume the same mold was used to make Mattel's Micky Mousegetar) and baritone-sized Beatles "New Beat" and "Elvis Presley" models, the latter featuring a portrait of "The King" on the headstock (Emenee made a very similar instrument that included the image of a hound dog and a heart with the words "Love Me Tender" atop the body). Instrument manufacturing juggernaut Harmony also ventured into the plastic uke market, producing a single, very unique looking model known as the "Modern Bali." It's shape and features were based on the US design patent (#162,521) granted to R.H. Crowle in March of 1951. Harmony's most extensive use of molded plastics was for producing the molded fingerboards fitted to the majority of the less expensive model ukes they produced in the 1950s and 1960s.

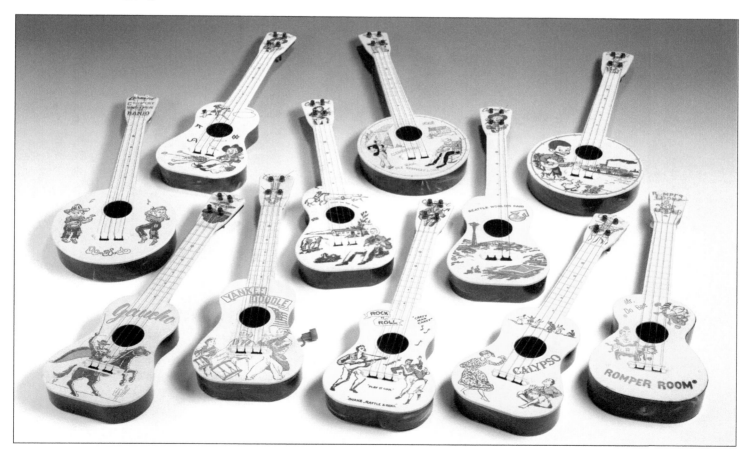

The Carnival Toy Mfg. Corp. of Bridgeport, Connecticut produced an extensive line of plastic ukettes, each with its own theme.

Three models from Carnival's line of plastic soprano-sized ukuleles include two different versions of their "Varsity" (left and center) and the 6-string "Gaucho."

THE ART OF VINTAGE UKULELES • SANDOR NAGYSZALANCZY

ABOVE: With a size that falls in between a regular soprano uke and a ukette, both Carnival's "Aloha" and "Davy Crocket" models feature wonderful decorative graphics.

LEFT: Founded in 1949, Emenee Industries' line of plastic ukuleles included the "Hootenanny Sing" model, which came with its own detachable automatic push button chord player.

Other popular Emenee soprano uke models include the "Howdy Doody" (foreground), "Bandstand" (left), Zorro (center) and Flamingo (right).

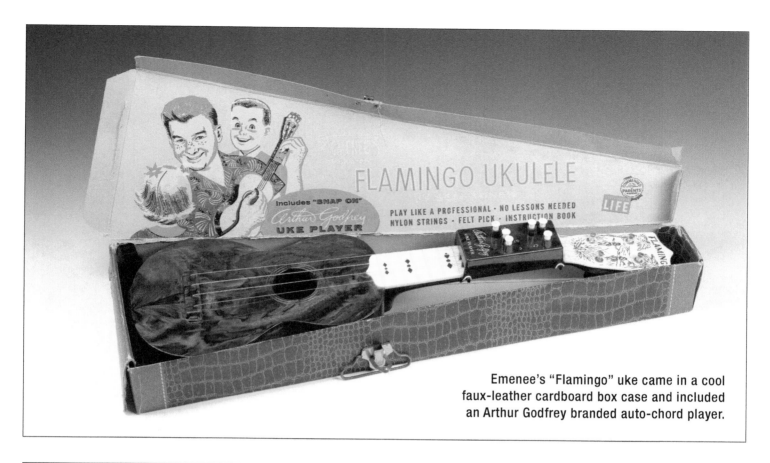

Emenee's "Flamingo" uke came in a cool faux-leather cardboard box case and included an Arthur Godfrey branded auto-chord player.

The molds used to make Emenee's Flamingo uke were also used for several other soprano models, including (left to right): the Jimmy Durate signature "Hot Cha Cha," the auto-uke-player-equipped "Automatic Uke" and the "Wai Ki Ki."

Other plastic uke manufacturers of the period include Reliable, which produced "Davy Crocket" and "Mod Guitar" model soprano ukes, and Lapin Products, which made the "Happy Tune" uke.

THE ART OF VINTAGE UKULELES • SANDOR NAGYSZALANCZY

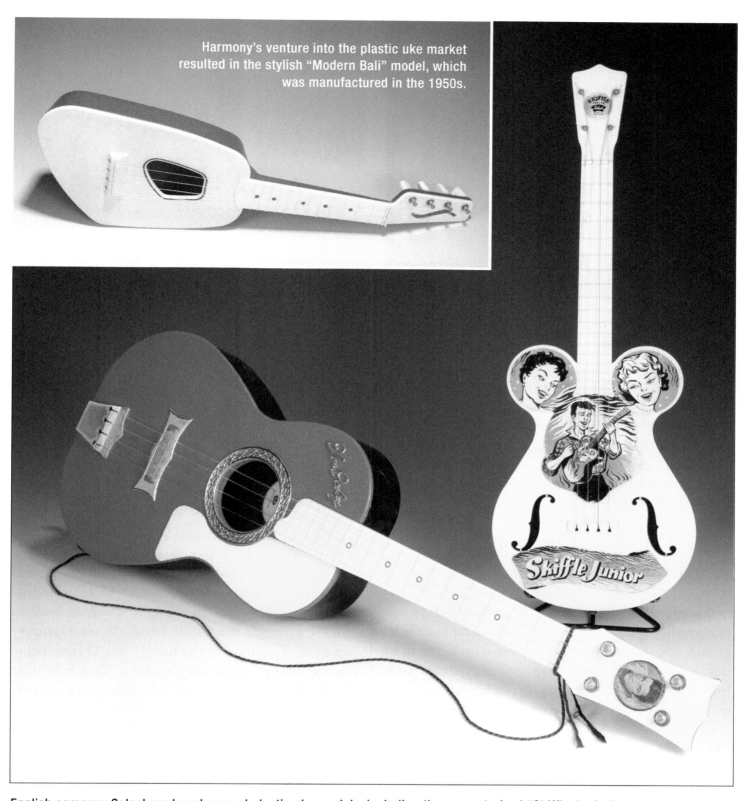

Harmony's venture into the plastic uke market resulted in the stylish "Modern Bali" model, which was manufactured in the 1950s.

English company Selcol produced several plastic uke models, including the concert-sized "Skiffle Junior" and baritone-sized "Elvis Presley."

By the mid-to-late 1960s, the tectonic plates of popular music had shifted. Baby boomers who once rejoiced at playing Hawaiian hapa haole tunes and novelty ditties they had learned from Arthur Godfrey now had a different beat thumping in their heads. Almost overnight, everybody wanted to play rock 'n roll music on guitars. To meet the demand, Maccaferri, like his competitors, did some clever slight-of-hand, producing six-string sopranos and re-branding some 4-string baritone ukes as "junior guitars," including Mastro's GTA-5 electric uke (see the photos on page 315).

Nova Scotian music educator J. Chalmers Doane not only invented an affordable student ukulele, he created a ukulele-based music teaching program that's been used in schools all across Canada and America.

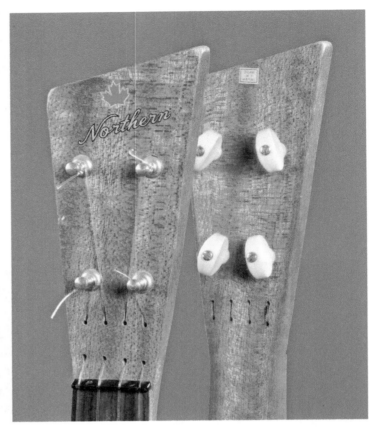

To save the trouble of having to add a slanted headstock to his ukulele, Doane, came up with idea of threading the strings through angled holes drilled between the nut and tuners.

7.4 J. Chalmers Doane's Northern Ukes

Whether they're made by artisan luthiers or manufactured in large factories, most ukuleles are born from a desire to build and sell the instrument itself. But that's not exactly the case with Canada's Northern brand ukuleles, which came about as the byproduct of one man's ambition to teach musical skills to the masses.

In the late 1960s, Nova-Scotia-born J. Chalmers Doane was director of music education for the city of Halifax. There, this experienced musician and teacher created a comprehensive music program designed to make students musically literate by the end of the sixth grade (there was a program for adults as well). Instead of relying on traditional instruments (violins, trumpets, etc.) to help his students learn basic musical skills—melody, harmony and rhythm—Doane taught them to play the ukulele. From his own studies in string methods at Boston University, he recognized that ukes were affordable, portable and easy to play.

To supply his students with inexpensive ukule-les, Doane initially bought them directly from the Harmony Musical Instrument Company of Chicago. These plain, white-wood ukes had plastic fingerboards and only cost around $6 each (their biggest shortcoming was that his enthusiastic students quickly wore out the plastic frets!). When Harmony went out of business in the mid 1970s, Doane had to come up with a new source of ukes. With help from his father and brother, he built his first prototype ukulele in his dad's basement. Since Doane didn't know how to bend the instrument's sides, he created a triangular body with straight sides. And in order to save the trouble of having to laminate a slanted headstock onto the end of the neck, he came up with idea of threading the strings through angled holes drilled between the nut and tuners (see the photo above). This not only created the necessary string break angle to keep the strings from slipping off the nut, it created a bit of friction that he said helped the strings stay in better tune. Doane was granted a U.S. patent (#4,041,830) for his unique "teaching ukulele" in 1977.

In a phone conversation I had with him some years

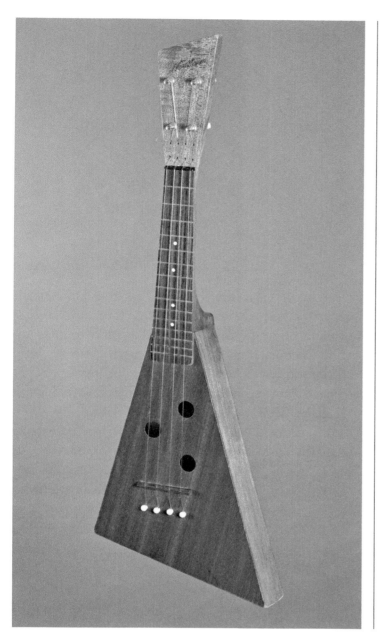

ago, Chalmers Doane told me that five or six different instrument makers tried to produce his triangle-bodied ukes before he finally struck a deal with the Northern company in Ontario. In order to produce the large numbers of ukes needed at a reasonable cost, Northern's operations manager Harry Dunnette had the instruments manufactured in Japan, most likely by the Nagoya Suzuki Violin Company. Initially, they produced a "standard" soprano-sized uke: the JCD-1 (Doane's initials). The JCD-2 soon followed; a concert-sized instrument Doane called a "tenor uke" (see the photo at left) with a larger body and longer scale length that better suited older students and adults. Both standard and concert ukes had mahogany plywood bodies, a trio of small round sound holes, solid mahogany necks, and rosewood fretboards and bridges. The strings were secured behind the uke's saddle-less bridge with guitar-style bridge pins. In later years, Northern also produced smaller numbers of fancier models, the JCD-3, -4 and -5, that sported solid rosewood bodies, spruce tops and various decorative appointments. They also made some ukes with regular Spanish-style bodies, such as the model UK-15. Even this simple student model incorporates a bit of Doane's ingenuity: Four screws on the headstock

LEFT: Doane's model JCD-2 Northen Uke was a concert-sized instrument with a large body and scale length that suited older students and adults.

BELOW: Northern also produced ukes with regular Spanish-style "figure of eight" bodies, such as this model UK-15.

A seasoned performer and recording artist, Chalmers Doane's albums include a recorded version of his teaching method as well as his "Uke Trio," album featuring ukulele and cello duets.

just behind the nut act as string trees, to increase the break angle of the strings, which helps keep them from slipping out of their slots on the nut.

In addition to creating ukuleles and teaching music, Chalmers Doane was also a seasoned performer and recording artist. His multiple albums include not only the record version of his teaching method, but " Uke Trio," which features ukulele and cello (as well as a cute pair of cartoon Northern ukes on the cover) and "Ukuleles East" an ensemble of Doane's "A list" senior uke students, most of whom are seen playing Northern ukuleles in the album's cover photo shown below.

By the time Northern stopped making Doane's triangular-bodied ukuleles in the mid 1980s, countless numbers of music students had learned to play on them. Doane's ukulele teaching methods have been used by music teachers all across Canada and the U.S. to instruct an estimated 50,000 students (see Section 8.1, page 327). Chalmers Doane retired in 1993, but his musical legacy lives on: The internationally acclaimed Langley Ukulele Ensemble of British Columbia got started as a result of Doane's music programs. You can see them performing, albeit briefly, in the 2006 Christmas movie "Deck the Halls," starring Mathew Broderick and Danny DeVito.

The cover photo of the "Ukuleles East" album features an ensemble of Doane's "A list" senior uke students, most of whom are playing Northern ukuleles.

7.5 Swagerty Kooky Ukes

One of my favorite images from the Swingin' Sixties is an iconic photo of Frank Sinatra's daughter Nancy wearing "These boots are made for walkin'" go-go boots and holding an exotic-looking stringed instrument. Its vaguely Asian appearance belies the fact that it was actually created by Southern California furniture maker, artist and woodworker Ancil Swagerty. From the late 1950s to the early 1970s, his "Swagerty Specialties Company" in San Clemente, CA manufactured a whole line of oddball four-string instruments collectively known as "Kooky Ukes.." The line included the tenor-uke-sized "Surf-A-lele," the 45-inch-long straight-necked, "Kook-a-lā-lee" and the curve-necked "Singing Treholipee" (pronounced Tree'-hole-i-pee).

Likely inspired by native instruments Swagerty saw while serving in the US Navy in the Pacific during WW II, all three Swagerty models feature shallow triangular bodies made from thin hardwood plywood and necks made of solid wood (probably ash). Each model was fitted with a fingerboard, bridge, string guides and friction tuners all made of molded hard black plastic. Swagerty Specialties obtained a design patent for the Treholipee in 1966, and copyrighted an 18-page book: "The Kooky Uke How-To Book," written by Sidney Clark, in 1967.

Swagerty's flagship model Treholipee has a 47-inch-

In this iconic photo of Nancy Sinatra, the exotic-looking stringed instrument she's holding is a Swagerty "Kook-a-lā-lee" ukulele.

From the late 1950s to the early 1970s, Ancil Swagerty's San Clemente, CA company manufactured a line of oddball four-string instruments collectively known as "Kooky Ukes."

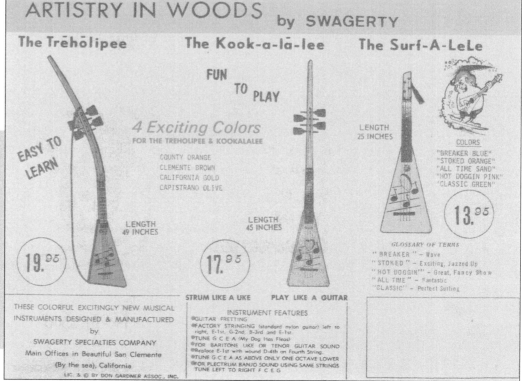

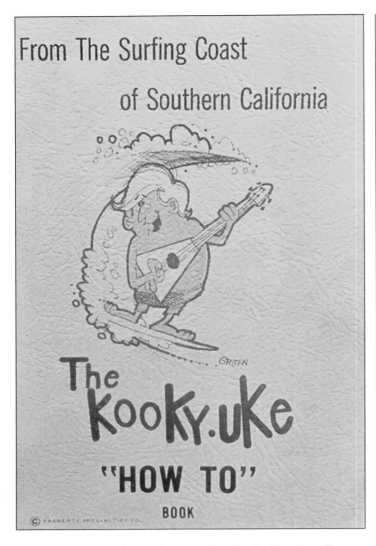

This is the cover of the 18-page "The Kooky Uke How-To Book," written by Sidney Clark in 1967.

Swagerty's flagship model "Singing Treholipee" has a long curved neck and a triangular body with three small sound holes that resemble musical notes.

long curved neck and a triangular body with three small sound holes with musical notes painted over them (that seems to account for the "Trehol" part of the Treholipee's name). The Kook-a-lā-lee is similar in overall size and features to the Treholipee, but has a straight neck and headstock. Its body has a single heart-shaped sound hole; it's the one Sinatra holds in the photo on the previous page. Both the Treholipee and Kook-a-lā-lee were fitted with large tuning "paddles" protruding from either side of their slender headstocks. Swagerty's Surf-A-LeLe model was basically a smaller, 25-inch-long, version of the Kook-a-lā-lee, with an oval (or sometimes heart shaped) sound hole, the same fingerboard as the other ukes, but smaller plastic friction tuners. They also produced a small number of 8-string versions of the Treholipee. All models were tenor-scale-length instruments that came factory tuned (low to high) to: "E-G-B-E," but could be tuned like a regular tenor uke (G-C-E-A), baritone uke/tenor guitar, plectrum banjo, or tenor banjo.

Allegedly, the long, extended headstocks on the Treholipee and Kook-a-lā-lee allowed the instruments to be stuck upside down into the sand at the beach whenever a player wanted to go surfing—less chance of getting sand in the sound hole! The smaller Surf-A-LeLe evidently could be played while riding a surfboard, as illustrated by the "Murf the Surf" character decal found on most Kooky Ukes. This cartoon figure was created by the famous California artist Rick Griffin, best known for his 1960s surf-related artwork, Zap comics, and posters and album covers for famous bands, including the Doors, Santana and the Grateful Dead.

In the 1960s, the $20. Treholipee and $18. Kook-a-la-lee came in 4 semi-transparent colors: "County orange," "Clemente brown," "California gold," and "Capistrano Olive." The $15. Surf-A-LeLe came in a few different colors, including "Breaker Blue,"

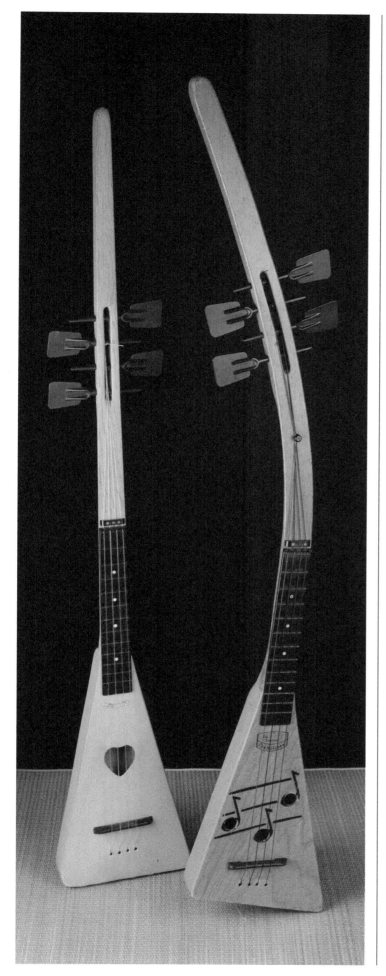

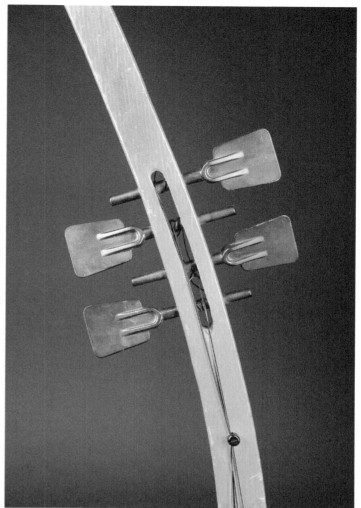

LEFT: The two longer versions of Swagerty's Kooky Ukes are the Kook-a-lā-lee (left) with its straight neck and heart-shaped sound hole and the Treholipee (right) with its signature 47-inch-long curved neck.

ABOVE: Both the Treholipee and Kook-a-lā-lee are fitted with large plastic tuning paddles which stick out of either side of the instruments' headstocks.

"Stoked orange," and "Hot doggin' pink." They also made a very small number of Kooky Ukes with dark brown/black bodies and red tuners and fingerboards. All the painting was done by an auto-body man Swagerty recruited for the task. Although actual production numbers are unknown (it's reputed that Swagerty may have made as many as 60,000 Treholipees!), Ancil Swagerty's nephew Bill Jr., who worked in his uncle's shop during the summers of 1968-1973, said that Holiday Inn was their largest customer. They ordered several thousand Kooky Ukes for all their hotels in Hawaii—a uke for every room! I'm pretty sure they were mounted as wall decorations, rather than left in the rooms for customers to play.

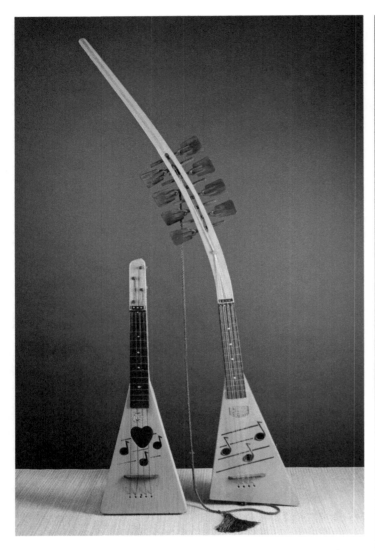

Surf-A-LeLe model (left) is basically a smaller version of the Kook-a-lā-lee. Swagerty made a small number of 8-string Treholipees (right).

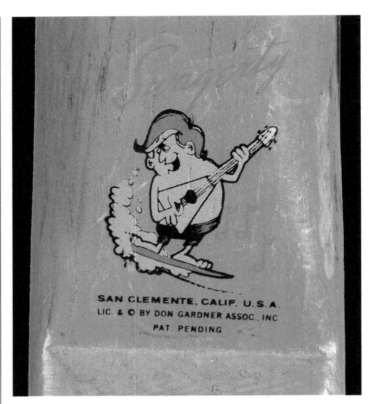

California artist Rick Griffin's "Murf the Surf" decal is found on most Kooky Ukes.

Besides the Kooky ukes, Swagerty produced a "Banana Bass" (yes, you guessed it, painted bright yellow and shaped like a big banana), a "Little Guitar," which was a Surf-A-LeLe-sized uke with an free form guitar-like body shape, and a double neck Kook-a-lā-lee. The double necks were supposedly only made specially for friends and never marketed to the public. They differ from standard Kook-a-Lā-Lees in that the instrument's twin sound holes are oval, not heart-shaped. Swagerty also made traditional harps and dulcimers on custom order.

At one point, Swagerty sold a small transistorized, battery-powered amplifier called the "Mini Amp Junior." Promoted by musician, comedian, television personality and one-time "Tonight Show" host Steve Allen (who also endorsed the entire Kooky Uke line), the amp required the uke to be fitted with a contact mic pickup which was sold separately.

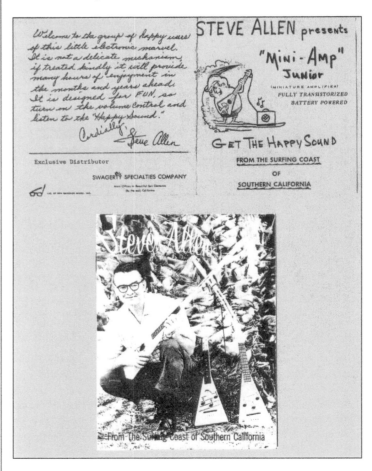

Swagerty's "Mini Amp Junior" was a small battery-powered amplifier once promoted by television personality Steve Allen.

This photo of photo of Princeton College Triangle Club Jazz Band shows two members playing tenor banjos, as they produced enough volume to be heard amidst the horn section and drums.

7.6 The Uke Goes Electric

As an iconic guitar riff launches the Southern Rock classic "Sweet Home Alabama," Lynyrd Skynyrd's vocalist Ronnie Van Zant tells us to "turn it up." He was certainly on to something: It's a scientific fact that human ears enjoy music more when it's played louder (within reason; I'm not talking about ear-splitting rock concert volumes). But then what of the lowly ukulele, one of the quietest stringed instruments on the planet? These days, making your uke loud enough to be heard in a noisy club or cavernous performance venue is no problem: If your instrument has a built-in pickup, just plug it in; if not, simply step up to a microphone and strum away.

But ukulele performers didn't always have it so easy. During the uke's first heyday in the 1920s, microphones were more commonly used for recording and radio broadcasting than for live performances, and electronic pickups were still in the experimental phase. In order to understand how ukulele amplification evolved in the decades to follow, we need to trace the history of the uke's 6-stringed cousin, the guitar.

In the 1910s and 20s, the rhythm sections of ragtime and Dixieland bands typically featured tenor banjos, as they naturally produced enough volume to be heard amidst the bands' much louder horn sections and drums (see the photo of Princeton College's Triangle Club Jazz Band, shown in the photo above). As popular band music evolved in the 1930s, banjo players traded their instruments for guitars, which had a mellower, less jangly sound more appropriate for the songs of the time. In lieu of traditional Spanish-style guitars, most players chose archtop guitars which possessed a crisp tone loud enough to be heard when played in the rhythm sections of small ensembles.

But as bands got larger in the big band era, guitarists struggled to be heard. One solution was provided by resophonic instruments developed by the Dopyera Brothers in the late 1920s (see Section 2.8) Resonator guitars employed one or more speaker-like aluminum cones to acoustically amplify the sound of their strings. Although they were notably louder than archtops, resonators possessed a metallic sound quality that limited their appeal on the mainland. The Hawaiian Territories were a different story: Native musicians, such

Native Hawaiian musicians of the 1920s embraced resonator instruments, both for their tone and volume, which was greater than regular acoustic instruments.

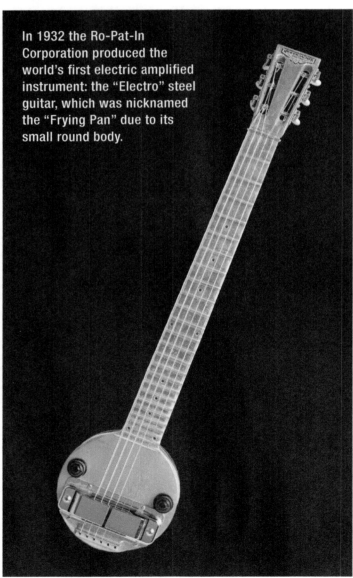

In 1932 the Ro-Pat-In Corporation produced the world's first electric amplified instrument: the "Electro" steel guitar, which was nicknamed the "Frying Pan" due to its small round body.

as slide guitar virtuoso Sol Hoopii (and his Novelty Trio band), quickly embraced the resonator guitar and developed a style of slide playing which gave popular Hawaiian music one of its signature sounds. Resonator ukuleles, both with metal and wood bodies, soon followed. Although resonator ukes were louder than regular ukuleles, they never achieved wide use in either Hawaiian or mainland bands.

Owing to the Hawaiian slide guitar's great popularity, in 1932 the Ro-Pat-In Corporation (later to become Rickenbacker) created and produced the world's first electric lap steel guitar: the "Electro" (nicknamed the "Frying Pan" due to its small round body). The Electro's horseshoe shaped electro-magnetic pickup employed coils that created a magnetic field. As its steel strings were played, their vibration caused changes in the magnetic field, thus producing an electrical current that could be amplified by plugging a cable into a small tube amplifier.

After introducing its own electric lap steel in 1936, the Gibson Instrument Company began production of the model ES-150 ("Electro Spanish") guitar: The first archtop guitar with a built-in magnetic pickup. These guitars were loud enough to be heard even in large bands. In the hands of talented guitarists such as Eddie Lang and Charlie Christian, an amplified electric guitar became a bona-fide solo instrument.

In 1949, Gibson started installing smaller versions of its magnetic pickups on their model TU tenor ukes.

Thus, the ETU-1 became the world's first electrically-amplified acoustic ukulele (they also produced and ETU-3, which had the same pickup and features of the ETU-1, but sported a triple-bound body). Unlike Gibson's standard tenors, ETU ukes were strung with metal strings, which made them sound more like electric guitars than acoustic ukes. Clearly, they were never very popular: Gibson produced only about 88 ETUs between 1949 and 1953. They did build one custom electric uke for TV and radio personality Arthur Godfrey. What made it special were its strings: Godfrey didn't like the sound or feel of steel strings, so Gibson created special polymer strings infused with iron powder, so that they would work with the uke's magnetic pickup.

In the early 1950s: DeArmond, an early pioneer of detachable guitar pickups, developed a contact pickup specifically for the ukulele. Their Model 750 pickup attached to the top of a uke by means of a large rubber band, thus allowing it to be installed on any regular acoustic ukulele. A microphone-like transducer inside the pickup amplified the vibration of the top as the uke was played. Thus amplified, a uke could sound loud, even if it were played softly. As the small booklet that

Gibson Instrument Company's model ES-150 was the first archtop guitar with a built-in magnetic pickup. Top player Charlie Christian is seen hear holding one.

First produced in 1949, Gibson's ETU-1 tenor ukulele became the world's first electrically-amplified acoustic ukulele.

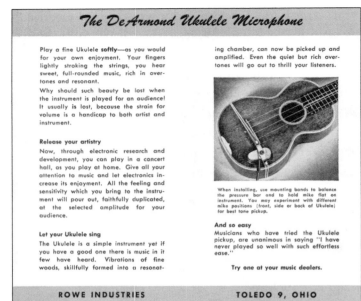

Unlike standard tenors, Gibson's ETU ukes had metal strings, necessary for them to work with the uke's built-in electric pickup.

The detachable DeArmond pickup attached to the top of a uke with a large rubber band, allowing installation on any regular acoustic ukulele.

DeArmond's "Ukulele Microphone" is a contact pickup that electrically amplified the vibration of the uke's top as it was played.

ABOVE AND BELOW:
Mastro's baritone-uke-sized model GTA-5 has a surface-mounted magnetic pickup and volume control and came with its own battery-powered amplifier.

THE ART OF VINTAGE UKULELES • SANDOR NAGYSZALANCZY

Tombo's Japanese-made "Ukelet," likely the world's first solid-bodied electric uke, came in a special case that contained an electric amplifier.

THE ART OF VINTAGE UKULELES • SANDOR NAGYSZALANCZY

The Ukelet's amplifier can run on either AC power or six D-sized batteries.

The controls for Tombo's 4-watt solid-state amplifier include volume and tone controls, as well as a switch for choosing either AC or battery power.

came with the pickup proclaimed: "All the feeling and sensitivity which you bring to the instrument will pour out, faithfully duplicated at the selected amplitude for your audience."

The electric guitar craze of the 1960s prompted the creation of some very interesting and unusual electric ukuleles that featured magnetic pickups. Mastro Industries, manufacturer of innumerable plastic ukes in the 50s, produced a baritone-sized ukulele made from "rosewood-swirl" styrene plastic. Fitted with steel strings and a surface-mounted magnetic pickup with a volume control, the Mastro GTA-5 came with its own gold-vinyl-covered, battery-powered TA-5 5-watt amplifier; no doubt part of Mario's attempt to keep step with the electric guitar craze. Can you imagine how cool it would've been to be a kid in 1965 and find this rock-ready plastic axe under the tree on Christmas morning?

The Japanese-made Tombo "Ukelet" was perhaps the world's first solid-bodied electric uke, with a shape suspiciously similar to a Fender Stratocaster. This tenor-sized instrument has four steel strings (they also made a 6-string model) and features a guitar-type magnetic pickup and volume and tone controls. It came in white, red or with a red-to-black sunburst finish. The coolest thing about the Ukelet is its rectangular case which contains a hidden surprise: Opening a hinged panel on the back of the case reveals a built-in 4-watt solid-state amplifier which runs on either six D-size batteries or regular household AC current. The design is somewhat like the Silvertone "Amp in Case" sold at Sears department stores in the 1960s.

Established in 1917, the Tombo Musical Instrument Company pioneered new electronic technologies in the early 1960's and implemented them in the electric guitars and organs they made. Tombo (which means "dragonfly" in Japanese) only produced the Ukelet for a couple of years in the mid 1960s. It was primarily sold in Asia and Hawaii. The company is still in business today and produces a line of harmonicas.

THE ART OF VINTAGE UKULELES • SANDOR NAGYSZALANCZY

Chapter Eight
Accessories & Ephemera

Ukulele accessories and ephemera are important elements in attaining a more complete understanding of the uke's history and influence on American popular culture in the 20th century.

Some of the best advice my mother gave me in regard to collecting was that the best time to buy something was when no one else wanted it. Being an antique dealer who bought and sold mostly European silver and porcelain, she knew exactly what she was talking about. Subsequently, I started collecting vintage ukuleles in the early 1980s, when the uke was considered the un-coolest instrument on the planet. (Personally, I blame Tiny Tim, or at least the managers/producers that encouraged him to perform as a rather ridiculous comic act).

Around the turn of the millennium, interest in the ukulele climbed once again. When prices went up, my uke collecting slowed to a trickle. Once that happened, I began to concentrate on collecting all manner of items associated with the ukulele: vintage sheet music, advertisements, trade catalogs, photographs, post cards, instruction and song books, 78 recordings, as well as various ukulele accessories including pitch-pipe tuners, capos, felt picks, etc. Not only did these things complement my instrument collection, but also help expand my knowledge and understanding of the history of the ukulele and its role in popular culture.

8.1 Instruction Method Books

Have you ever bought a musical instrument that you didn't know how to play? If you did so in the days before you could choose from dozens of different instructional books or a million how-to videos on the Internet, it's likely you sought instruction either from a music teacher or friend who already knew how to play.

But what if the instrument you chose was relatively

An assortment of vintage ukulele instruction books and playing methods.

new, so there were few friends or teachers who could give you lessons? Such was the case with the ukulele, the Hawaiian instrument that only came into existence in the late 1800s. The uke quickly became popular with both native Hawaiians and tourists visiting the islands. Music publishers recognized the need for instructional literature that could bring beginning players up to speed quickly. Because the ukulele was an affordable, simple instrument, most of the hundreds of instruction books printed in the early 1900s focused on how easy it was to learn to play.

One of the most popular early publications was the 1912 "Self Instructor for the Ukulele and Taro-Patch Fiddle" authored by Major Mekia Kealakai, which sold more than half a million copies. Its introduction claims that "…it is very easy for a child to master the ukulele without the slightest previous knowledge of music." Kealakai, an accomplished Hawaiian musician, com-

poser and leader of the Royal Hawaiian Band, created a method that included basic playing instructions, a selection of popular mainland and Hawaiian tunes arranged for the uke, and even a section of diagramed solos. Within five years, a dozen other ukulele instruction guides were available, including N.B. Bailey's 1914 booklet: "A Practical Method for Self Instruction on the Ukulele" and "The Kamiki Method" and "Guckert's Chords for the Ukulele At Sight Without Notes of Teacher," both published in 1917.

As popularity of the ukulele spread across the U.S. mainland in the 1920s, the publishing floodgates opened, unleashing a torrent of instructional booklets, many with colorful covers depicting happy groups of ukulele players in idyllic settings, take for example Kamiki's 1927 "The At-a-glance Illustrated Self Instructor for Ukulele and Ukulele Banjo" and Winn's "How to Play Melody on the Uke and Banjo Uke."

The 20s also saw the emergence of gimmicky quick-learning methods that touted how easy the ukulele was to play. The "Illustrated 5-Minute Guaranteed Ukulele Course" published in 1925 actually authorized music dealers to refund the booklet's 25-cent purchase price if the buyer was not fully satisfied! The booklet's foreword says: "For accompanying singing, the haunting harmony of the Ukulele has no superior... You can learn to play rich, harmonious accompaniment in a few minutes by this New Method." Such booklets were often promoted in newspaper ads and in the margins of popular sheet music. The booklets themselves often contained advertisements, promoting other instructional books or new ukulele models, such as Harmony's "Classmate" uke, which sold for $3.00 in the late 1920s.

Styles of Instruction Vary

Booklets typically began with instructions on how to tune a uke to the C-tuning (A-D-F#-B) that was commonly used with soprano and tenor ukes, as well as taro patches (modern G-C-E-A didn't become popular until the late 1940s). Tuning could be accomplished by use of a pitch pipe, a piano, or simply by ear. Drawn graphics or photographs were used to illustrate the tuning methods, as well as the proper way of holding a uke, using a felt pick and playing various strumming patterns, the latter referred to as "strokes." One 1927 booklet: "Strokes for the Ukulele" presented a "New 'Slow Motion' Method" which offered students the "secrets" of developing the right wrist motion for playing syncopated and Hawaiian strums.

A great many booklets included the rudimentary aspects of music theory: time signatures, keys, notes, etc. The exercises and songs presented in these books required players to read musical notation, even when playing chords. This approach was likely based on the fact that the piano was extremely popular in the early 20th century, and many ukulele newbies had previously taken piano lessons and were already familiar with standard musical notation.

TOP RIGHT: Major Mekia Kealakai's 1912 "Self Instructor for the Ukulele and Taro-Patch Fiddle" was one of the most popular early publications and sold more than half a million copies.

RIGHT: Innumerable ukulele instructional booklets were published in the 1920s, including Kamiki's 1927 "Self Instructor for Ukulele and Ukulele Banjo."

How to Hold Ukulele

Place neck of Ukulele between thumb and first finger of left hand. Bring fingers of left hand around and above Ukulele so that fingers fall *down* on the strings. This will make the chords easier. Do not grip the instrument tightly or your finger will quickly become tired. Hold Ukulele flat against body with right forearm so that right hand can strum across strings just above the sound hole.

How to Play With Pick

Until you have mastered the fingering of the chords, it is best to use the Felt Pick when playing the Ukulele. Later, when you can pay more attention to strumming, you can change from the Pick to using your finger tips as explained below. Always remember, however, that the Pick has the advantage of producing clearer and louder tones.

Grasp pick lightly between thumb and first finger of the right hand (see illustration). Do not pinch. Move tip of pick lightly back and forth across all four strings. Allow your wrist to hang loosely. Begin slowly and gradually increase speed until you can produce a smooth, even, continuous tone. The speed with which you move the pick across the strings will depend, of course, upon the tempo or time of the piece that you are accompanying.

How to Strum With Fingers

Do not attempt to strum with your fingers until you have mastered the chords on the following pages and until you can secure a smooth, even stroke with your Felt Pick. To strum with fingers, first practice striking the strings *downward,* diagonally, just above the sound hole of the instrument, with the *ball* of your thumb. Hold wrist loosely. Then strum downward, diagonally, with the tip of the nail of the index finger. Then bring the index finger up, using the *ball* of the finger. Next, combine the thumb and the index finger, going down diagonally with the ball of the thumb and the tip of the nail of the index finger and coming up with ball of the index finger alone. Practice this until you can do it smoothly. Then add the second finger, then the third, and finally the fourth. The secret in using the fingers lies in going down with *ball* of the thumb and the *nails* of the fingers, and coming up with the *balls* of the fingers.

Many ukulele instruction booklets featured quick-learning methods that touted the ease of learning to play the uke, including the "Illustrated 5-Minute Guaranteed Ukulele Course" published in 1925.

Most instruction booklets used graphics or photographs to illustrate tuning methods, the proper way of holding a uke, how to use a felt pick and how to play various strumming patterns.

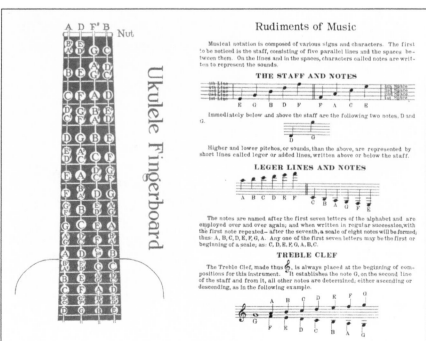

The rudimentary aspects of music theory—time signatures, keys, notes, etc.—were often covered in ukulele instruction booklets.

Over time, graphic diagrams replaced musical notation as a way of teaching not only ukulele chords, but song melodies and solos as well.

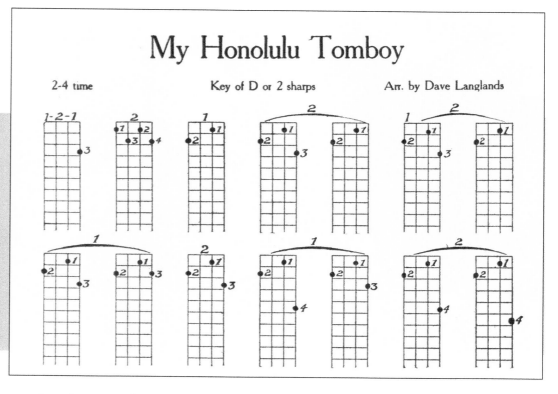

But it wasn't long before graphic diagrams began to replace musical notation as a way of teaching not only ukulele chords, but song melodies and solos as well. Whether hand drawn or illustrated through photographs, diagrams showed the fingering for chords, indicating the proper strings and frets where specific fingers designated by numbers (index=#1, middle=#2, etc.) were to be placed. Some booklets, such as J Kalani Peterson's 1924 Ukulele Method, displayed chords with both diagrams and musical notation.

Practically all booklets featured an assortment of songs to play using the simple chords just learned. Song selections often included obscure but fun to play novelty tunes such as "The Quilting Party," "They Like to Watch the Hose" and "Alice Where Art Thou?," although many featured songs that are still well known today, including "My Old Kentucky Home," "Santa Lucia" and "Aloha Oe."

Tunes were sometimes accompanied by piano notation and sometimes displayed with only chord diagrams or chord names (C, Gm, etc.) above the printed lyrics. Dan Nolan's "System of Playing the Ukulele" took a different approach: Instead of specific chords, the songs in Nolan's method employ the chord number system, where Roman numerals (I, III, IV, etc.) indicate chord intervals, thus allowing a song to be played in any chosen key. For example, in the key of C, a "C" is the I chord, the IV chord is "F" and the V chord is "G."

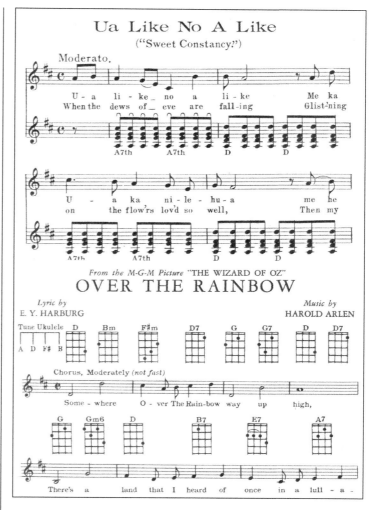

Popular tunes printed in booklets sometimes featured piano notation and sometimes displayed only chord diagrams or chord names (C, Gm, etc.) above the lyrics.

To aid with ukulele sales, many instrument manufacturers and music dealers included printed instructions with the ukes they sold.

Buy a Uke, Get an Instruction Booklet

To aid with sales, many ukulele makers and music dealers included printed instructions with the ukes they sold. The 20s vintage "Pep Leader" ukes included a single-page of instruction to help the purchaser get started. The sheet begins with the quote: "The richest child is poor without musical training." In Honolulu, ukulele teacher John Lai's Metronome Music store sold pineapple ukuleles under the Ka Lai brand name (the name was later changed to "Ka Lae" because it sounded more Hawaiian) Lai used his teaching experience to develop an eight-lesson booklet, "Ka Lae's Hawaiian Ukulele Instructions," which was included with the ukes he sold. On the mainland, Christy's Music House in San Jose, California printed their own small eight-page instruction booklet to help their customers learn to play the instruments they sold.

During the plastic uke era in the 1950s and 60s, most manufacturers included how-to-play booklets with their instruments, like the Fin-der "Beach Boy Uke Method," Carnival's "How to Play the Varsity Uke" and Mastro's self-teaching methods for their Islander and banjo ukes. Featuring a grass-skirted hula girl on the cover with the words "The Uke is Easy to Play," Selcol's booklet sets the standard for simple instruction: It teaches only three chords (C, F and G7) and concludes with "Now you can play hundreds of tunes!" The award for the cutest of booklet goes to Mastro's "Sparkle Plenty Ukette Method." Written by May Singhi Breen (see below), this booklet contains colorful cartoon imagery of Sparkle Plenty (a character from the Dick Tracy comic strip) on every page. In Sparkle's own words: "With my exciting instruction comic book you'll learn how to play in a jiffy!" Instead of printing a separate booklet for their toy-sized plastic cowboy-themed uke, Carnival printed playing instructions right on the back of the box the uke came in.

One of the cutest uke instruction booklets is Mastro's "Sparkle Plenty Ukette Method" which contains colorful cartoon images of Sparkle Plenty on every page.

The Easy Hawaiian Ukulele featured a fingerboard printed with the names of the notes for each string at each fret position.

One of the most novel approaches to ukulele instruction was developed by mail order novelty seller Johnson Smith & Co. of Racine, Wisconsin. Their "Easy Hawaiian Ukulele" made of "imitation koa" birch featured a fingerboard printed with the names of the notes for each string at each fret position, as well as a graphic showing the note in standard musical notation. The booklet that came with the uke explained how to finger chords and play melodies following the printed fingerboard notes.

Celebrity Uke Methods

A number of well-known performers of the era had their own uke method books, including Roy Smeck, Ukulele Hughes, Wendell Hall, May Singhi Breen and Arthur Godfrey. A fine performer and composer/arranger, "Ukulele Lady," May Singhi Breen not only created her own ukulele instruction method, but was instrumental (pun intended) in popularizing the use of standardized uke chord diagrams in books and sheet music. Breen convinced publishers to include small uke chord diagrams printed directly above the lines of lyrics. Her efforts were so successful that the majority of sheet music printed in the 1920s through the 40s features uke chord diagrams and arrangements.

In addition to the usual instructions for playing the uke and diagrams of common chords, each of these books contained an assortment of songs, typically arranged and (sometimes) written by the celebrity. Wendell Hall's "Know Your Ukulele" method booklet included a separate large chord chart featuring major, minor and diminished 7th chords, as well as chords dubbed as "unusual" including major 7ths, 7 flat 5, and minor 9th chords. Published in 1928, Roy Smeck's Ukulele and Ukulele Banjo method book promised to reveal all of Smeck's secrets of ukulele playing, including how to perform some of Smeck's famous "exhibi-

Many well-known performers had their own ukulele method books, including Roy Smeck, Ukulele Hughes, Wendell Hall and May Singhi Breen.

Exhibition Strokes

In the strokes described here, the plectrum movements require plenty of room for display, the right hand frequently moving from the bridge up to the 4th or 5th fret. For this reason all chords taken by the left hand must be in the first position, so as not to interfere with the right hand movements.

Repeat each stroke several times.

CIRCLE STROKE
(Winding the clock)

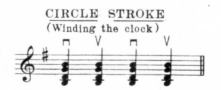

In executing this stroke the right hand moves in a circle.

Begin with a down stroke across the strings near the 8th fret, and then move the right hand in a circular manner, until it comes below the sound-hole, where the second stroke is made upward.

The position of the curved arrows in the adjoining sketch will show how the plectrum movements form a circle.

FIGURE EIGHT STROKE

A double circle is formed by this stroke.

The first down stroke is made across the strings near the 3rd fret, as shown by the arrow. The second stroke curves upward near the sound-hole. The third stroke is a down curve near the bridge, and the fourth stroke is an upward curve just above the sound-hole.

The curved arrows show how these movements form a figure eight.

Roy Smeck's 1928 "Ukulele and Ukulele Banjo Method" book described many of Smeck's unique playing techniques, including how to perform some of Smeck's flashy strumming patterns.

Some ukulele methods were specifically designed for group instruction, including Chicago schoolteacher Lucy Goodwin's Ukulele Course, published in 1931.

Group Instruction Methods

As stated in their titles, the majority of uke booklets were intended as self-instruction aids. But there were also ukulele methods specifically intended for group instruction. Chicago schoolteacher Lucy Goodwin created her own curriculum for teaching ukulele in her elementary school classes, the success of which led to Goodwin's Ukulele Course, published in 1931. Her book served as a guide for music teachers, playground directors and camp, club and group leaders and included exercises for group playing, instructions for arranging popular music for group play as well as suggestions for how to integrate the uke with other instruments, such as the guitar, mandolin and banjo. During World War II, the Gretsch Musical Instrument Company produced round-bodied, green-grey and blue "Army Ukes" which were sold to soldiers going off to war. To help soldiers learn to play their ukes,

First published in 1977, J. Chalmer Doane's "A Teacher's Guide to Classroom Ukulele" is a comprehensive teaching program that takes students through all the basics of music and uke playing.

tion strokes" such as the figure eight and zig-zag (AKA "Fan Tan"), as well as a collection of 100 novelty "jazz strokes" each presented in standard musical notation.

Quite a number of method books were written by ukulele players who were well known in their day, but now are mostly forgotten. There's J. Mace Wolff's "Complete Ukulele Instruction Course," Leon Coleman's "The Ukulele and How to Play it" and Hank Linet's "Ten Lesson Course in Ukulele Playing." Richard Konter, AKA "Ukulele Dick," is best remembered for taking his Martin ukulele on Rear Admiral Byrd's expeditionary flight to the North Pole in 1926. The instructions presented in Konter's 1924 "Improved Ukulele Method" book were developed by Konter as he taught shipmates how to play during his 20 years of service in the U.S. Navy. Beyond the basics, Konter's method included more advanced instruction for transposing, capoing and even using alternative tunings to change a uke's pitch.

Doug Smith's "Strum in Record Time" ukulele self-instructor combined a 45 record with a fold-out instructional printed sleeve.

Gretsch published large (38"x25") "Easy Play Ukulele" charts designed to aid in group instruction in barracks and USO clubs (see the photo on pg. 245).

In the 1970s, J. Chalmer Doane, a school teacher in Halifax, Nova Scotia, developed a group ukulele teaching method that was so successful, it provided the backbone of a music education program that's still in use today in schools all across Canada (also see Section 7.4) Doane's "A Teacher's Guide to Classroom Ukulele" first published in 1977, presents a comprehensive teaching program that takes students through all the basics of chromatic scales, intervals, rhythms, melody and harmony. Doane's program has taught countless students, including well-known Canadian ukulele virtuoso James Hill, who attended at the Langley School in British Columbia. That school is also famous for its renowned Langley Ukulele Ensemble, one of the top performing student ukulele troupes in the world.

Instructional Records

To supplement his ukulele teaching method book, J. Chalmers Doane recorded "An Introduction to Ukulele Basics" which was released as a vinyl LP record in 1976. The record provides audio instruction and examples of various strumming techniques, as well as major scales, bar chords, picking techniques and more. But Doane wasn't the first to use recordings to teach ukulele: In the 1940s, the Gotham Record Corp. of Philadelphia offered a combination instruction booklet and LP record created by uke virtuoso and "Wizard of the Strings" Roy Smeck. One side of the record is dedicated to tuning the uke, while the other covers playing instructions. Released in 1962, Don Rainey's "Read Listen Learn Tenor Uke" bundled a 45 RPM record in a paper sleeve that unfolded to reveal printed instructions that covered basic playing techniques. The record included tracks that taught tuning, simple chords and strumming rhythms. 1965's aptly named "Strum in Record Time" by Doug Smith also combined a 45 record with a fold-out instructional printed sleeve. Like Rainey's record, Smiths' provides a basic ukulele course, including more than a dozen easy-to-play tunes such as "On Top of Old Smokey," "Yellow Rose of Texas" and "Greensleeves."

The first big Hawaiian ukulele craze was partially fueled by the Hawaiian music and dance featured in the 1912 Broadway musical play "The Bird of Paradise."

The early 1900s saw the birth of many dozens of songs and sheet music designed to appeal to ukulele players and island music enthusiasts.

8.2 Ukulele Sheet Music

In the age of electronics, when playing just about any song is only a few clicks away on a Smart phone, tablet or other electronic device, it's hard to imagine a time when listenable music was much harder to come by. Before phonographs were common household items, if you wanted to hear a song, you either had to attend a musical concert or sing and/or play the song yourself. If you chose the latter option, the easiest way to learn one of the popular songs of the time was to buy the sheet music for it. Although musical compositions written out in standard notation date back many centuries, printed sheet music with both the words and music to popular songs didn't become commonplace until the 1800s.

Flash forward to the early 1900s the first big ukulele craze was initially fueled by Hawaiian exhibitions at the 1915 San Francisco's Panama Pacific International Exposition as well as the touring Broadway musical play "The Bird of Paradise" (well-known actor Clark

Gable said he was inspired to become an actor after seeing the play at the age of seventeen). With increasing tourism to the US's then-recently-acquired territory of Hawaii, millions of mainland Americans became fascinated with all things Hawaiian—including ukes and ukulele music. Songwriters were quick to take note (pun intended), and over the next couple of decades, composed tons of tunes tailor-made for ukulele players and island music enthusiasts.

Some early Hawaiian sheet music was written (appropriately enough) by native Hawaiian songwriters. Sonny Cunha, Henry Kailimai and Johnny Nobel all penned popular island tunes that were first published in Honolulu, including "My Honolulu Hula Girl" (Cunha, 1909), "On the Beach at Waikiki" (Kailimai/Stover, 1915) and "Hula Blues" (Cunha/Nobel, 1920). "Aloha 'Oe" is one of Hawaii's best-known songs, written by their last monarch, Queen Liliuokalani in 1878. The song later achieved world-wide renown when new sheet music editions, complete with English lyrics, were published in the 1930s.

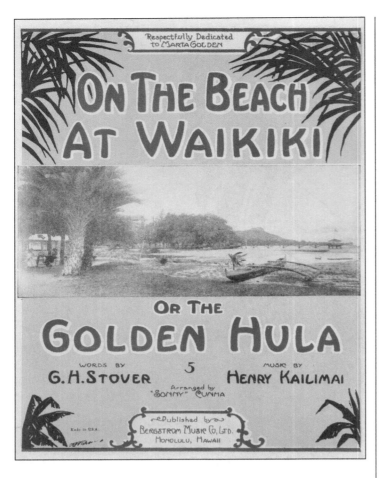

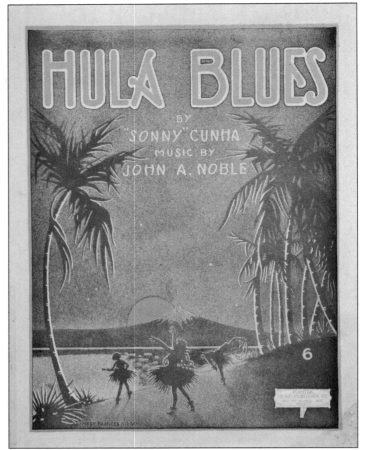

The popularity of Hawaiian songs didn't go unnoticed on the mainland, and it wasn't long before New York City became the commercial center of island-themed sheet music publishing. In the late 19th century, a concentration of music publishing firms formed in the western half of lower Manhattan, an area that came to be known as "Tin Pan Alley." Its nickname allegedly was coined by a songwriter who thought that the collective sound made by many cheap upright pianos all playing different tunes was reminiscent of the banging of tin pans in an alleyway.

In the early twentieth century, Tin Pan Alley was the hotbed of American popular song composition, pumping out countless hits by composers that included some of the best in the business: Irving Berlin, George Gershwin, Harold Arlen and Gus Kahn. Kahn alone wrote dozens of popular standards we still play today, including "Pretty Baby," "I'll See You in My Dreams," "Ain't We Got Fun," and "It Had to Be You." Tin Pan Alley's pool of composers also included many former vaudevillians, including Benny Davis ("Ukulele Moon" and "I'll Fly to Hawaii") and Harry Owens ("Sweet Leilani" and "The Hukilau Song"). Also a well-known bandleader, Owens later served as the musical director at Waikiki's Royal Hawaiian Hotel.

To capitalize on the Hawaiian uke craze, Tin Pan Alley published umpteen songs with exotic titles and lyrics devised to convey a sense of tropical adventure. Tunes like "Silver Sands of Love (Naughty Hawaii)" (Yellen/Sanders, 1921) and "On the Shores of Waikiki" (Ott, 1931) evoked images of secluded beaches, swaying palm trees and picturesque sunsets. Other songs sought to inspire romantic fantasies, with hula-dancing maidens: "Waiki-ki-ki Lou" (Jolson/Friend, 1920); or ukulele-strumming beach boys: "Aloha Honey Boy" (Carter/Smith, 1919). Of course, what could be more tantalizing to uke-crazed fans than sheet music that featured the ukulele in both the title and imagery: "That Ukalele Band" (Edelheit, Smith, Vanderveer, 1916; note the unorthodox spelling), "I Can Hear the Ukuleles Calling Me" (Vincent/Paley, 1916) "Ukulele Blues" (Lapham, Singhi Breen, Kors, 1924) and "Ukulele Lady" (Kahn/Whiting, 1925).

To better sell the fantasies that their song sheets promised, Tin Pan Alley publishers hired artists who created attractive sheet music covers which typically featured Hawaiian themes and paradisiacal island scenery. The ranks of these talented artists included Albert Barbelle ("Yaaka Hula Hickey Dula," Goetz/Young/Wendling, 1916; see photo on page 335),

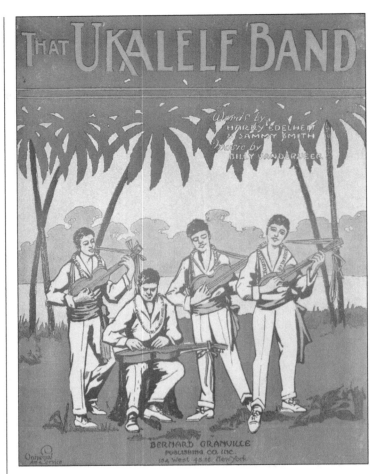

Leland Morgan ("My Waikiki Ukulele Girl," Glick/Smith, 1916) and prolific artist brothers William and Frederick Starmer. Between them, the Starmer brothers produced over a hundred covers between 1900 and 1940, including "My Honolulu Ukulele Baby" (Johnson/Kailimai, 1916) "Mo-Na-Lu" (Breau, 1922) and "Under the Ukulele Tree" (Dixon/Henderson, 1926). Truth be told, the beautiful images these artists created were often more inspiring than the lyrics of the songs themselves.

Speaking of lyrics, most Hawaiian-craze-era songs were written in the "hapa haole" style. Translated as "half foreign" or "half white," hapa haole songs combine a mix of Hawaiian and English words. Take, for example, the 1933 Cogswell/Harrison/Noble hit "My Little Grass Shack in Kealakekua, Hawaii." It includes the lyrics: "I want to be with all the kanes (men) and wahines (women) that I knew long ago" and "I can hear the Hawaiians saying "Komo mai no kaua ika hale welakahao." The latter phrase, loosely translated, means "welcome, stay a short time, experience hot time at my house." Lyricists often took liberties with the Hawaiian language and occasionally even made up words, as found in these song titles: "Oh, How She Could Yacki Hacki Wicki Wacki Woo: (That's Love in

Honolu)" (Murphy/McCarron/Von Tilzer, 1916) and "Yaddie Kaddie Kiddie Kaddie Koo," (Lewis/Young/Meyer, 1916). How do we know some of these words are made up? There's no "C" "D" or "Y" in the Hawaiian alphabet.

Musically, most hapa haole songs weren't based on traditional Hawaiian melodies, but rather employed trending musical styles of the time, including ragtime, blues and jazz. To adapt a songwriter's melodies for play on the ukulele, Tin Pan Alley hired top arrangers, the best being May Singhi Breen, aka "The Original Ukulele Lady" (see photo on page 334). Breen was an excellent uke player, composer and instructor. To make songs easier to play, Breen convinced publishers to include small uke chord diagrams printed directly above the lines of lyrics. A tuning diagram on

the song's first page showed the correct string pitches, which were typically in D tuning: A-D-F#-B. Why use tuning that's one-full-step higher than the C tuning (G-C-E-A) that's most common today? One explanation is that D tuning made it easier for ukes to play along with guitarists playing in the key of E or A. It's also said that the increased string tension made ukuleles sound brighter.

Among the many styles of songs it published, Tin Pan Alley was particularly well known for its "novelty songs." The sheet music typically featured eye-catching cover art, a wacky title and colorful lyrics. Memorable examples include "Since Maggie Dooley Learned the Hooley Hooley" (Leslie/Kalmar/Meyer, 1916), "The More I See of Hawaii the Better I Like New York" (Kalmar/Gottler, 1917), "On My Ukulele (tra la la

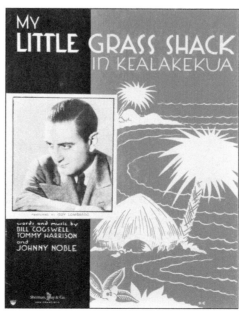

THE ART OF VINTAGE UKULELES • SANDOR NAGYSZALANCZY

333

HOW TO HOLD THE UKULELE

BACK VIEW

DO NOT SHOW THUMB

LEFT WRIST
FORWARD AND RELAXED

An image from May Singhi Breen's ukulele instruction booklet shows "Ukulele Lady" Breen demonstrating how to properly hold the ukulele.

Explanation of UKULELE DIAGRAMS

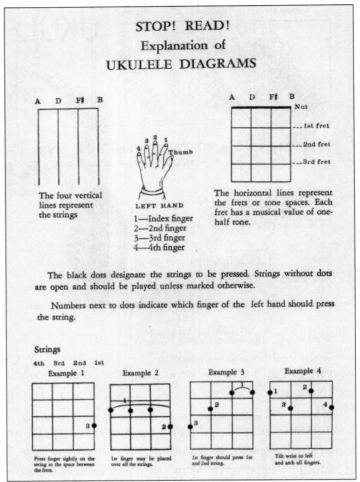

The four vertical lines represent the strings

LEFT HAND
1—Index finger
2—2nd finger
3—3rd finger
4—4th finger

The horizontal lines represent the frets or tone spaces. Each fret has a musical value of one-half tone.

The black dots designate the strings to be pressed. Strings without dots are open and should be played unless marked otherwise.

Numbers next to dots indicate which finger of the left hand should press the string.

Strings

4th 3rd 2nd 1st

Example 1 | Example 2 | Example 3 | Example 4

Press finger tightly on the string in the space between the frets. | 1st finger may be placed over all the strings. | 1st finger should press 1st and 2nd string. | Tilt wrist to left and arch all fingers.

An excellent uke player, composer and instructor, May Singhi Breen was instrumental in convincing music publishers to include small uke chord diagrams in printed sheet music.

la la)" (Parish/Morris/Herscher, 1926) and "Princess Poo-Poo-Ly Has Plenty Pa-Pa-Ya" (Owens, 1940). My personal favorite vintage novelty song: "Crazy Words, Crazy Tune" (Yellen/Ager, 1927) has a cover featuring a frenzied uke player and lyrics that I can only imagine express how folks who hate ukulele music must feel:

"There's a guy I'd like to kill, if he doesn't stop I will, got a ukulele and a voice that's loud and shrill."

Not all popular sheet music came from Tin Pan Alley or Honolulu; assorted titles were printed by pub-

lishing houses scattered throughout America, in cities including Chicago, Philadelphia and San Francisco. And as the ukulele craze spread around the globe, other countries got into the act. British publishers produced their share of Hawaiian-influenced song sheets, such as "Ukulele Dream Girl" (Keech, 1926), "Give me a Ukulele (and a ukulele baby) and Leave the Rest to Me" (Brown/Williams, 1926), and "He Played His Ukulele as the Ship Went Down" (Le Clero, 1932). British comedic actor, singer/songwriter and banjolele virtuoso George Formby performed in numerous WWII-era English films (See Section 6.1, pg. 252). One of his jauntiest tunes "The Ukulele Man" was featured both in the movie "Spare a Copper" and in sheet music printed in 1941.

After the first big Hawaiian ukulele craze ended during the depression, publishers continued to print island-inspired sheet music all the way through the 1930s. Although interest in Hawaiiana had declined, many memorable songs were written in this period, including: "When Hilo Hattie Does the Hilo Hop" (McDiarmid/ Noble, 1936), "Blue Hawaii" (Robin/Rainger, 1937) and "Lovely Hula Hands" (Anderson, 1940).

Ironically, it was the proliferation of affordable phonographs that contributed significantly to the demise of printed music publishing and its once prodigious output of ukulele-oriented sheet music. It's ironic because in the 1920s and 30s, phonograph and 78 rpm record sales actually helped boost sheet music sales. In fact, sheet music covers often featured a photo of a popular singer (Al Jolson, Bing Crosby, etc.) or band or group (Paul Whiteman and his orchestra, Jim and Bob; see the bottom photo on page 330) who had done a phonograph recording of the song. But by the time rock n' roll took over the airwaves and recording studios in the 1950s, sheet music featuring individual songs was pretty much a thing of the past.

Strings made from natural gut came standard on all ukuleles right up until WWII, when gut strings were in short supply.

8.3 Vintage Uke Strings

If you've ever had the privilege of playing a vintage ukulele strung with old-fashioned natural-gut strings, you know what a warm, mellifluous sound those strings can produce. It's distinctly different than the snappier—and much louder—sound created by modern uke strings made from synthetic materials.

Although steel instrument strings became available around 1900 (mostly for guitars), gut strings were a better choice for ukuleles, as most steel strings imparted too much tension on the thin, lightly braced tops used on traditionally built ukes. Hence, gut was the string material of choice for the vast majority of ukuleles sold up until the mid-1940s. Banjo ukes were an exception, as they were often strung with silver- or gold- plated steel strings, which made these instruments sound more like full-sized banjos. Silk was also used as a uke string material, but was far less prevalent than gut. To give them the increased thickness needed for the lower pitched strings, aluminum was wound onto a silk string core.

Long before the ukulele was born in the Hawaiian Islands, gut strings produced in Europe were used on all manner of stringed instruments—violins, cellos, harps, etc. Gut material has the perfect blend of strength and flexibility for not only instrument strings but also archery bow strings, tennis racket webbing, surgical sutures and more. Although sometimes called "catgut," these strings were typically made from the intestines of sheep and goats—nev-

Gut strings came packed in small glassine envelopes, like this Symphony brand string made in Germany.

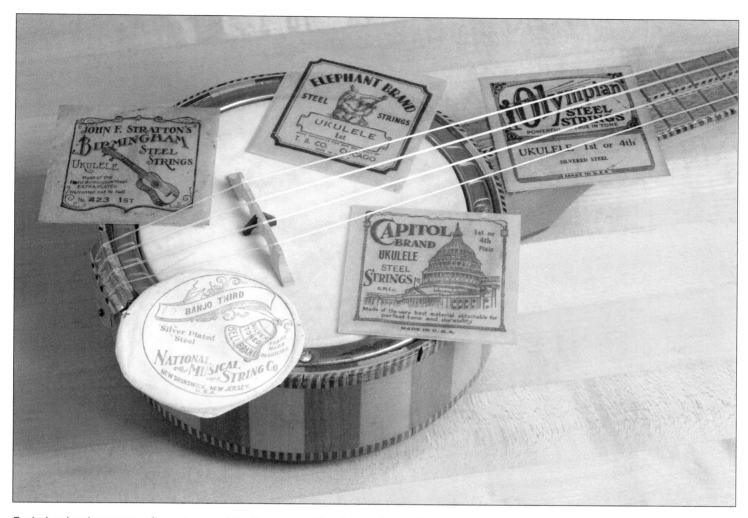

Early banjo ukes were often strung with silver- or gold- plated steel strings which made them sound more like full-sized banjos.

Silk ukulele strings were far less popular than gut strings; To give lower pitched strings the necessary thickness, aluminum was wound onto a silk string core.

Gut string envelopes were typically adorned with decorative graphics, to increase their sales appeal.

Many vintage gut string envelops featured Hawaiian-ish brand names and island themed graphics.

Uke strings were often given brand names that implied superior strength or tone, or that they were designed for professional players.

er felines. The process involved cleaning, scraping, soaking and drying the intestines, then twisting the fibers to form strings which were bleached, then ground and polished to the desired diameters. Sometimes the strings were colored with dye or coated with oil to make them feel slicker.

Gut strings made for ukuleles were sold under innumerable brand names and were packaged in small glassine envelopes often adorned with decorative graphics. Predictably, many of these envelops feature Hawaiian-ish brand names and/or island-themed graphics, including "Genuine Hawaiian," "Mauna Loa" "Perfecto," "Wai Ki Ki," "Wexel," and "Wapiti."

Uke strings were often given brand names that implied superior strength or tone, or that they were designed for professional players. Some string brand names suggest a country of origin, such as the French monikered "Tres Bon!" strings (made in Germany) and "La Preferita Highest Quality Genuine Italian Gut" strings, (made in the U.S.A.) Conversely, "La

Ukulele strings were not always made in the country implied by their brand name. For example, French-moniker "Tres Bon" strings were actually made in Germany.

Graziosa" strings were actually made in Italy. Quite a few ukulele manufacturers had their own brands of strings, including Martin, Gibson, Hollywood and Gretsch.

But the uke string scene changed during World War Two, when gut strings were in short supply; no doubt because the majority were made in Germany and Italy—both wartime enemies of the U.S. and its allied forces. A practical replacement for gut strings came about thanks to the efforts of Albert Augustine,

Uke manufacturers, including Martin, Gibson, Hollywood and Gretsch, often had their own brands of ukulele strings.

La Bella brand guitar strings made from Dupont nylon in 1948 were the first synthetic instrument strings.

an instrument maker from New York. Augustine happened upon some nylon line at an army surplus store in Greenwich Village and thought it would be a good material for classical guitar strings. The first synthetic guitar strings, made from Dupont nylon, were manufactured in 1948 under the La Bella brand name. Players praised the new nylon strings for their smoothness, durability and ability to stay in tune. Not only were they more affordable, but overcame the inherent problems of gut strings, which were harder to tune and became weak and brittle over time. It didn't take long for ukulele players to embrace the new strings and by the early 1950s, Dupont nylon strings were the new standard. In addition to clear, colored nylon strings were also available and were often used on plastic ukuleles in the 1950s and 60s (see the strings on the "Twist-Twist and Twist" uke in the photo shown below.

While most nylon uke strings are clear, they also came in colors which were often featured on plastic ukuleles produced in the 1950s and 60s.

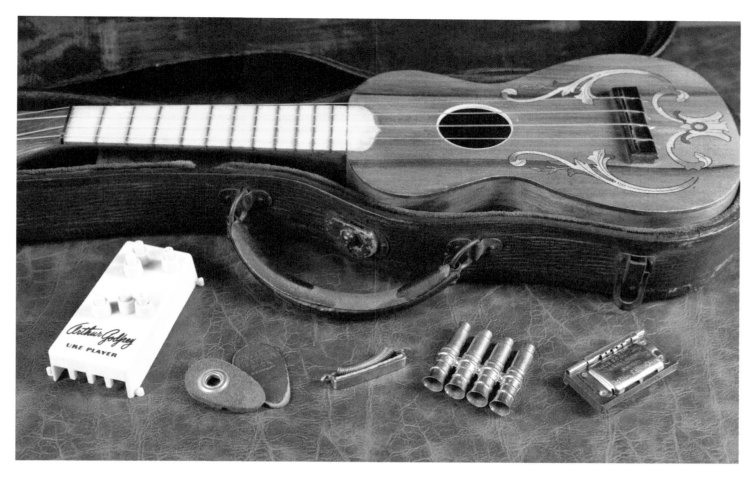

8.4 Important Accessories

What do you need in order to play a ukulele, besides fingers and a decent knowledge of where to put them on the fretboard in order to make musical sounds? Well, for starters, it's a good idea to have the instrument's strings in tune, which was usually accomplished in the first part of the last century by using a pitch pipe. Strumming with a good pick can change the sound you get from a uke, and a capo makes it easier to play in a higher key. For those who wish to take the easiest path to uke playing, there are push-button chord playing devices. And everyone needs a decent case to protect their prized ukulele from getting damaged.

Pitch Pipes

Long before electronic tuners were invented, pitch pipes were the common tool used for tuning stringed instruments, including ukuleles. Most ukulele pitch pipes feature four metal tubes, one for each note corresponding to a uke string. As the user blows into the end of a pipe, the air flows past a harmonica-style brass reed which oscillates to produce the desired mu-

sical note. Almost all these early tuners were made for the higher-pitched "D6" uke tuning (A – D – F# - B), the preferred tuning of the early era for soprano ukuleles and featured in songbooks and sheet music in the 1920s and 30s. The majority of pitch pipes shown here were manufactured in Germany or Czechoslovakia, with a few made in Italy or the U.S.A. More unusual tuners, like Leopold Muller's "Trutone" pitch pipe were built like small four-note harmonicas, complete with a sliding aperture that the user could set to the desired note.

Picks

While a ukulele can be strummed or picked with the fingers alone, players long ago discovered that a ukes tone could be altered by playing with a pick. Strumming with pick made of a hard material such as wood, ivory, horn, shell, metal or plastic generates a sharper, louder tone, while a softer pick made of felt, leather or rubber likewise creates a softer tone. Commercially made hard picks meant for use with guitars, mandolins or banjos were also commandeered by uke players. Felt picks were particularly popular, especially for strumming more delicate tunes, such as waltzes

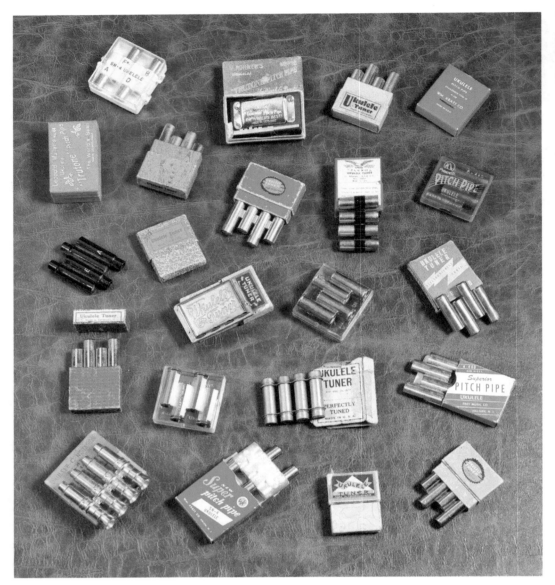

Tuning a ukulele with a pitch pipe was the most common tuning method up until the age of electronic tuners.

An assortment of metal ukulele pitch pipes, all of which contain harmonica-like reeds that create the notes needed for tuning.

THE ART OF VINTAGE UKULELES • SANDOR NAGYSZALANCZY

This attractive ukulele tuning pitch pipe was made in the shape of a small harmonica.

Like gut strings, uke pitch pipes were most commonly manufactured in either Czechoslovakia, Germany or Italy.

Leopold Muller's "Trutone" pitch pipe features a sliding aperture that's selectable for a particular tuning note.

This assortment of ukulele picks shows a wide range of materials, including felt, celluloid, horn and leather.

The Art of Vintage Ukuleles • Sandor Nagyszalanczy

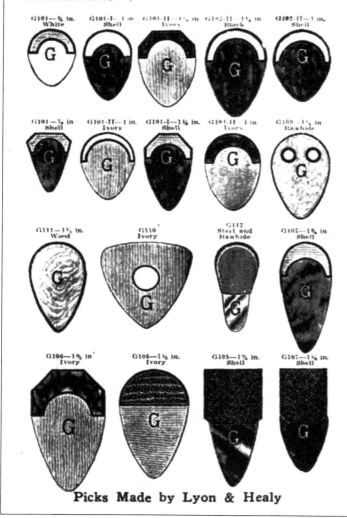
A 1918 catalog page showing picks made by Lyon & Healy.

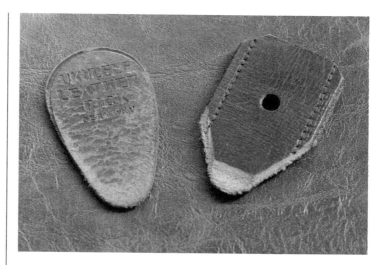

A German-made ukulele pick (left) and a home-made pick (right) crafted from a faux leather belt.

Capos

Like guitars, banjos, and similar fretted instruments, a ukulele can be fitted with a capo to raise the pitch of all of its strings. Of course, a small-sized capo is needed to accomplish this. At least one company produced a ukulele-specific capo in the 1920s/30s: The Elton #485 capo consists of a steel bar with a cork pad on its underside. The bent ends of the bar have hooks for attaching a small steel spring. In use, one end of the spring is unhooked, allowing the bar to be placed on the uke's fingerboard at the desired fret. The spring is then hooked back onto the bar, thus applying the tension that clamps the bar's cork pad down on the strings. A far less successful ukulele capo was patented by Norman M. Johnson in 1927: This quirky device had to be permanently screwed to the uke's headstock and could only reach as far as the 3rd fret.

Chord Players

For those who may not have the patience or finger coordination necessary to play a ukulele, a chord player is a welcome accessory. These devices mount to a uke's fingerboard directly over the strings and allow the user to play a variety of chords with just the push of a button, thus sparing the user the trouble of fretting the strings manually. Many early devices, originally intended for the guitar and then adapted for use with ukuleles, were designed to be permanently mounted to the instrument. Other chord players were made to be removeable, such as Reed's "Instant

and ballads, softly and gently. Felt picks came in many different sizes and harnesses' to suit a wide range of uke players. Some of the coolest ukulele picks I've seen are ones made by the players themselves, such as the pick seen in the photo (above, right) that was made from an old fake leather belt.

Elton's #485 capo consists of a steel bar with a cork pad on its underside and a detachable spring that allows the capo to be fitted to the neck of a uke.

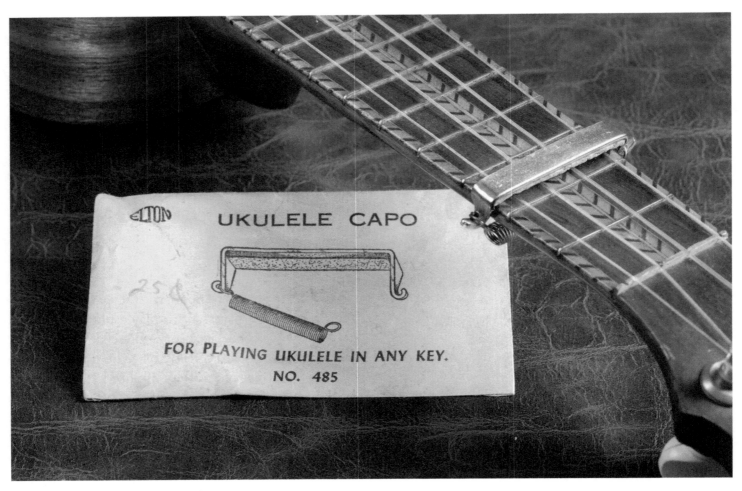

Once fitted to a uke, the Elton capo's spring provides the necessary tension to stop the strings at any given fret.

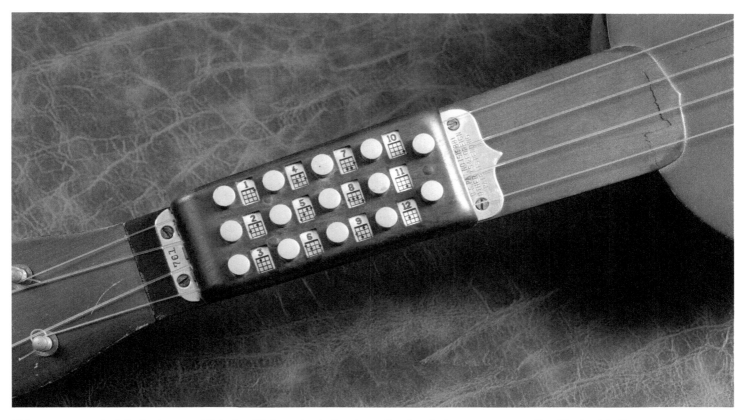

This no-name ukulele features a Nicholas Stein patented automatic chord player permanently attached to its fretless fingerboard.

Unlike other auto chord players, Jame's Reed's "Instant Noteless Player" required the player to push a button for each string/note to be fretted.

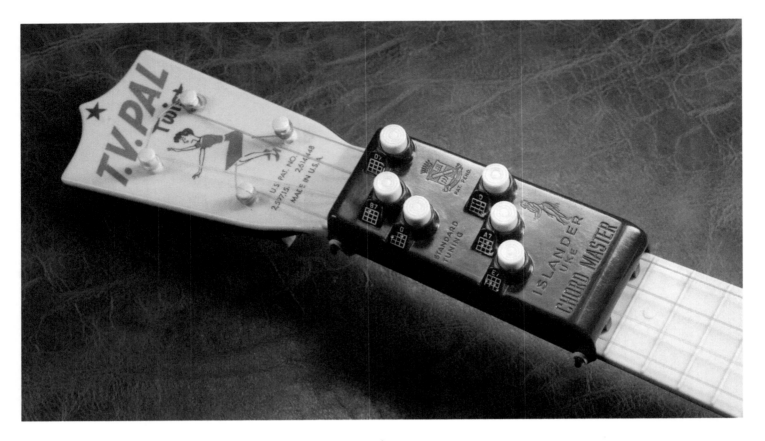

As this Tonk Brothers catalog page shows, cases for both regular ukuleles and banjo ukes came in a great many styles.

ABOVE: During the plastic uke craze of the 1950s and early 60s, Mastro produced their "Chord Master" automatic chord player that attached to a uke via a pair of rubber bands.

Noteless Player," patented in 1924. Made entirely of metal, this compact metal player came with a book containing (somewhat cryptic) diagrams that showed how to play "the latest popular songs" using Reed's device. The book also contains testimonials from Noteless Player users, including vaudeville star Trixie Friganza who was also a suffragette and early advocate for women's rights. Friganza claimed that, despite never having touched a stringed instrument before, she had learned to play a tune on the uke in just three minutes.

Chord players gained their greatest popularity during the plastic uke craze of the 1950s and early 60s. Designed to temporarily attach to a uke via a pair of rubber bands, most plastic players have six buttons that create only basic chords, such as C, F, and D7. Most were manufactured and sold by the same companies that produced their own brands of plastic ukes, most notably Mastro, which made the Islander "Chord Master" and Emenee, who produced the "Arthur Godfrey Uke Player." The small booklets that came with these players offered basic instructions and included a few simple tunes to play using only the player's push buttons.

Affordable ukulele cases made from stiff canvas were reinforced with "strawboard," a coarse yellow paperboard made of straw pulp.

Cases

Of course, safely transporting and storing a prized ukulele was just as important a hundred years ago as it is today. Like present day, ukulele cases in the 1920s and 30s ranged considerably both in terms of their cost and durability. The cheapest cases were simple felt bags, followed in price and protective quality by cases made from stiff canvas reinforced with "strawboard," a coarse yellow paperboard made of straw pulp commonly used for packing and box making. More expensive cases were made of leather, which was often deco-rated with tooled designs. Some of the best canvas and leather cases were manufactured in Chicago by Geib & Schaefer, who fitted them with heavy fleece linings and edges bound with Keratol, a type of imitation leath-er. The majority of these cases were "end loaders" with a hinged, latched flap at the bottom. While relatively sturdy, such cases were sometimes known as "bottom dumpers," as it was all too easy for the flap to open unexpectedly, thus spilling the precious contents onto the ground. Geib & Schaefer also manufactured "Kant Krack" brand soft shell cases, made of several thick-nesses of fabric treated with chemicals and baked into

End loader cases that feature a single hinged flap at the bottom were sometimes known as "bottom dumpers," as the flap could open unexpectedly allowing the uke to fall out.

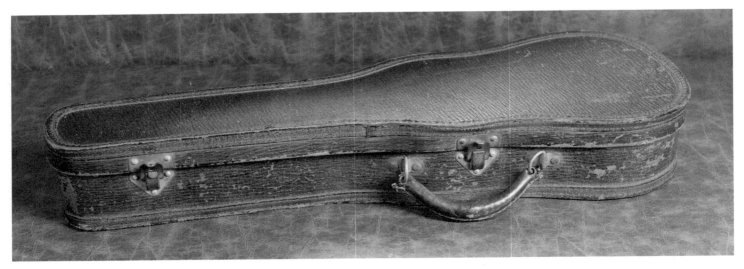

Cases made from chipboard, a type of fiberboard made of multiple layers of rigid cardstock, were typically covered with a waterproof synthetic material such as Keratol.

shape under high pressure.

By the late 1920s, chipboard, a type of fiberboard made of multiple layers of rigid cardstock, had largely replaced canvas and leather as a soft-shell case material. Chipboard cases were typically of a "side opening" design, featuring a full length hinged lid that locked with several latches. Construction wise, these cases were built from several laminated layers of chipboard covered outside with a waterproof material, such as Keratol and inside with cotton flannel. Semi-flexible chipboard cases offered a uke little more protection than canvas or leather cases.

Hard-shell cases were a big step up in terms of the protection they afforded an instrument. Not only were they made from sturdier materials, typically several layers of wood veneers molded to the shape of the ukulele, but they were both lined and padded. The best hard cases had velvet or velour plush lining and a built-in lidded pick box. Their only drawback was cost: In 1930, a soprano-size Martin "Style D" hard case made of three wood plys covered with Keratol and lined with plush silk cost $12.— $1 more than the cost of their Style 0 mahogany soprano uke! The earliest of Martin's hard cases were made by the Felsberg Company, which became the Harptone Company in 1928.

Some of the most interesting cases are those that were made for instruments with non-standard-shape bodies. The most common of these were cases made for pineapple ukes (most notably, those made by Kamaka; see Section 1.4) and the rarest were custom-shape cases for specific instruments, such as the Roy Smeck "Vita Uke" and Lyon & Healys' "Shrine" uke (see the photo on page 68).

Although they were expensive, hard shell cases made from wood veneers molded to the shape of the ukulele and lined inside with velvet or velour provided the best protection for a prized instrument.

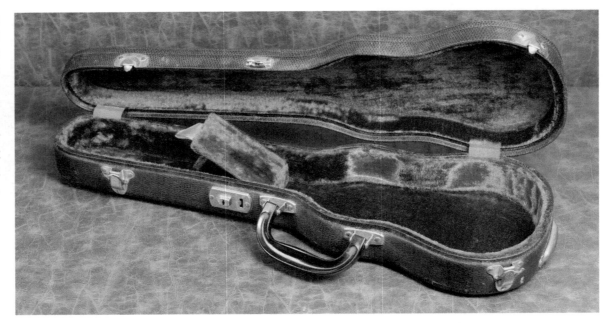

Hula Girl Nodders

8.5 Ukulele Ephemera

The stuff I've collected over the years includes all manner of Hawaiian souvenirs and mainland-made memorabilia ranging from small sculptures and figurines to glassware and ceramics to various promotional items. Some of these items are practical, albeit a bit odd; a uke parakeet toy, for example. Others are purely whimsical, like Franklin Mint's rowboat sculpture. Just about the only thing these items have in common is that they all feature the ukulele.

There's plenty of zany ukulele ephemera that's come out in more recent years—a slew of bobble heads: Betty Boop, Tiny Tim, President Obama, Olaf from Frozen, etc. Also, uke sunglasses, keychains, picture frames, earrings, mugs, bottle openers, tote bags & tee shirts and even a plastic uke-shaped hard-boiled egg slicer. However, our focus here is on vintage items made between the 1920s and the mid-1960s.

Hula Girl Nodders

The first Hawaiian hula dolls appeared in the 1920s, made of unglazed bisque ceramic or earthenware. These hand-painted figures typically had fake grass skirts, floral halter tops, and cloth leis and were enormously popular tourist items. The hula nodders, aka "dashboard dolls,"

Chalkware Piggy Bank

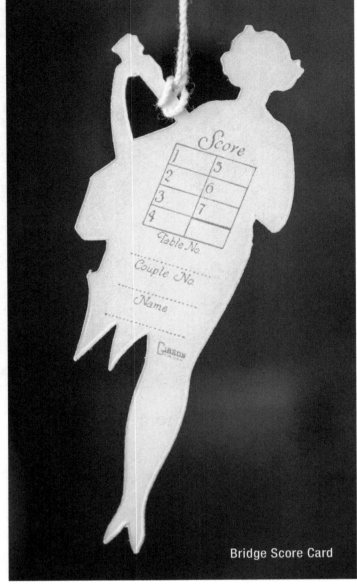

Bridge Score Card

produced in the late 40s were chalkware, cast from plaster of Paris formed in a mold, then painted. The torso of the figure joined to the legs and base via a flexible metal spring that allowed the top portion to bounce back and forth with a hula-like motion. A fringed fabric skirt hides the joint between the halves.

Chalkware Piggy Bank

This charming uke-playing piggy bank is my favorite piece of Hawaiiana. Like the vintage hula girl nodders, the 8-inch-tall hollow pig is chalkware, adorned with a cloth lei and hat. The bank's coin slot is located in the middle of the ukulele that the pig is playing. The back of the bank's base says "Hawaii" in raised letters. A removeable rubber plug at the bottom of the hollow pig provides a means of removing the change that's collected inside the bank.

Bridge Score Card

Printed and punched out of thick cardboard, this stylishly dressed, ukulele-strumming red head is actually a card for keeping score while playing contract bridge, an enormously popular card game in America during the 1930s, just after the peak of the uke's first wave of popularity. The back side of the card is printed with places for a couple playing as a team to write their names and table number, as well as a grid for keeping track of their game score.

B&E 1928 Ukulele Medal

Cast from beautiful bronze, this medal appears to be an award given to the best female ukulele player of 1928. The medal's pin bears the initials "B of E," which

B&E 1928 Ukulele Medal

Blind Mice" and the blue one plays "London Bridge is Falling Down." Each is fitted with nylon strings and working multi-colored tuners. Starting in the 1940s, Knickerbocker Plastics manufactured all manner of injection-molded hard plastic toys, including dolls, bathtub duckies, squirt guns, baby rattles and other toys for small children.

Parakeet Uke Toy

Just like humans during the time of COVID-19 lockdown, parakeets evidently need toys to keep themselves entertained when they're confined in small cages. Made by the Inland & Coastal Products Company in Rumson New Jersey, this circa 1940s-50s parakeet toy is in the form of a uke made from molded plastic. It has two metal "strings" fitted with loose beads for Polly to peck at. The top of the uke houses a mirror. Evidently, parakeets mistake their own image in the mirror for that of another bird. They can spend hours preening and chattering with their reflection, which helps cheer

possibly stand for "board of education." The back of the medal is stamped "Chicago, Ill.," so it's likely that the school—perhaps a girl's prep school—which awarded it was somewhere in the northern Midwest.

Uke Music Boxes

Made by the Knickerbocker Plastic Company of North Hollywood California, both of these ukulele-shaped toys house small mechanical music boxes. Turning the hand crank rotates a drum with small tines which pluck the 12 tiny metal bars each of which sound a different note. The pink uke plays "Three

Parakeet Uke Toy

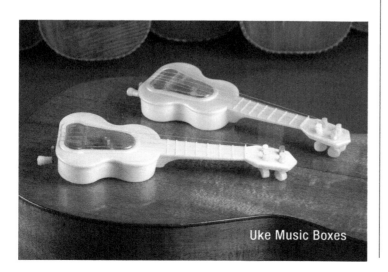

Uke Music Boxes

up a lonely bird, making them feel like they have a friend in the cage with them. Who knew?

The Carnation Milk Cardboard Ukulele

The Carnation Evaporated Milk Company was founded in 1901 and sold condensed milk that came in cans and had a long shelf life; a great product for a time when household refrigerators weren't all that common. To promote their products, Carnation published dozens of cookbooks and recipe brochures from the 1930s through the 1950s. It's likely that the cardboard ukulele shown here was a bonus featured attached to one of their publications; note the old tape marks in the corners. The lithographed cardboard uke was meant to be pressed out, folded up and fitted with rubber-band strings. As the strings can't be tuned or fretted, the Carnation uke was meant to be more of a noisemaking toy than a functional musical instrument.

Student Ukulele Pencil Case

Student Ukulele Pencil Case

Produced by the Hassenfeld Brothers of Pawtucket Rhode Island, this plastic pencil case was probably made in the 1950s for young school children. It originally included three "Surprise" brand #2 pencils and a 6" plastic ruler. The cases' black and blue top pulls off to allow access to the contents, and doubles as an eraser.

Ukulele Lounge Gaming Token

A one-time Las Vegas bar and hangout called the "Ukulele Lounge" issued this one-dollar gaming to-

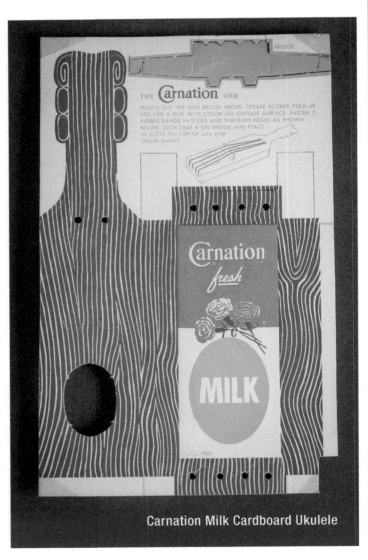

Carnation Milk Cardboard Ukulele

Ukulele Lounge Gaming Token

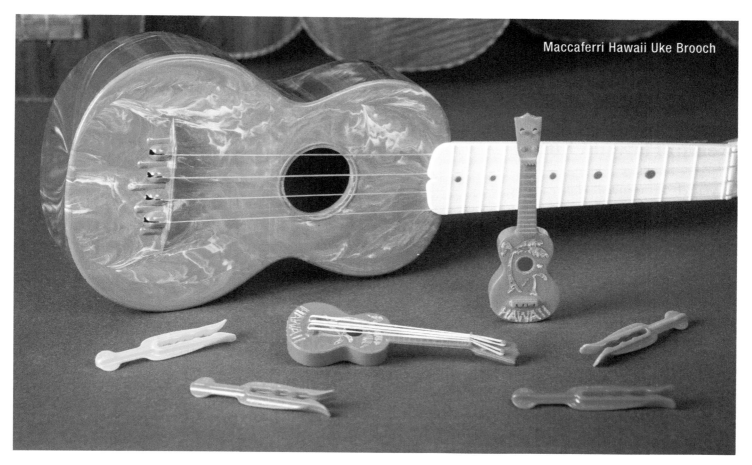

ken used for slot machines and other gambling endeavors. The tropically-themed lounge was located at 620 Las Vegas Boulevard in North Las Vegas. While it may seem strange to have a Hawaiian-themed bar in the middle of the Nevada desert, the fact is that native Hawaiians such as Johnny Ka'aihue (aka "Johnny Ukulele") pioneered Las Vegas' lounge entertainment scene in the 1950s. The Ukulele Lounge closed in 1980, but the building is still there, its exterior currently adorned with a vibrant mural painted by local artist Eric Vozzola.

Maccaferri Hawaii Uke Brooch

Mario Maccaferri is the man responsible for manufacturing more than 9 million plastic ukuleles in the 1950s and 60s, single-handedly fueling a resurgence of interest in the instrument. The line featured several popular models including the Islander, TV Pal and the Playtune Senior (the swirly-red-topped soprano uke shown here). To help promote his instruments, Maccaferri created 5-in.-long red plastic "Hawaii" ukes which he gave away at trade shows. Each had a small clip on the back, allowing it to be worn as a brooch. Tabs at the bridge and nut held a pair of thin rubber

Ken in Hawaii Outfit

band "strings." The plastic clothes pins in the photo are present as a reminder that they were Maccaferri's first mass-produced products, made and sold during World War II when traditional wooden clothes pins were in short supply.

Ken in Hawaii Outfit

Mattel introduced their iconic doll "Barbie" in March of 1959, and two years later they created a boyfriend for her named Ken. In following years, Mattel produced dozens of accessory outfits for the couple. The "Ken in Hawaii" outfit (accessory #1404, first released in 1963) included a blue and white sarong, a floral lei, cork sandals, a straw hat decorated with flowers and a plastic ukulele. A tag that came with the outfit proclaimed: "Barbie and Ken laughed when they found out that ukulele in Hawaiian means 'leaping flea'! So Ken just had to buy a 'uke' to make his Hawaiian costume perfect!"

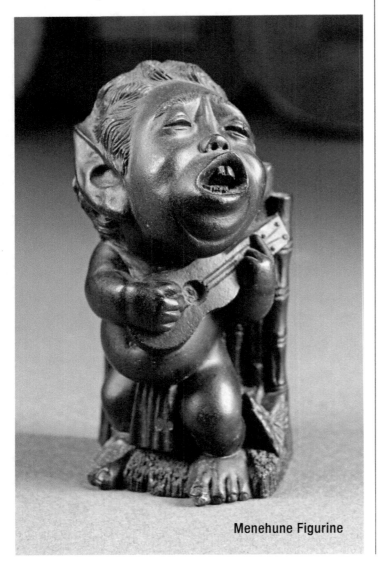

Menehune Figurine

Menehune Figurine

This ukulele-playing character is a Menehune, who in Hawaiian tradition, are mythical little people who live in the island's forests and hidden valleys. The small figurine was made around 1965 by Coco Joe, a Hawaiian artist who mixed ground-up lava into resin which he used to cast small sculptures and objects sold to tourists as souvenirs. The company was started in 1960 by returning WWII veteran Donald R. Gallacher who ran a shop in the town of Punaluu on the northeast coast of the island of Oahu. In 1973 his business had 50 employees and produced more than 400 different items including jewelry, children's books, ashtrays, statues, plaques, keychain fobs and more.

Franklin Mint Boat Sculpture

The "Ukulele Serenade" is a pewter sculpture created by artist Norman Nemeth which shows a 20s era couple in a rented rowboat identified on the prow as "Crystal Lake 12." The man in the straw hat plunks out a tune on his ukulele for a parasol-wielding lady whose facial expression indicates that she's not exactly enraptured (hopefully the lunch packed in the woven picnic basket on the boat's seat will please her more). The sculpture was produced in a limited edition by the Franklin Mint in 1980. Originally located in Wawa Pennsylvania, The Franklin Mint is well known for producing mass-marketed collectibles sold through magazine ads and television commercials. After initially minting gold and silver commemorative coins and medallions, Franklin expanded their operations, producing all manner of items including plates, knives, die-cast model cars and planes, sculptures. They even produced a porcelain Marilyn Monroe doll dressed as the uke-playing character "Sugar Plenty" she portrayed in the popular movie Some Like it Hot.

Souvenir Glassware

Souvenir glassware and dishes were very popular items for tourists to bring back as gifts from their Hawaiian adventures (grandma was always grateful). Glassware typically had decals or painted images of hula dancers, tropical birds, beach scenes, etc. More uncommon and unusual is the glass shown in the upper-right-hand corner of the photo on pg. 319, which

Franklin Mint Boat Sculpture

Sparkie likes to
sing a song
And play
the Ukulele,
On Musical Glasses
play along
and tinkle tunes
so gaily

G.P.G. Co. CIN. O

Souvenir Glassware

depicts a jaunty uke-strumming character named "Sparkie." This glass was part of a series produced by the G.C.G. Company of Cincinnati, Ohio, which manufactured soda fountain glassware. Each glass in the series has Sparkie playing a different musical instrument: piano, saxophone, drum, xylophone, trombone, or ukulele. A scale on the side of the glass shows how high to fill the glass. With the set of glasses all filled to different levels producing different notes when tapped, a simple tune can be plunked out. The glasses also have poems on their reverse sides; this is the rhyme on the uke-playing Sparkie glass: "Sparkie likes to sing a song and play the Ukulele, On Musical Glasses play along and tinkle tunes so gaily."

About The Author

Sandor Nagyszalanczy was born in Budapest Hungary and immigrated to the United States with his parents when he was a child. Sandor started playing guitar in his early teens and performed with a number of garage bands as a rhythm guitarist and lead singer in the late 60s and early 70s. Upon receiving a soprano uke as a gift, he developed a repertoire of Hawaiian hapa haole songs and Tin Pan Alley novelty tunes from the 1920s. Between 1995 and 2015, Sandor sang and played tenor and baritone ukes with two bands: The UkeAholics and Uke Ellington.

Sandor began collecting ukuleles in the mid-1980s, eventually acquiring a collection of nearly 500 instruments along with innumerable pieces of uke-related ephemera. As a writer for Ukulele Magazine, he did deep research into the history of vintage ukuleles, writing dozens of articles about uke builders and players as well as the instruments themselves. Sandor currently lives in the Santa Cruz mountains in coastal California and works as a writer, photographer and recording engineer and producer.